Copyright © 2017 Zoe Lambreas

The images used in this book were free to use commercially, were out of copyright, belonged to the author or were used by permission obtained by the author.

Editing: Zoe Lambreas
Typographic Design: Zoe Lambreas

All rights reserved. No part of this publication may be reproduced, stored in a retrieval system or transmitted in any form or by any means; for example electronic, photocopy and recording without the prior permission of the author. The only exception is brief quotations in printed reviews.

According to the *Copyright Act 1968* of Australia, one chapter or 10% of the book may be copied for educational purposes when the institution has given a remuneration notice to CAL (Copyright Agency Limited). For details contact: CAL via email: info@copyright.com.au or phone (02) 93947600

ISBN:978-0-9946333-3-0

First published June 2017, Melbourne, by ZR Enterprises
Second Edition: published May 2018, Melbourne, by ZR Enterprises
Edited & reprinted: Jan., 2022; Aug., Oct. & Dec. 2023; May, July & August 2024

SELA Books
www.speaklikeaustralians.com

The front cover shows Theo and Argyro with baby Voula in "sheep country" — from the novel "Speak English like Australians!"

Speak English Like Australians!
EAL/EFL Grammar & Activities
TEXTBOOK 1

Zoe Lambreas

To improve your Aussie pronunciation and listening skills, you can watch videos and listen to the chapters being read in various Australian voices. Go to YouTube: Home, and search for the author Zoe Lambreas. Or scan this QR code with your mobile .

Alternately, go to Zoe's website www.speaklikeaustralians.com to hear the audios and to complete the listening clozes and dictations which are in this EAL/EFL Grammar & Activities Textbook 1. Or scan with your mobile QR Scanner for the website.

To place a book order or for more information please go to the website above and click on ORDERS. Or scan here:

Dear Reader,

I hope you enjoy the activities and ideas in this book. Should you wish to offer any comments, please contact me on my website, as I would love to hear from you.

Kind regards,

Zoe Lambreas

Contents

1 Chapter 1 Coming to Australia

1	Reading Comprehension
2	Reading: word attack skills
7	Speaking: I don't understand
8	Speaking: cultural misunderstandings ACSF 2.07 & 2.08
9	Chant: Cultural Misunderstandings
10	Listening: a jig-saw activity
11	Listening: write the missing words
12	Listening: continued
14	Dictation: aural
15	Pronunciation: using IPA symbols for sounds
17	Pronunciation: the Schwa
18	Phonograms: how used in this series of text books
18	Tongue Twisters: "a"
19	Conversation Bits: she'll be right; oodles; no worries
20	Spelling: plural nouns
21	Vocabulary: crossword
22	Vocabulary: synonyms
23	Figures of Speech: simile
24	Proverbs: short, well-known expressions that share advice and truth
25	Writing: building sentences (simple & complex sentences etc.)
27	Writing: joining sentences together
28	Parts of Speech: a definition of nouns & determiners
30	Grammar: uncount/mass and count nouns
31	Grammar: words to use with count & uncount nouns
32	Verb Tenses: to be, to have & to do
33	Verb Tenses: the base verb for questions & negatives
35	Verb Tenses: "do" and "have" in questions
36	Verb Tenses: "Do you ever...?" & "Have you ever...?"
37	Verb Tenses: "Would you ever...?" & "Would you have ever...if...?"

38 Chapter 2 Becoming an Aussie

38	Reading Comprehension
39	Speaking: sharing opinions about cultures
40	Expressions for opinion
40	Being a good listener
41	Speaking: sharing personal information
42	Chant: Assimilation

43	Listening: aural text cloze
46	Listening to a song for general meaning
47	Dictation: listening to "chunks" of prose
48	Pronunciation: plural nouns & present simple verbs
49	Pronunciation: reminder
49	Pronunciation: minimal pairs /s/ and /z/
50	Phonograms: "ar", "ai" & "au"
51	Conversation Bits: a fair go
52	Spelling: the 350 most commonly used words in English
55	Vocabulary: unfamiliar words
56	Figures of Speech: allusion
57	Proverbs: know and do
58	Writing: a paragraph
59	Parts of Speech: nouns
60	Grammar: word order in sentences
62	Verb Tenses: present simple tense
63	Verb Tenses: list of irregular verbs, bases & participles

69 Chapter 3 The Marriage Proposal

69	Reading Comprehension
70	Speaking: arranged marriages ACSF 2.07
71	Speaking: reading about arranged marriages
72	Chant: Proxy Marriage
73	Listening: text cloze
74	Dictation: running dictation
75	Pronunciation: stressing and grouping words together when you are reading
77	Phonograms: "augh" and "ough"
77	Tongue Twisters: "f"
78	Conversation Bits: What a coincidence! What a fluke!
79	Spelling: adding suffixes to silent "e" words
80	Vocabulary: synonyms
84	Figures of Speech: antithesis
85	Proverbs: travel
86	Writing: two contrasting paragraphs (persuasive genre)
87	Parts of Speech: infinitives & gerunds
89	Grammar: gerunds & infinitives
91	Verb Tenses: present participles
92	Verb Tenses: present simple & present continuous tenses

94 Chapter 4   Family

94	Reading Comprehension

95	Speaking: getting a listener's attention
96	Chant: Family
97	Listening: cloze activity
98	Dictation: aural
98	Dictation: in pairs
99	Pronunciation: linking sounds /w/ & /n/
101	Phonograms: "aw", "ay", "c"
101	Tongue Twisters: "r"
102	Conversation Bits: what a stereotype; no surprises there
103	Spelling: when to use double "s"
104	Vocabulary: synonyms
105	Figures of Speech: synecdoche
106	Proverbs: woman
107	Writing: a childhood recount or an imaginary recount (narrative genre)
108	Writing: imaginary recount (narrative genre)
112	Parts of Speech: determiners
113	Parts of Speech: verb and preposition
115	Grammar: determiners
116	Verb Tenses: have got/gotta
117	Verb Tenses: making questions with the simple tenses–conjugation

118 Chapter 5   School

118	Reading Comprehension
119	Speaking: learning and school
120	Speaking: board game
121	Chant: Going to School
122	Listening: follow the text along
123	Dictation: a different running dictation
124	Pronunciation: plural "s"
125	Phonogram: "ch"
125	Tongue Twisters: "s" & "ch"
126	Conversation Bits: dilly-dally! lift my game! I was mortified!
127	Spelling: silent "e" rules
129	Vocabulary: crossword
130	Figures of Speech: simile revised
131	Proverbs: relationships
132	Writing: Two Supporting paragraphs (persuasive genre)
134	Writing: application for a course (persuasive genre)
136	Parts of Speech: count and uncount nouns revision
139	Grammar: the patterns of sentences

141	Verb Tenses: present simple & present continuous

143 Chapter 6 School Ceremonies and Rituals

143	Reading Comprehension
144	Speaking: modals express possibility
145	Speaking: indirect questions–to ask politely
146	Chant: School Rituals
147	Listening: text cloze
148	Dictations: aural & running dictation
149	Pronunciation: reminder
149	Pronunciation: minimal pairs /ʃ/ and /tʃ/
150	Phonogram: "ci"
150	Tongue Twisters: "ci"
151	Conversation Bits: it's up to you!
152	Spelling: "c" spelling rules and pronunciation
153	Vocabulary: crossword
154	Vocabulary: word families
155	Figures of Speech: merisms
156	Proverbs: learning
157	Writing: a personal letter (transactional genre) ACSF 1.05 & 1.06
159	Parts of Speech: collective nouns
160	Parts of Speech: collective nouns & male/female/young animals
161	Grammar: indirect questions–polite questions
164	Grammar: determiners (articles and specific & non-specific determiners)
165	Verb Tenses: revision present continuous tense
166	Verb Tenses: use the correct forms of the verbs

167 Chapter 7 Imperial Australia

167	Reading Comprehension Chapter 7 ACSF 2.03 & 2.04
168	Speaking: class debate–monarchy or republic? ACSF 3.07 & 3.08
169	Expressions for Polite Disagreement
170	Speaking: public speaking in a debate
174	Speaking: sharing points of view
175	Chant: old English nursery rhymes
176	Listening: text cloze
176	Listening: shadow reading in chunks
177	Listening: on the Internet watch and listen to a YouTube video
178	Dictation: dictogloss
179	Pronunciation: reminder
179	Pronunciation: minimal pairs /i:/ and /I/
180	Phonogram: "i"

180	Tongue Twisters: "i"
181	Conversation Bits: photobombed! some random!
182	Spelling: "er", "en", "est" and "y" suffixes (word endings)
183	Vocabulary: crossword
184	Figures of Speech: tautology
185	Proverbs: birds
186	Writing: a letter to a friend (transactional genre) ACSF 2.05 & 2.06
187	Writing: comparing & contrasting (persuasive genre) ACSF 3.05 & 3.06
188	Writing: genres–six types
190	Parts of Speech: compound nouns
192	Grammar: linking or copula verbs
193	Verb Tenses: conjugation of "to study"

194 Chapter 8 Anzac Day

194	Reading Comprehension
195	Reading: opinions, facts and statistics
197	Speaking: jig-saw activity
198	Speaking: discussion & sharing opinions
200	Chant: Soldiers Marching
201	Listening: video of ANZAC Day
202	Listening: text cloze
203	Listening: dictogloss
204	Dictations: aural & running dictation
204	Alternative Dictation: running dictation
205	Pronunciation: linking sound /dʒ/
206	Pronunciation: minimal pairs /tʃ/ and /dʒ/
207	Phonogram: "dge"
207	Tongue Twisters: "dge"
208	Conversation Bits: fleet-footed! stalking me? milestone! Guinness Records! leisure!
209	Spelling: adding a suffix to word with a final "l"
210	Vocabulary: match words to meanings
211	Vocabulary: acronyms and make a crossword
212	Figures of speech: anaphora
214	Proverbs: comfortable
215	Writing: opinion – organising your own two or three paragraphs (persuasive genre)
217	Writing: a speech (transactional genre)
219	Parts of Speech: infinitive and distributive nouns
221	Grammar: informal use of "though" & "but"
222	Verb Tenses: the 12 verb tenses
223	Verb Tenses: stative verbs cannot be used in the continuous tense

Dear Learner,
Please use the following spare pages for notes to yourself and for writing new vocabulary.
Regards,
Zoe

Chapter 1 Coming to Australia
Reading Comprehension

After reading the first chapter of *Speak English Like Australians!*, answer the following questions in full sentences. This requires a good understanding of sentence structure and is a skill worth practising. In other words include the question words in your answers.

1. What was the Assisted Passage Programme?
___
___
___

2. Why did Theo decide to leave Greece?
___
___
___

3. What did Theo have to do for the Australian Government?
___
___
___

4. Why did Theo's co-workers tell him to *take it easy*?
___
___
___

5. What had Theo learnt to drink in Australia?
___
___

6. Why did Theo get upset with the man who winked at him?
___
___
___

---

1 Assisted Passage was a programme of the Australian Government that paid for migrant men to come here by ship to work wherever the Government sent them in order to build Australia's infrastructure. 2 Theo decided to leave Greece for a chance at a better life overseas and he could send money back to his brothers and his mother. 3 Theo had to pay back the Australian Government, because the Government had paid for him to travel to Australia, so he had to work at whatever the Government decided. 4 Theo's co-workers told him to take it easy because he was working too hard. 5 Theo had learnt to drink beer in Australia. 6 Theo got upset when the man winked at him because in Greece men only wink at women.

Reading: word attack skills

What do you do when you are trying to read and you see a word you don't know? Don't lose your confidence! Here are some ideas that you can try to help you pronounce unfamiliar words.

1. Learn the sounds of the alphabet letters and also learn the most used sounds of two and three letters together like "oo" and "ee". These are called *blends* of letters. Digraphs are two letter blends and trigraphs are three letter ones. Phonograms are the sounds that written letters make. Often a letter may have several possible pronunciations. Please refer to the next few pages and the sections "Phonograms".

2. If you can't read a word "sound it out" by beginning with the first letter and saying its sound. Then say the sound of each following letter. Finally join or *blend* all the sounds in the word, slowly and smoothly together. Can you hear a word you know now? Does it make sense in the sentence?

3. Read the sentence again and try to understand the meaning of the word.

4. Don't stop reading but read the next sentence to see if you can understand better what the first sentence might mean.

5. Compare the word you don't know to a word that it looks like, that you know. Is it said the same way? Is it part of the same word that you know? Does it have the same meaning? The word you know could help you understand the meaning of the sentence.

6. Look at pictures for context and try to understand what idea the word or sentence is about? Think about your own experiences in life. Does it make sense to you now?

Reading: word attack skills—phonics

When reading, try to "sound out" (say out loud) unfamiliar words. Knowing these common blends and their sounds will help you to read out aloud any new words. Most often there are two letters to make a sound (digraphs) but sometimes there are three of them (trigraphs).

Consonant Digraphs – Two Letters Make One Sound
[* trigraphs - 3 letters making 1 sound]

ck	ch	*dge	kn
duck	church	hedge	kneel
ph	sh	th	*tch
elephant	shout	thunder	catch
wh	wr	ng	
wheel	wring	ring	

Make words by using the trigraph "tch" with the following letters: a, e, i, o, u, b, c, h, p, r, w

Answers: batch, butcher, bitch, botch, bewitch, catch, catch-up, crotch, crutch, etch, hatch, hatchet, hitch, patch, patcher, pitch, pitcher, ratch, retch, watch, watcher, witch, wretch.

Consonant Digraphs – Two Letters Make Two Sounds
[* trigraphs - 3 letters making 3 sounds]

bl bloke 	br bricks 	cl clown 	cr crown 	dr drive 
fl flag 	fr friends 	gl glitter 	gr grandma 	pl plank 
pr prince 	qu queen 	sc scan 	*scr scrub 	sk skinny 
sl slippers 	sm smell 	sn sneeze 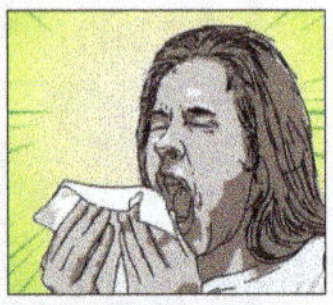	sp splash 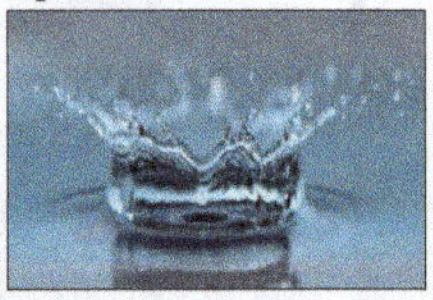	*spr spring 
st stop 	*str string 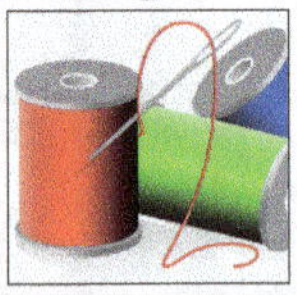	sw sweet 	tr train 	

Consonant Monograph – One Letter Makes Two Sounds
[* trigraph – 3 letters making 2 sounds]

x box 	*cks selfie-sticks 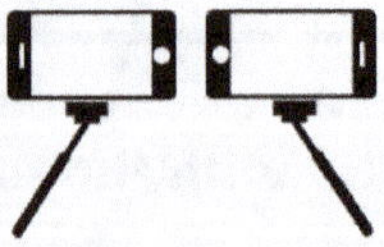

Make words by using the trigraph "str" with the following letters: a, e, i, o, u, g, n, p

Answers: strap, strip, strain, string, stripe, strong, strung, strange.

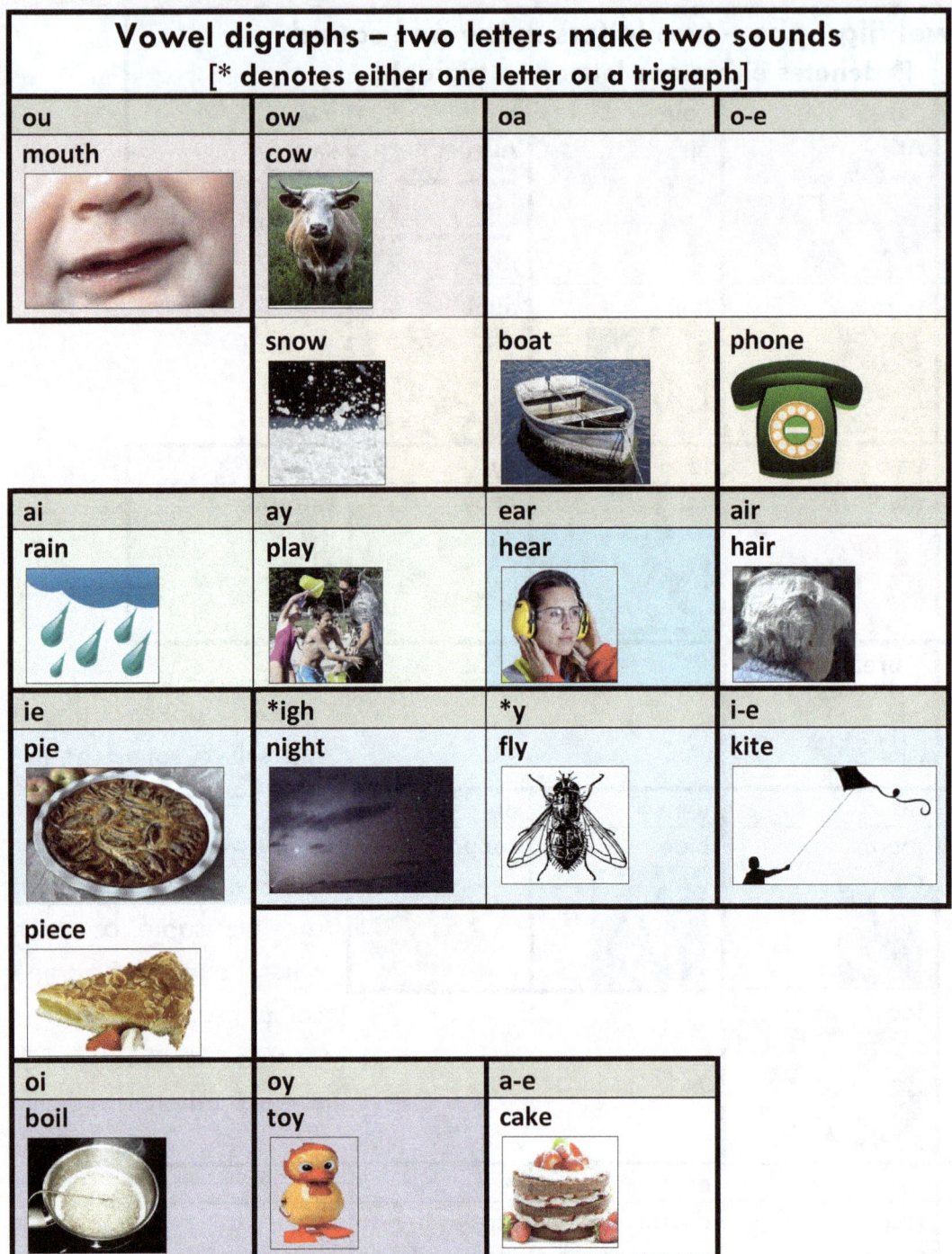

Similar coloured boxes show sounds that are the same as each other. Boxes of the same colour as the page have no relationship to each other.

1. Underline the words that have the same vowel sounds as *cow*.   blow   mouth   brow
2. Underline the words that have the same vowel sound as *cake*.   steak   like   say   hi
3. Underline the words that have the same vowel sound as *fly*.   bye   blind   guy   pie

Answers: 1. mouth, brow 2. steak, say 3. bye, blind, guy, pie

Speaking: I don't understand

Expressions to use when you don't understand

FORMAL (spoken in a polite voice)

Pardon me?   Excuse me?   Sorry?   What was that?
I'm sorry I don't quite get that.
Ah, sorry could you re-phrase that please?
Sorry, I'm afraid I don't follow you.
I'm confused. Could you tell me again please?

INFORMAL

Huh? What was that? I don't get it. Come again? Say again?

VERY INFORMAL IDIOMS (for close relationships)

It's all Greek to me.
I can't make head nor tail of what you're telling me.
Sorry but what you're saying is as clear as mud to me.

Pair Work: ROLE PLAY

1. Pretend that you are working at McDonald's and your partner is a customer who comes to order some food.

2. Write a conversation with your partner and use some of the expressions to say you don't understand what the 'customer' is telling you for his/her food order. (i.e. Pretend you don't understand and use some of the expressions above.)

3. Practise the conversation together and if possible perform your role play to the class.

Speaking: cultural misunderstandings ACSF 2.07 & 2.08

Group Work

Poor Theo experienced some problems because of the differences between his culture and the Australian culture. He misunderstood why a man winked at him! Also, in the beginning, he thought he had to work extra-hard to impress his workmates. This was the culture in his home country.

Discuss the questions and share your experiences. Ask each other questions to make sure you understand and to show you are interested.

1. What cultural differences did you see when you first came to Australia?
2. Have you ever had a cultural misunderstanding like Theo did? What happened to you and how did you feel?

Now, ask each other the questions below, or think of your own to ask. Use the present simple tense because you are discussing habitual behaviour.

a) Do you have different rules about dating in your mother country?
b) In your culture, what colour clothes do you wear to go to a wedding or to a funeral?
c) Are there any different traditions about what you do when a baby is born?
d) In your culture how do you find a spouse?
e) How do you celebrate a marriage?

Ask someone in your group to share one or two of your group's ideas with the rest of the class.

Chant: Cultural Misunderstandings

Practise saying the song until you can sing it easily and keep the rhythm going. You will find it useful to stress the bold text.

Theo left his country
To **start** a brand new **life**.
Australia was so **different**
He **got** himself in **strife**.

In the **pub** with other **blokes**
One **winked** to tell him "**Hi!**"
Theo **grabbed** him by the **collar**
To **punch** him in the **eye**.

Men **stopped** him in his **anger**
And **asked** him what was **wrong**.
He **explained** the serious **matter**
Alas!
His **thoughts** were *not*, spot-**on**!

Listening: a jig-saw activity

Divide the class into four groups and give each group member the same part of the story to read together and to discuss sentence by sentence and to look up any words they don't know. Slang may need instructor explanation. Then re-group learners so each of the four parts can be shared in the new group. Although learners may refer to their written part, in order to help their memories, they are to speak their part and not to read it out. Learners listen to each speaker in turn and ask him/her questions to clarify their understanding.

Part 1
His father was in the boat with his two grandchildren who had been holidaying with their grandparents. Their grandfather was taking them back home to their parents when they all fell into the sea; their bodies were carried out of the sea and put on a cart for their last trip home. Theo was just twenty years old when that happened. He was the eldest son in his family, born in 1920. He had two brothers and three sisters. Theo's father had sent him to the city of Kalamata to help out at his sister's bakery without pay.

Part 2
When the bodies of her two children arrived in the cart, Theo was there to see and to share their grief and pain. The children's father lost his mind and was hospitalised. Now that his own father had died, Theo felt he had to find work to help support his family, but it was hard to find a job in Greece after the Second World War, in 1945. Then, something terrible happened! There was another war in Greece, from 1946 to 1949. It was a civil war between neighbours and brothers. This war was very bad and many Greeks killed each other.

Part 3
Even Theo had been captured and kept prisoner in a three-storey brick building, where he was tied up and had to lie down on a concrete floor, but he wasn't killed. Lucky! After the Second World War and the civil war that came after that, Greece was a very poor country and the government had little control. Theo looked for different ways to make money and he felt lucky when he got a job as a policeman, at about thirty years of age.

Part 4
At that time, young men were walking around the streets of Athens wearing only one arm in their sleeve. The other sleeve was left empty! Maybe it was a new fashion, or a political demonstration. The government was trying to stop young people from doing this. They gave each policeman a pair of scissors and told them to cut the empty sleeve off. After being through wars, Theo thought this was a bit funny: when he used his scissors to cut the empty sleeves off jumpers and jackets. He didn't mind doing it.

Listening: write the missing words

Open YouTube. Search by typing Zoe *Lambreas-chapter 1*. Open the video "Speak English Like Australians! Chapter 1 Coming to Australia". Alternatively go to: www.speaklikeaustralians.com and click on Audio. Find Chapter 1. Then listen to the video without stopping it and write the missing words in the passage. Listen to the end to improve your confidence in listening to English. Replay it again if you need to. Have fun!

Theo wanted to help his mother, because his father had died when a boat he was travelling in, tipped over. His father was in the boat with his two grandchildren who had been holidaying with their grandparents. Their grandfather was taking them back home to their parents when they ¹_____ fell into the sea and all three died. The grandfather's body was never found, but the children's bodies were carried out of the sea and put on a cart pulled by a horse, for their last trip home. Theo was just twenty years old when that happened. He was the eldest son in the family, born in 1920. He had two brothers and three sisters. He had an older married sister, Panayiota married to Stavros, who owned a ²_____ in the city of Kalamata. Theo's father had sent him to the city of Kalamata to help out at his sister's bakery without pay. When the bodies of her two children arrived in the cart, Theo was there to see and to share his sister's grief and pain. The children's father was so shocked that he lost his mind and was put in hospital. He never got better! Now that his own father had died, Theo felt he had to find work to ³_____ support his family, but it was hard to find a job in Greece during and after the Second World War, in 1945. Then, something terrible happened! There was another war in Greece, from 1946 to 1949. It was a civil war between neighbours and brothers. This war was very bad and many Greeks killed each other. Even Theo had been captured and was a prisoner in a three-storey brick building. For some months, he was tied up and had to lay ⁴_____ on a concrete floor to sleep. This gave him back pain, but he wasn't killed. They let him go free. Lucky!

After these wars Greece was a very poor country and the government had little control. Theo looked hard to find work and he felt lucky when he got a job as a policeman, at about thirty years of age.

At that time, young men were ⁵_____ around the streets of Athens wearing only one arm in their sleeve. The other sleeve was left empty! Maybe it was a new fashion, or maybe they were complaining about the government. The government wanted to stop young men from doing this. They gave all policemen a pair of scissors and told them to cut off empty sleeves. After being through wars, Theo thought this was a bit funny—when he used his scissors to cut the empty sleeves off jumpers and jackets. He didn't mind doing it.

Another thing the Greek Government wanted was to make sure cafes and restaurants were clean places. They ordered policemen to check the businesses that sold food. If a policeman found any dust, they had to give a warning to the owners. On the ⁶_____ visit, if the dust was still there, when the policeman came back to check, the business was closed down! Theo did not like doing this job. He did not like closing down shops and making it hard for people to run a business. Theo's job was a good one and he got good money. But when he saw how unhappy people were, and how hard it was for them when he closed down their shops, Theo felt bad. He didn't want to do this job anymore, so he quit his ⁷_____ as a policeman!

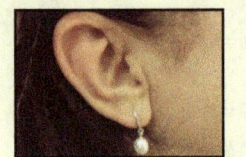

Listening: continued

By this time Theo was in his early thirties. He was tall, handsome and full of hope for the future. What could he do now to get some ⁸_____? He had already helped his sisters find husbands and built houses for them, but now he wanted to help his two younger brothers. Theo knew the olive trees the family owned in their fields were not enough for all three brothers. When each brother got married and had kids, the olives and the oil, from the olive trees, would not bring in enough money. The olive trees were enough for only ⁹_____ family. Theo loved his brothers and decided to help them by leaving the fields for his two brothers. He decided to go overseas for a chance at a better life. Also he knew he would have a job and could send money back to his bothers and his mother. Many migrants had this idea. Theo did not really want to leave Greece, but it would help his family to go and find work ¹⁰_____. Where did he go? To Australia!

So, in October 1953, he got on the ship called Fairstar, which was going to Melbourne. That year, Theo was one of about 75,000 new migrants, who left with much hope, to live in Australia. The Australian Government needed migrants, so it paid for Theo to go to Australia by ship. After that, Theo had to pay back the money by working for two years for the Australian Government. Theo had to work ¹¹_____ the Government told him to go. He had to do any job the Government needed to get done. It was called the Assisted Passage Programme, because they helped people to go to Australia. These men, who came from Europe, built Australia. It was hard work. They built roads, railways, telephone lines, electricity and water dams.

When Theo ¹²_____ in Melbourne he was taken to a place called Bonegilla. Many migrants went there for two or three weeks to learn a bit of English until they got a job from the government. It is still there and is about 300 km north-east of Melbourne. Theo's first job was to make railway lines for the trains in Victoria. He worked like a dog, to show the men he was working with, that he was not lazy. However, the workers, who were all Australians, told him to take it easy. "Just relax a little," they told him. "Take it easy! There's no hurry!" That was the ¹³_____ time he heard the Australian idea of taking it easy and she'll be right mate. Theo soon learnt about tea-breaks and when it was time for a smoko. Theo's job was not easy, but everyone worked hard to build-up young Australia.

His next job was to take the bark off Black Wattle trees in Western Australia. The bark was used for burning and drying animal skins to make shoes. Some left-over ¹⁴_____ was put on paths. "The Tan", the 4 km path around the Royal Botanic Gardens in Melbourne, got its name because tan bark was put on top of it.

When Theo finished his two years of work for the Government he went back to Melbourne. What job could he find? He took a train out of Melbourne to the end of the railway line. His journey ended in Hamilton, in the western part of Victoria. Theo had been to Hamilton before, so he knew 11,000 people lived there. (An ex-Prime Minister, Mr. Malcolm Fraser, lived on a farm there too.) It is a country place and everyone knows it has the ¹⁵_____ sheep in Australia: the Merino sheep. Hamilton has two main streets of shops: in Gray Street and in Thompson Street. Theo got off the train and walked along Gray Street and down Thompson Street, looking at the shops.

Working with Aussies, Theo had learnt to drink beer. He enjoyed drinking one or two glasses. When he saw the Commercial Hotel, he went in to buy a glass of beer. It felt good to be off the train and to sit in a cool place with other men. In those days it was against the ¹⁶_____ for women to drink at a pub: it was only for men.

As he was drinking his beer, he looked around and saw a man wink at him. Theo became very angry and his face turned a red colour. In his country, men only winked at women. Theo didn't want anyone to have any wrong ideas about him. He got up, walked to the man, and was going to punch him in his face! Quickly some men near there stopped him. They asked him what was ¹⁷_____. With his little English Theo told them that the man had winked at him and that it was very rude! He was going to teach this man a lesson! The men explained to Theo that in Australia, a wink can sometimes mean "Good day!" or "How are you going mate?" Theo felt ashamed and said sorry to the man who had winked at him. They shook ¹⁸_____. It had all been a mistake because of their different cultures.

As Theo left the hotel he heard the men laughing at him. His face went ¹⁹_____ again. He knew he must learn many new things about life in Australia. After two years he still had a lot to learn. He must learn to speak English like Australians! It is true that when we don't know things, we make mistakes, but by mistakes we can also learn. Unlucky Theo thought he had heard "How are you going Mike?" After his mistake in the hotel, Theo usually said ²⁰_____ to people and winked at them too. To be extra friendly he often said, "How you going Mike?" All his life, Theo did not know it was "mate", because he thought he had heard "Mike". He just did not know the words were different. His future family did not correct him, because they thought it was his way of ²¹_____ funny! (1601 words)

The answers are below the photo.

Answers: 1. all 2. bakery 3. help 4. down 5. walking 6. next 7. job 8. money 9. one 10. overseas 11. anywhere 12. arrived 13. first 14. bark 15. best 16. law 17. wrong 18. hands 19. red 20. hello 21. being

Page 13

Dictation: aural

Ask the students to take this passage home and to read it and learn how to write the words for a dictation during the next lesson. Alternatively it may be used as an impromptu dictation.

When Theo arrived in Melbourne he was taken to a place called *Bonegilla*. Many migrants went there for two or three weeks to learn a bit of English until they got a job from the government. It is still there and is about 300 km north-east of Melbourne. Theo's first job was to make railway lines for the trains in Victoria. He worked very, very hard to show the workers he was working with that he was not lazy. However, the workers, who were all Australians, told him to take it easy. "Just relax a little," they told him.

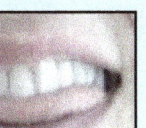

Pronunciation: using IPA symbols for sounds

When you check the meaning of a word in a dictionary, using a book or an app. on your smart phone, the word is usually followed by how to pronounce it. The pronunciation is different from the spelling of the word and is shown in slashes or brackets. The stressed syllable has an accent mark in front of it. For instance, in a dictionary you would find the following for the word "student":

student /ˈstjuːdənt/, n. **1. a** a person who is learning at a college or university etc.
b. a pupil at a secondary school: *Teachers use a variety of materials to inspire their students.*
2. someone who studies a subject with depth and persistence: *a student of insects*

There is an internationally recognised *list of symbols* to represent each sound/phoneme. It is used by linguists and language learners all over the world and is known as **The International Phonetic Alphabet**. The symbols of this alphabet are usually explained using common words that contain each sound. Most often the IPA explanation is located in the front or the back of a dictionary. It looks like this:

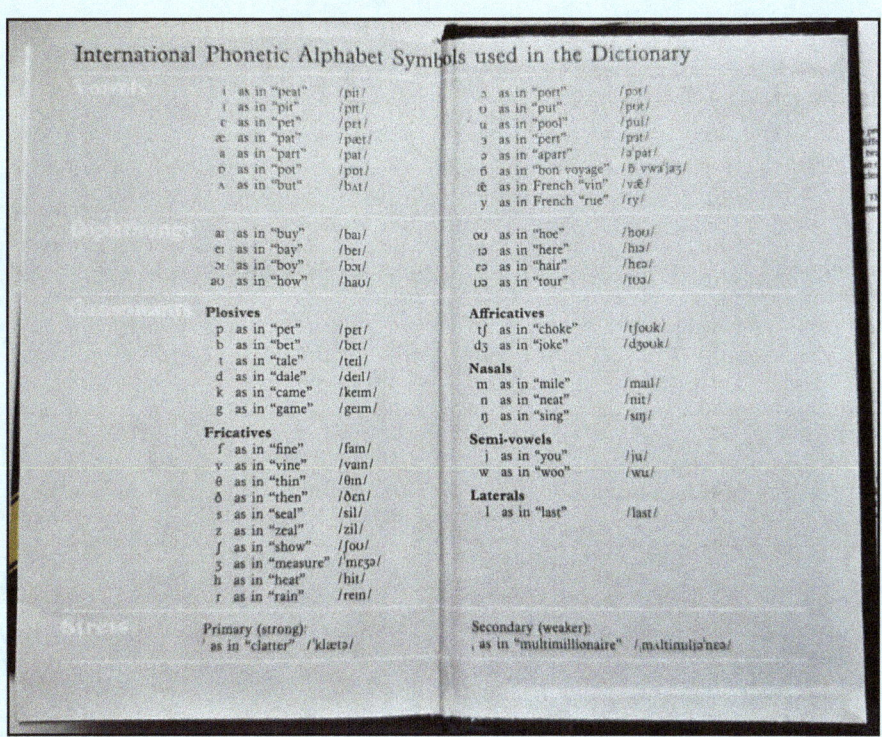

Each language has its own sounds and the **Australian** English Phonemes are on the following page.

Practice for you

For each word, use the IPA to write its pronunciation inside the slashes. The first one is done for you.

1. mother /ˈmʌðə/   2. oven /   /   3. father /   /   4. understand /   /
5. neck /   /   6. *your name* /   /

Answers: 1. /ˈmʌðə/ 2. /ˈʌvən/ 3. /ˈfɑːðə/ 4. /ˌʌndəˈstænd/ 5. /nek/ 6. varying answers

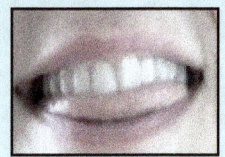

To hear and see how to make these Aussie sounds, use the QR code to my website or go to YouTube. Search for *Zoe Lambreas* and watch the Pronunciation video. I have altered and introduced some International Phonetic Alphabet symbols to more closely resemble Australian sounds; specifically numbers: 4, 8, 15, 20, 21, 22 & 23.

Practise using the general Australian accent by listening to AUDIO of 32 stories from the novel "Speak English Like Australians! by Zoe Lambreas" on the website www.speaklikeaustralians.com This will help learners to practise vocabulary, pronunciation and intonation as they listen to and repeat the stories.

You can order the novel on the website, or buy it from anywhere that sells books. Perhaps your local library has a copy.

Of course, learners can remind themselves which sounds they must practise, by writing the number of these sounds in the box on the top right of the chart below.

The Aussie English Phonemes

Unless whispered, all sounds are voiced, except for the 8 consonants underlined in green.
The symbols are based on the International Phonetic Alphabet (IPA), but are adapted to suit Aussie general pronunciation.

Also, there are 9 non-rhotic /r/ phonemes in teal, as explained below the chart.

The sounds I need to practise are numbers:

Vowels: monophthongs 1–13   Vowels: diphthongs 14–21   Vowels: triphthongs 22–23

1 iː eat	2 ɪ it	3 ʊ put	4 ʊː pool	5 uː blew	14 ɪə near	15 ʌɪ day	
6 e egg	7 ə mother /the schwa/	8 ɜː burn /eː/	9 ɔː born	16 ʊə tour	17 ɔɪ soy	18 ɒuː own	22 ɑɪə iron
10 æ ant	11 ʌ up	12 ɑː barn /ʌː/	13 ɒ on	19 eə hair	20 əɪ my	21 æʊ down	23 æʊə power
24 p pea	25 b be	26 t ten	27 d den	28 tʃ chin	29 dʒ jin	30 k cod	31 g god
32 f fan	33 v van	34 θ thank	35 ð this	36 s sip	37 z zip	38 ʃ show	39 ʒ Asia
40 m met	41 n net	42 ŋ sing	43 h hip	44 l lip	45 r rip	46 w wet	47 j yet

Consonants: all single phonemes 24 – 47
9 non-rhotic /r/ phonemes 7, 8, 9, 12, 14, 16, 19, 22, 23 = /r/ is silent at the end of a syllable or before a consonant.
7 mother /mʌdə/   8 burn /bɜːn/   9 born /bɔːn/   12 barn /bɑːn/   14 near /nɪə/   16 tour /tʊə/   19 hair /heə/   22 iron /ɑɪən/   23 our /æʊə/

Layout based on Adrian Underhill's 44 phonemes of Received Pronunciation from https://www.englishclub.com/images/pronunciation/Phonemic-Chart.jpg adapted by Zoe & used by permission

Pronunciation: the Schwa

One of the most common Australian English sounds is the schwa. This is the phonetic symbol for a shwa /ə/.

It is a soft, unstressed sound. The voice does not go up.
The pitch of the voice is lowish.

1. Listen to your instructor say the words below. Can you hear the shwa in the second syllable of each word?

/ə/	/ə/	/ə/
per / son	cul / ture	wo / man
person	culture	woman

2. Is the syllable with the schwa a stressed or unstressed sound?

3. Listen a second time as your teacher says the words. Notice that each syllable is clearly heard. Each word is said in one breath smoothly and without stopping.

4. Now listen to your teacher say each word and repeat it exactly the same way.

Many Australian English words that end with "r"; "re"; "er" /ɜː/; "ar" /aː/ and "or" /ɔː/ have a schwa sound instead of the /r/ end sound. This makes it a bit confusing for spelling. The "d" ending after a schwa is very soft too in words ending with "ed". The syllable **without** the schwa is stressed and has a higher pitch (because the voice goes up a little bit).

5. Listen for the stressed syllables and the unstressed schwa syllables, as your teacher says these words. Underline the stressed syllables. Circle the unstressed schwa syllables.

however	wanted	sugar
worker	painted	motor
father	decided	wherever
insulted	schooner	later

6. Listen to your instructor say the words again. Repeat each word smoothly in one breath. Say the schwa clearly.

Phonograms: how used in this series of text books

Each **sound** in a word can be **spelt** by a single letter (e, t, f) or by multiple letters (ea, ee, ph). These **written spellings** are called **phonograms**.

A sound can also be written as a **pronunciation/phoneme**. The International Phonetic Alphabet (IPA) is a well-known alphabet used to explain pronunciation and these are written in square brackets [ ] or in slashes / /, as in the first row of the table below. Phonograms are the written sounds we use when we **spell**. Although the phonogram "a" remains the same, there are 7 phonemes (pronunciations). The table shows the phonemes for the letter "a".

Say the words out loud as you read each column.

International Phonetic Alphabet for "a" pronunciation (Refer to page 16.)	/æ/	/ɑ:/	/ʌɪ/	/eə/	/ɔ:/	/ɒ/	/ə/
The phonogram letter "a" can have 7 different possible sounds/phonemes. Please add to this list as you learn more words.	jam	ask	cake	care	call	salt	annual
	mat	class	lake	dare	fall	wander	cathedral
	mash	fast	mate	flare	walk	want	festival
	slap	last	rate	rare	talk	what	several
	splash	pass	skate	stare	stall	was	usual

Tongue Twisters: "a"

Say each tongue twister until you can say it easily and smoothly.

1. Arriving at the Melbourne Art Festival, Arthur and Amy asked for water and then walked to their stall.

2. Aren't Arnold and Alistair annoyed anymore?

3. Anne always arranges her apples and apricots in appealing ways.

4. Apples and almonds always taste awesome after meals.

5. Adam ate almost all the apricots and didn't care!

Conversation Bits: she'll be right; oodles; no worries

The instructor says the conversation, pausing after each "chunk" so the learners can repeat after the instructor, imitating intonation and stress patterns. Repeat the conversation until learners feel comfortable with the colloquial expressions and their intonation is native-like. Ensure learners feel confident when to use the colloquial expressions during an informal conversation.

Learners may then practise in pairs, checking one another's pronunciation and saying the expressions in one breath.

Denis	I can't wait to go to Europe.
Glenys	Yes, I've been looking forward to it for years. I can't believe we're actually going!
Denis	Yep. The plane tickets are in my pocket and the suitcases are packed.
Glenys	Do you think we should've booked our hotel in Paris? Are you sure we'll find something once we get there?
Denis	Oh, don't worry so much. She'll be right! There are oodles of hotels with vacancies. I checked on the Internet.
Glenys	Well if you say so…..
Denis	Yeah, no worries Glenys. Relax!
Glenys	There's our taxi. Let's get to the airport!

Explanations:
she'll be right=everything will be okay
oodles=lots and lots of something
no worries=it's alright, don't be anxious

Spelling: plural nouns

Rule 1 Normally to make a single noun into a plural noun, add "s."
E.g. dad→dads   student→students   house→houses   dog→dogs

Rule 2 But when nouns end with a consonant and a "y" substitute the "y" with "ies."
E.g. country→countries   curry→curries   property→properties   cherry→cherries

Rule 3 When a noun ends with a vowel and a "y" just add "s."
E.g. day→days   valley→valleys   toy→toys   birthday→birthdays   tray→trays

Rule 4 Some nouns ending with "f" or "fe" - replace these endings with "ves."
E.g. leaf→leaves   knife→knives   calf→calves   ourself→ourselves

Rule 5 For nouns ending with "o", we usually just add an "s" but some take "es."
E.g. photo→photos   avocado→avocados   radio→radios   piano→pianos
mosquito→mosquitoes   potato→potatoes   hero→heroes   tomato→tomatoes

Rule 6 When a noun ends with "ss" add "es."
E.g. business → businesses   cross→crosses   boss→bosses   class→classes

Rule 7 Some nouns have irregular plurals.
E.g. man→men   tooth→teeth   basis→bases   axis→axes
aquarium→aquaria   vertebra→vertebrae   die→dice   woman→women

Rule 8 Uncount nouns do not take a plural "s."
E.g. advice, alcohol, anger, butter, coffee, eternity, heat, ice, knowledge, luggage, milk, news, oxygen, politics, psychology, water, weather, wine, work, sugar, salt

Spelling Rule Practice

Next to each word write the number of its rule. The first three words have been done for you.

a) businesses (6)	b) cultures (1)	c) leaves (4)
d) wives	e) governments	f) Australians
g) companies	h) teeth	i) countries
j) glasses	k) keys	l) potatoes
m) organizations	n) collars	o) jobs
p) interests	q) misunderstandings	r) work
s) Aussies	t) deals	u) photos

Answers: d) 4 e) 1 f) 1 g) 1 h) 7 i) 2 j) 6 k) 3 l) 5 m) 1 n) 1 o) 1 p) 1 q) 1 r) 8 s) 1 t) 1 u) 5

Vocabulary: crossword

IDIOM for punching a man = to punch out his lights or to give him a knuckle sandwich

Complete the crossword using vocabulary from Chapter 1 of *Speak English Like Australians!*.

Clues

Across
3. to quickly close and open one eye as you look at someone
6. great feeling of sadness and loss
7. people from overseas who decide to live in another country
9. the name of the Greek immigrant who arrived in Australia in 1953
10. Greece is famous for its _____ oil
11. Proverb or expression for working hard "work like a ____"
12. The Australian Government paid for migrants to come to work and it was called the Assisted _____ Programme.

Down
1. a _____ war is one where people in the same country fight one another
2. to leave your job, to stop doing something, to leave
4. Theo went overseas for a chance at a _____ life.
5. If a policeman found any dust in a café, they had to give a _____ to the owners.
8. slang word for "having a smoke/cigarette"

Answers: Across: 3. wink 6. grief 7. migrants 9. Theo 10. olive 11. dog 12. Passage Down: civil 2. quit 4. better 5. warning 8. smoko

Vocabulary: synonyms

Use the words from the box to replace the words in red, with words of similar meaning.

mum whose husband had died	event	tool	fighting between Greek and Greek
similar feeling	poor	gave	strong decision	make people obey	left
died	hanging down	what people liked wearing at that time	work	destroyed
giving what was needed	funny	very strict and serious	cleanliness and health rules
wealth and comfort of society	really hated	found	more than necessary area
brothers and sisters	not what he believed was right to do	what he thought was funny
young people	unbending	plans for action	looked for	cut	owners
closed for always	lucky	making of these rules to happen	damaged	danger
possible	property	unfair and harsh	what his conscience told him to do

Theo, being the eldest son, keenly felt the responsibility of ¹providing for his ²widowed mother and five ³siblings. Ever since his twentieth year, when his father ⁴perished in a drowning ⁵incident, Theo had ⁶sought ways to establish a ⁷viable future in an ⁸impoverished country, ⁹devastated by the Second World War, and by the ¹⁰civil war that followed. He felt ¹¹fortunate to obtain a policeman's job.

At that time, the ¹²youth were often seen wearing jumpers or jackets with one sleeve unworn and left ¹³dangling: for some reason it had become ¹⁴a fashion fad, or perhaps it was a political protest. The Government ¹⁵issued policemen scissors, to ¹⁶snip off the sleeves left loose by young males. Theo rather found this ¹⁷amusing as it found a ¹⁸resonant chord with ¹⁹his humour. Another Greek Government ²⁰determination was to ²¹enforce strict food and ²²hygiene laws for cafes and restaurants to lift the ²³standards of living. Therefore, much of the police work involved the inspection and a strict ²⁴implementation of these laws. ²⁵Proprietors of public buildings, such as motels and restaurants, were given only one warning if a white-gloved police officer ²⁶detected any dust whatsoever, on their ²⁷premises. If any dust was observed on a second visit, the business was ²⁸permanently shut-down by the police.

This was Theo's job but he ²⁹abhorred the ³⁰draconian and ³¹excessive aspect of this part of his work. To put someone's ³²livelihood in ³³jeopardy by being the means of enforcing ³⁴rigid and ³⁵extreme government ³⁶policies was ³⁷beyond his sense of justice. Although his job was easy and well-paid, Theo lived by ³⁸the dictates of his conscience. If he was to be the ³⁹instrument by which others were ⁴⁰ruined thus unfairly, he would rather suffer himself. He ⁴¹quit his job.

Answers: 1. giving what was needed 2. mum whose husband had died 3. brothers and sisters 4. died 5. event 6. looked for 7. possible 8. poor 9. destroyed 10. fighting between Greek and Greek 11. lucky 12. young people 13. hanging down 14. what people liked wearing at that time 15. gave 16. cut 17. funny 18. similar feeling 19. what he thought was funny 20. strong decision 21. make people obey 22. cleanliness and health rules 23. wealth and comfort of society 24. making of these rules to happen 25. owners 26. found 27. property 28. closed for always 29. really hated 30. unfair and harsh 31. more than necessary area 32. work 33. danger 34. unbending 35. very strict and serious 36. plans for action 37. not what he believed was right to do 38. what his conscience told him to do 39. tool 40. damaged 41. left

Figures of Speech: simile

Similes are a *figure of speech* that use words which don't actually mean exactly what they say. For example: *She was as big as an elephant!* Really, literally, the lady would never be as large as an elephant, but it forms a picture, in the mind, of a very fat person! That is how *figures of speech* are used: to decorate and adorn communication. You can make up your own similes to create an image in your reader's mind, but be aware that there are common or traditional similes too. Other types of figures of speech, allusion, anaphora, etc. will be discussed in the following chapters.

Similes /sɪ məliːz/ help us to picture one thing as being similar to another thing. Similes use the words: "as", "than" or "like" to compare two things together. E.g. ...high **as** a kite; ...thinner **than** a rake; ...slept **like** a log/baby.

Complete the following traditional similes.

1. The old man was as _____ as a bat.
2. Her wicked heart is as _____ as coal.
3. She felt as happy as a _____ at high tide.
4. They were as quick as _____.
5. The children were as _____ as mice.
6. as warm as _____
7. as cunning as a _____.
8. as brave as a _____.
9. as sick as a _____.
10. as strong as an _____.
11. eat like a _____
12. sleep like a _____
13. She was so scared she became as white as a ___.
14. as white as _____
15. They ran as if for their _____.
16. as thin as a _____
17. sing like an _____
18. swim like a _____
19. as wise as an _____
20. fighting like cats and _____
21. He ran as fast as the _____.
22. He is larger than _____.
23. as timid as a _____

Underline the simile in the text.

When Theo arrived in Melbourne he was taken to a place called Bonegilla. Many migrants went there for two or three weeks to learn a bit of English until they got a job from the government. It is still there and is about 300 km north-east of Melbourne. Theo's first job was to make railway lines for the trains in Victoria. He worked like a dog, to show the men he was working with, that he was not lazy. However, the workers, who were all Australians, told him to take it easy. "Just relax a little," they told him. "Take it easy! There's no hurry!"

Answers: 1. blind 2. black 3. clam 4. lightning 5. quiet 6. toast 7. fox 8. lion 9. dog 10. ox 11. horse/pig 12. lamb/log 13. ghost/sheet 14. snow 15. lives 16. rake 17. angel 18. fish 19. owl 20. dogs 21. wind 22. life 23. mouse   The simile is: he worked like a dog

Proverbs: short, well-known expressions that share advice and truth

You can't teach an old dog new tricks.
It is difficult to make someone learn a new way of doing things when they are older. "Your mum will find it difficult to learn to use a mobile now that she is 85 years old!"

It's never too late to learn.
You can always learn something new. "After our children were married, my husband decided to learn how to sail a yacht saying that it was never too late to learn!"

Better the devil you know than the devil you don't know.
It is better to deal with a person or thing you know, although you do not like them, than to deal with a new person or thing because it might be even worse than the person or thing you don't like!

He who does not travel does not know the value of men.
Travelling helps you to appreciate and to understand other people.

Travel is the only thing you buy that makes you richer.
When you travel you see and learn new things that enrich your knowledge and life experience.

Nothing for nothing!
You don't get something without any effort or cost.

There is always a catch!
If someone helps you they expect something in return, even if you think it is free, there is always a cost, something to pay or do in return.

Red sky at night, sailors' delight. Red sky in morning, sailors take warning.
The reddish glow of the morning caused by haze or clouds bring storms.

Locate the proverb in the text and explain its meaning.
Theo left the pub ashamed of himself and shaking his head in wonder. Australia certainly would take some getting used to, even after two years he still felt alienated. It is true that through ignorance we make mistakes, but by mistakes we can also learn. However, would he ever learn?

Answers: The proverb in the text is: "through ignorance we make mistakes, but by mistakes we can also learn". It means that when we are unaware or inexperienced we make errors but we learn from our mistakes.

Writing: building sentences (simple & complex sentences etc.)

To communicate, words must have meaning and make sense. Words are the smallest blocks of communication, just as bricks are the basic parts of a building. To make a sentence, words are organised together to give meaning.

1. The smallest meaningful communication can be as small as a **single word**. Some people would say it is not a proper sentence as the verb is missing. These are **minor sentences**. For instance:

What? Really? Beautiful! Cosy! Thanks.

Minor sentences can include more words to make a meaningful phrase that still does not include a verb.

a) *What house?*
b) *Really very nice.*
c) *How very beautiful!*
d) *How cosy!*
e) *Thanks so very much for your friendship.*

2. After that we can grow the phrase into a clause, by adding one or more **verbs**. It is now a proper sentence. A sentence with one independent clause (that has meaning/a complete thought), is called a **simple sentence**. For example, adding to the above phrases:

a) *What house did you live in last year?*
b) *It was really very nice of you to help me yesterday.*
c) *How very beautiful she looked on her wedding day!*
d) *How cosy you have made your home!*
e) *I want to say thanks so very much for your friendship.*

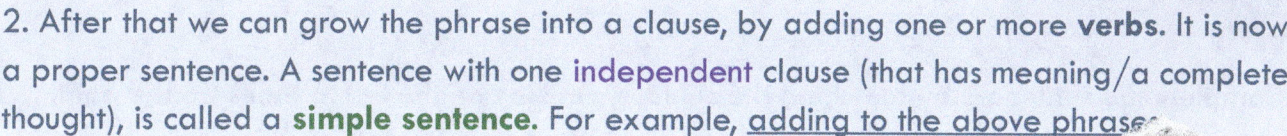

3. We may add *another clause using a conjunction* like "and", "because", "while", "so", "if", "when" etc. When a clause cannot stand alone (a subordinate clause or dependent clause) and depends on the other independent clause to give it complete meaning, the sentence is called a **complex sentence**. Examples follow:

a) *What house did you live in last year while you were studying?*
b) *It was really very nice of you to help me yesterday, so I thank you again.*
c) *Because she had put her hair up, how very beautiful she looked on her wedding day!*
d) *For the first time I realise how cosy you have made your home!*
e) *I want to say thanks so very much for your friendship when I needed it the most.*

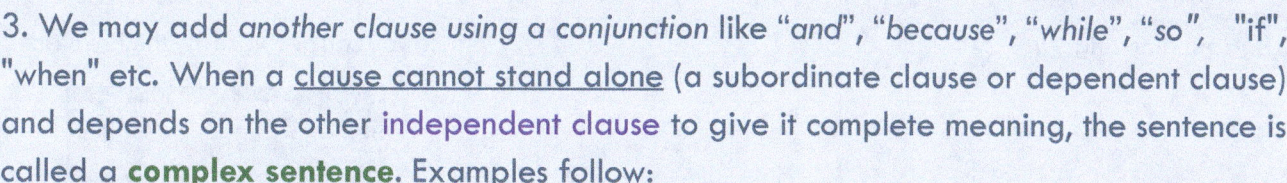

4. When we use two or more independent clauses connected into a sentence with a <u>conjunction</u>, it is a **compound sentence**. Each clause has complete meaning and can stand alone as a simple sentence by itself. For example:

a) *What house did you live in last year <u>when</u> your family moved from Sydney to Melbourne?*

b) *It was really very nice of you to help me yesterday <u>as</u> I couldn't have done it without you.*

c) *How very beautiful she looked on her wedding day <u>and also</u>, the groom was very handsome.*

d) *How cosy you have made your home <u>and</u> the colours are very relaxing.*

e) *I want to say thanks so very much for your friendship <u>because</u> you have helped me in my time of need.*

5. For a **compound-complex sentence** we can add another clause with a conjunction. The sentence has two or more independent clauses <u>and one or more dependent clause</u>/s. Examples are:

a) *What house did you live in last year <u>when</u> your family moved from Sydney to Melbourne, <u>while</u> I was overseas.*

b) *It was really very nice of you to help me yesterday <u>as</u> I couldn't have done it without you <u>even if</u> I worked all day.*

c) *<u>Because she had put her hair up</u>, how very beautiful she looked on her wedding day <u>and</u> the groom was very handsome, <u>although</u> he had not shaved.*

d) *<u>For the first time I realise</u> how cosy you have made your home <u>and</u> the colours are very relaxing.*

e) *I want to say thanks so very much for your friendship, <u>because</u> you have helped me in my time of need, <u>when I needed it the most</u> and no one else stepped up.*

Complete the sentences by matching the clauses/phrases on the left to those on the right.

1. Come into the house
2. He drove in a hurry
3. You are very kind
4. Won't you take some cake
5. It's too late now
6. My friend flew out yesterday
7. What a very cute
8. How amazing

a. and thoughtful as always!
b. to see you after all this time!
c. with your tea?
d. to go shopping for Christmas.
e. and I am leaving tomorrow.
f. little baby!
g. and broke the speed limit.
h. so you can get warm by the fireplace.

Which completed sentences in the table above are:

9. simple?
10. complex?
11. minor?
12. compound?

Writing: joining sentences together

I like ice-cream. Every Friday I buy a Cornetto from the petrol station. I go there to fill up with petrol for the week. My favourite is the vanilla one. I also like the raspberry flavour too.

These sentences are correct and even interesting but they are disjointed (they don't seem connected). What can we do to improve them? Use conjunctions to connect the sentences (and, but, so, because, as, since, although, though, even though). Or use linking words to connect the ideas between sentences (Furthermore,... Also,... However,... Next,... Therefore,... etc.)

Use the conjunctions or linking words in the boxes to better connect the sentences. You might need to remove some words and punctuate the sentence using full stops, commas, capitals or lower case letters.

> however   when   while   as   because
> which   when

Looking out of the window I saw a tall man walk to our front door. ____ It was around dinner time. ____ Who could it be? ____ We weren't expecting anyone. ____ My father answered his persistent knocking. We heard him cry out in delight. ____ It was his brother from Spain! It was a huge surprise for everyone!

Use the words in the box to connect the *ideas* between the sentences in the paragraph.

> indeed   undoubtedly   yet   but   as
> and   since   furthermore   which

____ Martha was feeling very happy. ____ Today was her wedding day. ____ she and Ted had been planning it for months! She could hardly believe it had finally arrived! ____ Surprisingly, she felt relaxed and contented. She wasn't nervous at all. ____, she had had a good night's sleep ____ felt rejuvenated!

Answers: Looking out of the window I saw a tall man walk to our front door, when it was around dinner time. However, who could it be as we weren't expecting anyone? When my father answered his persistent knocking, we heard him cry out in delight, because it was his brother from Spain. It was a huge surprise for everyone!

Undoubtedly, Martha was feeling very happy, since/as today was her wedding day. Indeed she and Ted had been planning it for months! She could hardly believe it had finally arrived! Yet/But surprisingly, she felt relaxed and contented. She wasn't nervous at all. Furthermore, she had had a good night's sleep and felt rejuvenated.

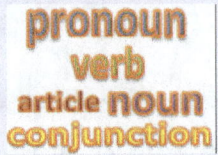

Parts of Speech: a definition of nouns & determiners

There are different types of nouns and determiners. Their main purpose is to identify people, places and things. We will discuss these further in the sections headed *Grammar* as well as *Parts of Speech* throughout this book, easily found on following pages of this colour.

	Parts of Speech			
name	**definition**	**purpose**	**type**	**examples**
NOUNS	names of all things, people, places, ideas	to identify people, places and things	common	student, river, country
			proper	Wantirna, Sunday, Australia, Tom
			abstract	hope, intelligence, loyalty, kindness, love, hate, patience
			collective	flock, choir, team, school, pack
			compound	raindrop, chopstick, homework
			uncount	advice, knowledge, furniture, ice
			gerund	thinking, writing, swimming, cooking
			infinitive	to work; to be; to sing; to do
DETERMINERS	used together with nouns	placed in front of or after a noun to make it clear what the noun refers to	definite article	the
			indefinite article	a, an—before nouns starting with a vowel SOUND
			demonstrative	this, that, these, those
			possessive	my, your, his, her, its, our, their
			quantifier	a few, some, a little, much, many, a lot of, lots of, enough, any, another, other, several, no
			number	one, five, a hundred
			distributive	every, each, all, both, half, neither, either, none
			pre-determiner (used before determiners especially the, a, an) multipliers, fractions, intensifiers, other	twice, three times, multiple times, half, one-third, quite, such, rather, what, all, both
			interrogative	what, whose, which

Page 28

Parts of Speech: determiners

With the help of the table on the previous page, underline and name the types of nouns and determiners in the sentences.

1. Winding its way along the border of NSW and Victoria, is the Murray River.
2. Eva, is the name of the baby.
3. Melbourne, is rated the best place to live in the world.
4. My husband has a lot of knowledge in his field and loves to work.
5. Our neighbours' family, have a holiday house in Frankston.
6. As a student I hated doing homework!
7. I have five siblings who are younger than I.
8. Neither of them is an accountant.
9. There is enough of food for everyone.
10. My mother is nearly 100 years old!

Read the following information and then complete the sentences below by using a determiner.

11. _____ chairs need to be repaired.

12. _____ maiden name was "Heeding".

13. Our house is across the road from _____ place.

14. My son invited _____ of his friends to his birthday celebrations.

15. Do you have _____ book I can read?

Articles and pronouns that go in front of nouns are all generally called **DETERMINERS**

- **Specific** determiners are used when we can identify who/what we are talking about.

    the, this, that, these, those, my, your, his, her, its, our, their

    E.g. The dog ran towards my cat.
    These flowers are his gift to our mum.

- **General** determiners are for speaking about no particular person or thing.

    a, an, all, another, any, both, every, little, much, other, each, few, fewer, many, neither, several, either, more, most, no, some, enough, less, other

    E.g. You can come at any time you like. They have other ideas.
    There is a fly in my soup. I have several black shoes.

Answers: 1. Winding/gerund; border/common; NSW/proper; Victoria/proper; Murray River/proper; 2. Eva/proper; name/common; baby/common 3. Melbourne/proper; place/common; world/common; 4. husband/common; knowledge/uncount & abstract; field/common; to work/infinitive 5. neighbour/common; family/collective; house/common; Frankston/proper; 6. student/common; doing/gerund; homework/compound 7. five/number; siblings/common; 8. neither/distributive; accountant/common 9. enough/quantifier; food/common 10. mother/common 11. These/Those 12. Her 13. their 14. all 15. a

Page 29

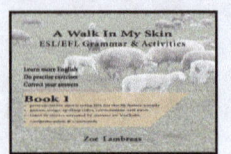

Grammar: uncount/mass and count nouns

There are some similarities and some differences between countable and uncountable nouns. The main difference is that uncount or mass nouns do not take a plural "s" although a few actually end with an "s", but it is part of the word. Some words like "some, a lot of, lots of" can be used with both count and uncount nouns, but "much" & "less" are *only used with uncount nouns* and "many" & "fewer" *with count nouns.*

Write the nouns from the box into their correct columns, for count and uncount nouns.

accommodation	bottle	cash	desk	education	fridge
gold	house	information	jelly	knowledge	language
music	net	oxygen	pen	quality	river	sugar	truck
usage	van	weather	x-ray	yoga	zebra

COUNT NOUNS	UNCOUNT NOUNS

Complete the sentences using "many" or "much".

1. There is not _____ sand in my daughter's sand-pit.
2. When I toured the palace during my overseas trip I saw _____ traditional furniture.
3. Yes thank you, I would love to take home _____ lovely, juicy oranges from your tree!
4. I love to have as _____ ice as possible in my drinks during summertime.
5. I'd like _____ ice cubes in my glass please!
6. Sonia and Jason received _____ sets of dishes as wedding gifts!

Answers: count nouns: bottle, desk, fridge, house, language, net, pen, river, truck, van, x-rays, zebra uncount nouns: accommodation, cash, education, gold, information, jelly, knowledge, music, oxygen, quality, sugar, usage, weather, yoga 1. much 2. much 3. many 4. much 5. many 6. many

Grammar: words to use with count & uncount nouns

Note that some uncount nouns end with "s" but it is not the plural "s". For example: acoustics, aerobics, athletics, classics, diabetes, genetics, gymnastics, linguistics, maths, measles, mumps, news, physics, politics, shingles, etc.

Write suitable words that can be used before each noun like *fewer, less, much, many, your, several, 3 or 4, any etc*. Try not to use "lots of/a lot of" and "some" as these are always possible anyway.

1. Thanks for _____ advice. It was very useful.
2. How _____ houses do you own?
3. He is working very hard. He has ____ jobs.
4. We have _____ work at the moment, so I'm getting heaps of overtime!
5. How _____ countries have you visited?
6. Can I please have _____ apples?
7. I have _____ bread for my sandwich every day.
8. Do you use _____ butter on your bread?
9. How _____ sugar do you take in your coffee?
10. I'm going outside to get _____ fresh air.
11. Our teacher gives us _____ homework, so I work hard.
12. Do you do _____ housework on the weekends?
13. My son likes _____ cheese on his spaghetti.
14. There are _____ fruit trees in our back yard.
15. My husband reads _____ newspaper every morning.
16. Would you like _____ milk in your coffee?
17. I was very happy to hear _____ news about your son's marriage.
18. Do you have _____ memories of your parents?
19. When I travel I only take _____ luggage with me.
20. If I had _____ worries I would reduce my blood pressure!
21. If I had _____ cent for every time I heard you say that, I would be rich!
22. How _____ money do you make in an hour?
23. If I ate _____ sugar and ate _____ more fibre, I would improve my health.

Cross out the incorrect word.

a) I have a lot of work / works to do when I get back home.

b) How many pieces of luggage / luggages are you taking on abroad with you?

c) On his résumé, he wrote down all his previous job / jobs that were relevant to his application.

d) The children asked for their mum's permission / permissions to go to the local milk bar.

e) I asked my neighbour if she had any new / news to share with me.

Answers: 1. the/your 2. many 3. 2, 3, 4 etc./several 4. a lot of/much 5. many 6. some/2, 3, 4 etc. 7. two slices of /2 kilos of etc. 8. any/some/much 9. much 10. some 11. a lot of/lots of/much 12. any/some/much 13. some/lots of/a lot of/a bit of/a little 14. 2, 3, 4 etc./many/a few/a lot of/lots of/several 15. the 16. some/a bit of/a little/any 17. the 18. any/some/many 19. a bit of/a little/a few pieces of 20. fewer 21. a/one 22. much 23. less; some/much/a bit more/a little more CORRECT words are: a) work b) luggage c) jobs d) permission e) news

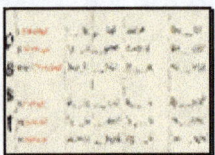

Verb Tenses: to be, to have & to do

The most commonly used verbs in English are: "be", "have" and "do".
Conjugate the verbs in the tables, so you can be confident using them.

TENSES		Present Simple	Present Continuous	Past Simple	Past Continuous	Future Simple
1st person singular	I	I am				
2nd person singular	you		you are living			
3rd person singular	she/he/it			she was		
1st person plural	we				we were living	
2nd person plural	you					you will
3rd person plural	they					

TENSES		Present Simple	Present Continuous	Past Simple	Past Continuous	Future Simple
1st person singular	I	I have				
2nd person singular	you		you are having			
3rd person singular	she/he/it			he had		
1st person plural	we				we were having	
2nd person plural	you					you will have
3rd person plural	they					

TENSES		Present Simple	Present Continuous	Past Simple	Past Continuous	Future Simple
1st person singular	I	I do				
2nd person singular	you		you are doing			
3rd person singular	she/he/it			she did		
1st person plural	we				we were doing	
2nd person plural	you					you will do
3rd person plural	they					

Answers: for the previous page: Conjugate the verbs   BE present simple-you are; she is; we are; you are; they are present continuous-I am living; she is living; we are living; you are living; they are living past simple- I was; you were; we were; you were; they were past continuous-I was living; you were living; she was living; you were living; they were living future simple-I will; she/he/it will; we will; they will; you will. HAVE present simple-you have; she has; we have; you have; they have present continuous-I am having; she is having; we are having; you are having; they are having past simple-I had; you had; we had; you had; they had past continuous-I was having; you were having; he was having; you were having; they were having future simple-I will have; he/she/it will have; we will have; they will have. DO present simple-you do; she/he/it does; we do; you do; they do present continuous-I am doing; she is doing; we are doing; they are doing; you are doing Past simple-I did; you did; we did; you did; they did past continuous-I was doing; you were doing; he was doing; you were doing; they were doing future simple- I will do; you will do; it will do; we will do; they will do

Verb Tenses: the base verb for questions & negatives

1. The *base verb* is the basic form of a verb. It has no tense and is formed from the infinitive verb but without the "to". For example:

infinitive verb	base verb
to do	*do*
to study	*study*
to see	*see*
to drive	*drive*
to walk	*walk*

*The infinitive has no tense and can act as a noun, adjective, adverb and verb.

2. Use the *base verb* to make questions for the present simple and the past simple tenses using the helping/auxiliary verb "to do". It is this verb that makes the tense. For Example:

statement (in present or past simple tenses)	question	negative
She does the cooking.	Does she *do* the cooking? (present tense)	She doesn't *do* the cooking.
We study a lot.	Do we *study* a lot?	We don't *study* a lot.
I saw him yesterday.	Did you *see* him yesterday? (past tense)	She didn't *see* him yesterday.
They drove to the beach.	Did they *drive* to the beach?	They didn't *drive* to the beach.
We walked a long way.	Did we *walk* a long way?	We didn't *walk* a long way.

3. We also use the **base verb** with *modals* like:

        must, should, can, could, will, would, ought to, may, might.

Use the base verb of the one in brackets.

a) They *should* _____ (to be) at the airport an hour before their flight.

b) You *ought to* _____ (to check) the weather before going out!

c) I *didn't* _____ (to grow) tall until I was sixteen years old.

d) You *may* _____ (to come) in now.

e) She *doesn't* _____ (to know) where to go.

f) They *will* _____ (to arrive) tomorrow afternoon.

g) Why *don't* we _____ (to go) out tonight.

h) They *wouldn't* _____ (to be) able to attend if the dinner was on Monday.

Answers: a) be b) check c) grow d) come e) know f) arrive g) go h) be

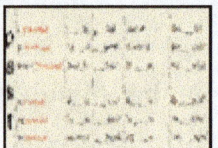

Verb Tenses: the base verb for instructions & directions

Use the **base verb** when giving instructions about making or doing something. For example:

1. To get a phone app, **go** to "Play Store" and **open** it.
2. **Move** down the screen until you **find** the app. you want.
3. **Tap** on the app.
4. **Look** for the words "install" and "decline".
5. **Tap** "install".

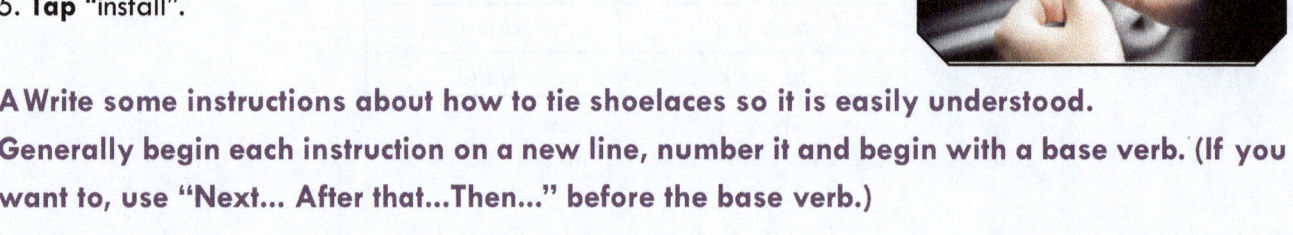

A Write some instructions about how to tie shoelaces so it is easily understood. Generally begin each instruction on a new line, number it and begin with a base verb. (If you want to, use "Next... After that...Then..." before the base verb.)

_____
_____
_____
_____

B Read out your instructions to a friend to see if they are clear and easy to follow.

The **base verb** is also used when giving directions about going somewhere.

For example:

E.g. **Turn** left at the corner and **take** the next right. <u>Next</u> **go** straight ahead until you reach the intersection. <u>Then</u> **take** a left. **Go** down/up the road until the roundabout and **turn** left. <u>After that</u> you will **see** the shops on your right.

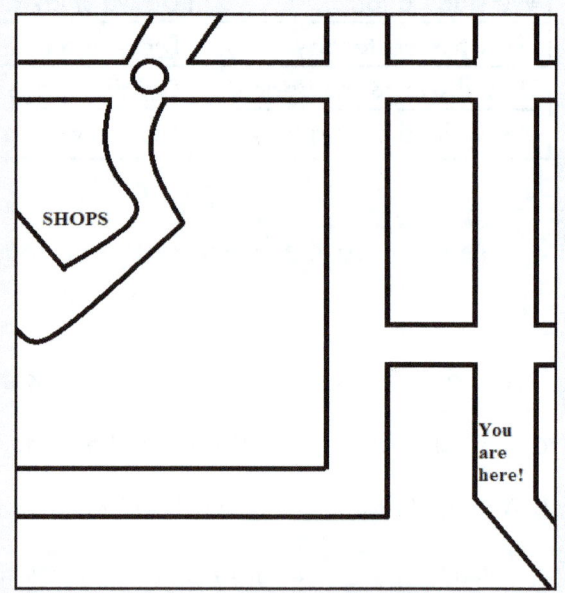

On the map (right) find "You are here!" and follow the directions (above) to draw a line, with arrows, showing the way to go.

A. Write some directions about how to walk from your room to the nearest library.

_____
_____
_____

B. Read out your directions to a friend. Were your directions clear and easy for your friend to understand?

Verb Tenses: "do" and "have" in questions

Conversation Bingo
(DO YOU...? HAVE YOU EVER...? questions)

The instructor practises the pronunciation of the questions and explains the grammar. For example, using the base verb with DO, DOES, so there is no "s" verb ending. With "have" use the past participle to form the present perfect tense. E.g. Have you ever been to Europe?" "Yes, I have been to Europe. I was there in 2019."

Then students mingle and talk to each other. Each student signs the square of the question they have answered "YES" to. Answers must be full, not just "Yes." E.g. "Yes I do like fishing." or "No I don't like fishing."

The first person to get four in a row <u>and</u> five in a column yells, "Bingo!" and the game stops.

Do you like gardening?	Have you ever been to the footy?	Have you ever gone to a circus?	Do you eat sushi?
Do you have a dog or a cat at home?	Do you like speaking English in class?	Do you ride a bicycle these days?	Does your car give you trouble?
Have you ever baked a birthday cake for someone?	Do you go to the beach in the summer?	Does your teacher usually smile in class?	Do you work full-time?
Do you go overseas every year or two?	Does your neighbour talk to you?	Do you feel sea-sick when you go on a small boat?	Do you prefer tea to coffee?
Does your spouse cook almost every day for you?	Do you own your house?	Do you have a garden?	Have you ever smoked?

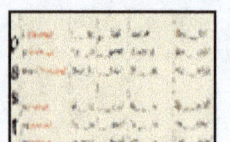

Verb Tenses: "Do you ever...?" & "Have you ever...?"

The word "ever" is used in expressions like: "I have never, ever thought of that!" and "Perry is *ever* so grateful for your help." However, "ever" is most commonly used in questions. "Do you ever...?" (present simple) and "Have you ever...? (present perfect) are both present tenses, but they have different meanings.

"Do you ever...?" refers to what you are doing *these days*, in your normal life. "Do you ever go out for walks after dinner?" would be asking if it is something you do nowadays.
"Have you ever...?" is used to ask about something that could have happened in your *entire* life, from birth until the present time! "Have you ever been skiing?" is asking whether or not you have had this experience in your life.

In the first column, write the correct question beginning for each ending. i.e. "Have you ever..." or "Do you ever..." The first one has been done for you.

Have you ever...	a. liked the same jokes as your brother?
	b. drunk any alcohol?
	c. enjoy horror movies?
	d. been overseas?
	e. feel awkward going to business functions?
	f. forgotten a friend's name?
	g. think about life after death?
	h. miss working now that you are retired?
	i. eaten oysters?
	j. become lost navigating somewhere new?
	k. shop at Fountain Gate Shopping Centre?

Answers: b. Have you ever. c. Do you ever. d. Have you ever. e. Do you ever. f. Have you ever. g. Do you ever. h. Do you ever. i. Have you ever. j. Have you ever. k. Do you ever.

Verb Tenses: "Would you ever...?" & "Would you have ever...if...?"

The word "ever" can also be used with modals like "could, can, should, ought to, would, may, might" to form questions. "Would you ever...?" is for present day possibilities and under what conditions or circumstances. One might ask their friend: "Would you ever consider marrying him?" The answer might be, "Yes, *if/when* he stops smoking."

"Would you have ever...if...?" is for *past life experience possibilities* if you could go back in time and change your behaviour. Of course, this is not possible! But the person asking wants to know *what if*. "Would you have ever trained in swimming if your parents had encouraged you?" (Your parents did not encourage you in the past, but **if** they had, would you have wanted to train for swimming? Consider it now and tell me what you might have done in those past days.) "No I would not have wanted to train, because I was too lazy to get up early every morning and swim for hours before school! I could never have done it!"

Complete the sentences. Then say if it is still a possibility or if it is impossible, because it's about an event already in the past. (And you cannot change what has already happened.)

1. Would you have _____ wanted to find your birth mother _____ you had been given her name?
2. Should you _____ live at home alone since you feel so lonely?
3. Ought _____ ever to lift your grandchildren when you have back problems?
4. Might you _____ ever learnt another language if you _____ lived in another country?
5. Can you ever forgive your husband for _____ so bossy and stubborn?

Answers: 1. ever, if; impossible 2. ever; possible 3. you; possible 4. have, had; impossible 5. being; possible

Chapter 2 Becoming an Aussie
Reading Comprehension

After reading *Speak English Like Australians!*, Chapter 2, answer the following questions in full sentences. Do this by using some of the question for each answer. This will take more writing skill, as sometimes you will need to re-order the words. Answers are below.

1. What did Theo think was different in Australia?
_____
_____

2. Who was the owner of the café and where was he from?
_____
_____

3. What did Andy ask Theo when they first met?
_____
_____

4. Do you think Theo was entirely happy in Australia? Explain.
_____
_____
_____

5. Why didn't Theo ask Argyro to marry him when he was in Greece?
_____
_____

6. What is the meaning of the words "average height"?
_____
_____

7. Circle the correct answer. A dowry is a:-

a) present   b) a large wedding gift given by the bride's family   c) a piece of paper

Answers: 1. In Australia people did things differently, dressed differently and the food was different too. 2. The owner of the cafe was Andy and he was from Cyprus. 3. When they first met, Andy asked Theo where he came from. 4. Theo was not entirely happy in Australia as he felt lonely and wanted to get married. 5. Theo didn't ask Argyro to marry him because she didn't have a dowry and since he had worked hard to provide his sisters with dowries he felt it was only fair that he receive a dowry himself. 6. "Average height" means not too tall and not too short.

Speaking: sharing opinions about cultures

In some cultures young people don't find their own husband or wife. It is arranged by their parents or someone who has the job of "marriage maker". For example, in Australia young Koori men wait for their father's brother to find them a wife. In Ireland young people used to talk to a "match maker" to find them a husband or a wife. The match maker would introduce the young man and woman and then sit between them as they talked and got to know each other. They were never left alone until after their wedding day.

Many Asian and Middle-Eastern cultures still promote arranged marriages. Surveys have shown that these types of marriages are often very successful and happy. Also, divorce is not common in these cultures, but it might be because divorce is thought of as "bad" and it is a stigma to be divorced.

In Western cultures the young people themselves choose their partner. It might be because they feel it is embarrassing that they would need parents to find someone for them! Sometimes they don't even marry, but just live together, not as husband and wife, but as "partners".

During your speaking time, use the ideas on the *following page* for "Being a good listener" and the "Expressions for opinion". These show skills that are very important in the Australian workplace and are highly valued by employers as part of good communication and team work.

Pair Work
Share your opinions regarding arranged marriages with another person.
A. Was yours an arranged marriage, or, do you intend to have an arranged marriage?
B. Would you marry a first cousin? Explain.

Group Work
Talk together in groups and share your opinions about arranged marriages.
1. How should a person choose their future spouse?
2. What things should a person look for in a person they want to marry?
3. Who should decide about the marriage—the kids or the parents or someone else?
4. Theo had to **assimilate,** that is he tried to become like a native Australian. Do you think migrants should **assimilate** into Australian society, or retain their customs as part of a **multi-cultural** society?

Speaking: sharing opinions about cultures (continued)

5. Theo was fortunate to find a job *cold canvassing, or asking for a job even though there is no advertisement asking for workers*. Most jobs (85%) are not advertised and are filled by people "networking" and speaking to each other. How did you or a friend find a previous job?

6. Ask the quietest person in the group to share some opinions of group members with the rest of the class.

Expressions for opinion

I personally feel/believe that….
I suppose….
I reckon….
To my mind….
As I see it….
As far as I can tell…
To my way of thinking….
Quite frankly,…

I honestly feel….
In my opinion….
From my point of view….
It seems to me….
It appears to me that….
Personally, I think….
Really? I don't see it that way because….
As a matter-of-fact I think…

Being a good listener

1. When someone in the group is speaking, the listeners should encourage the speaker. This is an important conversation skill. You can do it by:
   - looking at them and nodding to show you are listening.
   - smiling and nodding.
   - making agreeable noises like yeah/yes, uh huh, mmm.
   (If you remain still and don't say or do anything the speaker will feel uncomfortable. You could experiment with this idea and remain silent listening to someone and note what happens.)

2. Use reflective listening skills: when the speaker pauses, repeat what they have said in your own words (paraphrase) to show you were actively listening and understood what was said. This helps the speaker feel understood and comfortable.

Speaking: sharing personal information

When we ask for personal information, the present tense is often used.

Group Work

1. Practise using the present simple tense. Look at the table below and read the questions. Notice the tense of the questions is the *present simple*. The last is *present perfect*.

2. Answer the questions about yourself in the "Questions" column.

3. In groups of four, spend time speaking and listening to each other. Take turns to ask the other people in your group the questions and then write their answers, along with their names.

Survey your friends for their information.

Questions	Person's Name & Answer	Person's Name & Answer	Person's Name & Answer
Where <u>do</u> you come from? (nationality) What <u>do</u> you do in your free time?	Shadia I <u>come</u> from Iraq. In my free time I <u>like</u> to do gardening.		
<u>Do</u> you want to do more study after English classes? What <u>is</u> your age?			
<u>Do</u> you have any relatives in Australia? Where <u>do</u> you live?			
Why <u>do</u> you want to improve your English? <u>Have</u> you <u>made</u> some friends in Australia? Explain.			

Chant: Assimilation

Practise saying the song until you can sing it easily and keep the rhythm going. Stress the bold text. Practise until you feel it is easy for your tongue to make the sounds and you can stress the correct words to hear the beat of the poem.

First I changed my **language**

Then I changed my **dress**

Next I changed my **accent**

I **sounded** like a **mess**!

So I enrolled in **night** school

My **English** to **improve**

But!!

I **couldn't** get out the **driveway**

My **car** just wouldn't **move**!

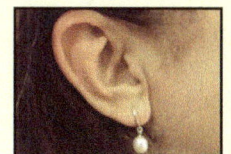

Listening: aural text cloze

The instructor reads the text below, from *Speak English Like Australians!* Chapter 2 Becoming an Aussie. It should be read at normal speed and, if need be, re-read. Learners write the missing words from the text. Alternately, the text is available to listen to, by clicking on *YouTube: Home*. In the search bar, type *Zoe Lambreas-Chapter 2*. Or you could go to the website: www.speaklikeaustralians.com and click *Audio & VIDEO* on the top tab. Click *Chapter 2*. Or use the QR code on your phone. The answers are at the end of the next page and up-side-down.

Theo left the hotel smiling to himself and shaking his ¹_____. Australia sure was a strange place! The people had different ²_____ of doing things and food like olives and feta cheese were unavailable in the local shops, in 1953! In those days the Australian Government wanted ³_____ to change their culture and become like other Australians. They did not want *New Australians* to keep their old ⁴_____. Migrants had to change their old ways and become Australians. That was the law. Theo felt uncomfortable because his thinking and the Greek culture were different from the Aussie culture! He wanted to fit in.

As Theo walked down Gray Street, the main street, he felt hungry. Then he saw the "Lucas Café" ⁵_____. What he did not see was that there was a Greek flag flying on top of the shop. Anyway, a nice smell came from the ⁶_____. Theo knew the smell of "chips". He went inside to buy some. The ⁷_____ was long and cool and there were tables and chairs on the left and right sides. At the front, ⁸_____ the door there was a bench. Behind this bench Theo could see there were lollies, chocolates, cigarettes and ice-creams for sale. There was a ⁹_____ standing who was looking at him with interest. (continued on the next page)

Page 43

Listening cloze: continued

"Chips plis," said Theo. The man smiled at Theo's accent and asked him where he was from. They talked for a little time and got to know each other. The man behind the bench was ¹⁰_____ and he was the owner of Lucas Café. Andy was a Greek from Cyprus, a British Colony. His ¹¹_____ was pretty good, because he learned it in ¹²_____, in primary school. While they talked, Theo told Andy he needed a job. Lucky for Theo, Andy needed a worker and gave Theo a job, peeling potatoes and helping in the ¹³_____. After a few months, Theo was chopping potatoes and grilling ¹⁴_____ like an expert! As the months passed, Andy's two business partners left the café to live in ¹⁵_____. When this happened, Theo asked to be Andy's new partner and a part owner of the business. Andy, who spoke good English would be the front man speaking with the customers, while ¹⁶_____ would do most of the cooking and cleaning at the back of the shop. (The two men worked well together for fifteen years, before the shop closed.)

The café was very busy and Theo had to work ¹⁷_____ hours: from 7 or 8am until 8 or 9pm. By the time he had ¹⁸_____ up and locked up the shop, he sometimes didn't get home till 10pm! Theo always walked home, about 900 metres. He could not drive and the cool night air felt good, after working inside all day. Theo lived with Andy and his small family in French Street, across the road from the Botanical Gardens.

Theo was doing well in his new country. He was trying to be like an ¹⁹_____ and learn about the Aussie culture. But something was missing! He did not feel okay with his life! He was feeling alone. He found he was always thinking about a lovely girl, Argyro, he had met in Greece. He had only spoken to her a few times. She had not ²⁰_____ with him as some girls did. Theo remembered the funeral of her uncle when he spoke to her and she was serious and polite. She was also beautiful. He had thought about marrying her, but he did not ask her to marry him, because her family was very ²¹_____. He did not have much money to take a wife. In those days a girl needed a dowry to help her marry. Theo had worked hard in Greece to give two of his sisters dowries, so they could find husbands. At that time he thought it was right to get a dowry himself, from his wife's family. In the villages in Kalamata where he had lived, the dowry custom was ²²_____. Everyone gave dowries to their daughters. But poor Argyro had no dowry.

What was Argyro like? She was honest, hard-working and nine years younger than Theo. She was of average height and build. Her hair was shortish, wavy and dark brown. Her eyes were ²³_____.

Now in Australia, four years after he had met Argyro, Theo wanted to start a family. He felt lonely. He wanted to write a letter to Argyro's father to ask him a question. Did Argyro want to come to Australia to get married to him? By now Theo did not want a dowry, but would Argyro leave her country, and all the people she loved to marry him? Would she take a ²⁴_____ at a new life in a strange country?

(796 words)

Answers: 1. head 2. ways 3. migrants 4. culture 5. sign 6. door 7. shop 8. beside 9. man 10. Andy 11. English 12. Cyprus 13. kitchen 14. steaks 15. Melbourne 16. Theo 17. long 18. cleaned 19. Aussie 20. flirted 21. poor 22. common 23. hazel 24. chance

the gates of the Botanical Gardens in Hamilton

Argyro aged 25 years

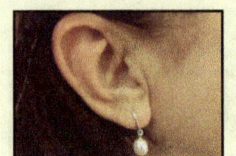

Listening to a song for general meaning

Go to YouTube and listen to the song "I'm all out of love, I'm so lost without you" sung by Air Supply on
https://www.youtube.com/watch?v=ySg2H0KzjjE

1. Which answer best describes the song:

a) he wants to renew their love   b) he doesn't want her back   c) he feels happy not to feel lost

2. Would you say the mood of the song is:

d) happy   e) exciting   f) sad   g) angry

3. "I'm all out of love" means:

h) he hates the person he used to love

i) he feels glad to be free

j) he is so full of love for this person that he can't feel love for anyone else

Answers: 1a) 2f) 3j)

Page 46

Dictation: listening to "chunks" of prose

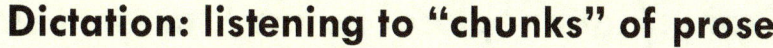

Words in sentences naturally belong together and are referred to as "chunks" of words. Chunks may be longer or shorter, depending on the decision and preference of the person reading. For instance, from the dictation below, **"Theo asked to be Andy's new partner"** you may use shorter chunks like:

Theo asked to be (one chunk)

Andy's new partner (one chunk)

While reading, a pause should not come in the middle of a chunk, as the meaning becomes obscure. You would **not** say "Theo asked to" because the "be" belongs with the chunk.

The instructor or learner reads a chunk of text in one breath, repeating as necessary. When the dictation is completed, correct the dictation as suits the learners.

As the months passed,
Andy's two business partners
left the café to live in Melbourne.
When this happened,
Theo asked to be Andy's new partner
and a part owner
of the business.
Andy, who spoke good English
would be the front man
speaking with the customers,
while Theo would do
most of the cooking and cleaning
at the back of the shop.
The two men worked well together
for fifteen years,
before the shop closed.
The café was very busy
and Theo had to work long hours:
from 7 or 8am until 8 or 9pm.
By the time he had cleaned up
and locked up the shop,
he sometimes didn't get home till 10pm!
Theo always walked home,
about 900 metres.
He could not drive
and the cool night air felt good,
after working inside all day.

Pronunciation: plural nouns & present simple verbs

Refer to *The Aussie English Sounds Chart* in Chapter 1.

At the **beginning of a word** "s" can only be pronounced /s/ and "z" is pronounced /z/. For example: sunny, subway, zero, zebra

But at the **ends of words**, "s" has 3 sounds: unvoiced /s/, voiced /z/ and voiced /əz/. For example: cats, dogs, businesses.

Therefore, when there is a plural "s" at the **end of a noun/verb**, it sounds like /s/ in words ending with the unvoiced sounds /p/, /t/, & /k/. For example: lips, students, rocks.

However, when the **end of a noun/verb** has a voiced sound, then the plural "s" is pronounced the voiced /z/. For example: means, wigs, clothes, loves, digs, involves.

Finally, if a noun/verb **already ends with** / ʃ/, /tʃ/, /s/, /dʒ/, then the plural must end with "es" and makes the sound /əz/.
For example: buses, boxes, confuses, faces, churches, matches, dishes, garages, badges.

Pronunciation practice
For plural "s" there are three possible sounds. Practise saying each column of noun words. Can you think of some nouns to add?

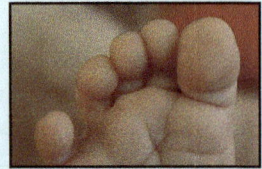

/s/ after unvoiced sounds /p/, /t/, /k/, /f/, /θ/	/z/ for all voiced sounds except for /dʒ/	/əz/ after /ʃ/, /tʃ/, /s/, /dʒ/
creeps	toys	dishes
mops	mows	washes
sheets	moves	bunches
adults	girls	churches
blocks	kababs	munches
comics	lads	dresses
chefs	toes	dismisses
graphs	roars	boxes
cloths	clothes	foxes
broths	rims	circuses
deaths	thins	fridges

Pronunciation: reminder
Practise the pronunciations of the Aussie Sounds in Chapter 1 Pronunciation.

Pronunciation: minimal pairs /s/ and /z/

Learners take turns to say one word twice from each pair. The listener tells the speaker which word was said, either the first or the second word in the pair. If the pronunciation was clear and the hearer could discern the sounds, the correct word is chosen. The instructor can help with pronunciation and discerning of sounds as required by learners.

Learner A to say learner B to listen

1. sap   zap
2. loose   lose (not win)
3. sip   zip
4. Sue   zoo
5. said   zed
6. mossy   mozzie (slang = mosquito)
7. cease   seize
8. face   phase

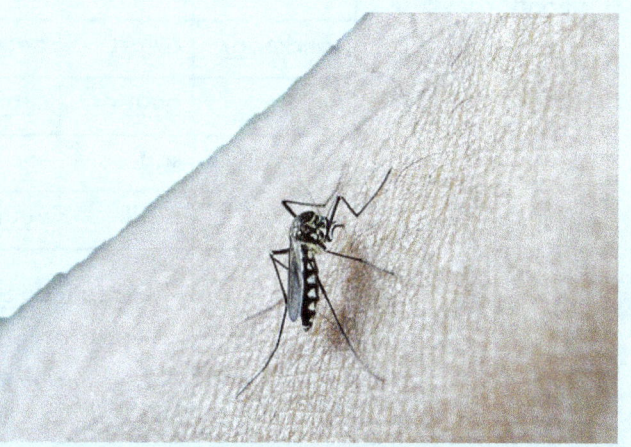

Learner B to say learner A to listen

A) advice   advise (verb)
B) price   prize
C) Lisa   Liza
D) ice   eyes
E) lice   lies
F) buses   buzzes
G) seal   zeal
H) close (to me)   close (the door)

Tongue Twisters: "s" and "z"

Try these sentences. Say them smoothly in one breath and keep practising until you do not get *tongue tied*!

1. Bob's businesses sell hoses, clothes, scissors and numerous sundry items.
2. You might lose your coins if the clip is loose on your purse.
3. Smiling and sitting, relaxing with Sam, Susan saw some haze and smelled smoke on Sunday.
4. So Samantha, did Sally sell Simon's surfing stuff during Saturday's sale since we last met?

Phonograms: "ar", "au" & "ai"

The pronunciations for the letter combinations "ar", "ai", and "au" are explained in the table.

IPA for "ar", "au" & "ai" pronunciations	/aː/	/ɔː/	/ɒ/	/ʌɪ/	/e/	/ə/
The phonogram "ar" can have two sounds and the phonogram "au" can have two different sounds too. Spellings using the letters "ai", can have three sounds.	arm	warm	sausage	rain	air	bargain
	carpet	wharf	Aussie	claim	again	captain
	seminar	warn	Australia	complain	against	certain
	handlebar	dwarf	because	explain	said	curtain
	jaguar	quarter	cauliflower	raise	hairy	fountain
	guitar	sauce	somersault	waist	pair	portrait
	party	audit	vault	strain	stair	mountain
		Exceptions: aunty, chauffer, gauge, mauve		*Exceptions:* plait, aisle		

Use the words from the table above to label these 7 photos.

Tongue Twisters: "ai"

Try these sentences. Say them smoothly in one breath.

1. Abigail aims not to fail but to gain praise as a maid.
2. Gail said she sprained her arm and complained she was in pain as she played in the rain!
3. The rain in Spain falls mainly on the plain.

Conversation Bits: a fair go

Theo had struggled to provide his own sisters with their dowries, therefore, he had thought it only fair to receive a dowry himself, from his intended's family. However, her family could not provide her with a dowry as they were very poor. Consequently, he had decided not to propose to her. It was his sense of a "fair go" that had dampened his marriage plans!

Repeat the conversation until your intonation is native-like. Say the expression in one breath. Ensure you feel confident when to use the colloquial expression "a fair go" during informal conversation.

Denis	Tomorrow I'm going to Sydney for work!
Glenys	Really! But I thought your boss always wanted you here in Melbourne!
Denis	That's true but I told him to give me **a fair go**. I wanted a chance to show him I could get some good results if he gave me a chance.
Glenys	Well that's great. Who normally goes?
Denis	He does himself, or he sends Robert.
Glenys	Well it shows that he finally trusts you. He thinks you will do a good job.
Denis	Yes, I'm sure I will. I know all our clients in Sydney because I always dine with them when they're here on business.
Glenys	Let me help you pack your bag!
Explanation: a fair go = used to ask someone to be reasonable or fair, to be treated equally and fairly	

Spelling: the 350 most commonly used words in English
http://www.world-english.org/english500.htm (used by permission)

Make sure you can spell these words because they are repeatedly and commonly used daily.

Rank	Word								
1	the	26	from	51	which	76	more	101	any
2	of	27	or	52	do	77	day	102	new
3	to	28	had	53	their	78	could	103	work
4	and	29	by	54	time	79	go	104	part
5	a	30	hot	55	if	80	come	105	take
6	in	31	but	56	will	81	did	106	get
7	is	32	some	57	way	82	my	107	place
8	it	33	what	58	about	83	sound	108	made
9	you	34	there	59	many	84	no	109	live
10	that	35	we	60	then	85	most	110	where
11	he	36	can	61	them	86	number	111	after
12	was	37	out	62	would	87	who	112	back
13	for	38	other	63	write	88	over	113	little
14	on	39	were	64	like	89	know	114	only
15	are	40	all	65	so	90	water	115	round
16	with	41	your	66	these	91	than	116	man
17	as	42	when	67	her	92	call	117	year
18	I	43	up	68	long	93	first	118	came
19	his	44	use	69	make	94	people	119	show
20	they	45	word	70	thing	95	may	120	every
21	be	46	how	71	see	96	down	121	good
22	at	47	said	72	him	97	side	122	me
23	one	48	an	73	two	98	been	123	give
24	have	49	each	74	has	99	now	124	our
25	this	50	she	75	look	100	find	125	under

Page 52

Spelling: the 350 most commonly used words in English

To help you remember these words, read and then write them every day for one week.

126	name	151	sentence	176	follow	201	head	226	between
127	very	152	set	177	act	202	stand	227	city
128	through	153	three	178	why	203	own	228	tree
129	just	154	want	179	ask	204	page	229	cross
130	form	155	air	180	men	205	should	230	since
131	much	156	well	181	change	206	country	231	hard
132	great	157	also	182	went	207	found	232	start
133	think	158	play	183	light	208	answer	233	might
134	say	159	small	184	kind	209	school	234	story
135	help	160	end	185	off	210	grow	235	saw
136	low	161	put	186	need	211	study	236	far
137	line	162	home	187	house	212	still	237	sea
138	before	163	read	188	picture	213	learn	238	draw
139	turn	164	hand	189	try	214	plant	239	left
140	cause	165	port	190	us	215	cover	240	late
141	same	166	large	191	again	216	food	241	run
142	mean	167	spell	192	animal	217	sun	242	don't
143	differ	168	add	193	point	218	four	243	while
144	move	169	even	194	mother	219	thought	244	press
145	right	170	land	195	world	220	let	245	close
146	boy	171	here	196	near	221	keep	246	night
147	old	172	must	197	build	222	eye	247	real
148	too	173	big	198	self	223	never	248	life
149	does	174	high	199	earth	224	last	249	few
150	tell	175	such	200	father	225	door	250	stop

Spelling: the 350 most commonly used words in English

251	open	276	care	301	enough	326	black
252	seem	277	second	302	plain	327	short
253	together	278	group	303	girl	328	numeral
254	next	279	carry	304	usual	329	class
255	white	280	took	305	young	330	wind
256	children	281	rain	306	ready	331	question
257	begin	282	eat	307	above	332	happen
258	got	283	room	308	ever	333	complete
259	walk	284	friend	309	red	334	ship
260	example	285	began	310	list	335	area
261	ease	286	idea	311	though	336	half
262	paper	287	fish	312	feel	337	rock
263	often	288	mountain	313	talk	338	order
264	always	289	north	314	bird	339	fire
265	music	290	once	315	soon	340	south
266	those	291	base	316	body	341	problem
267	both	292	hear	317	dog	342	piece
268	mark	293	horse	318	family	343	told
269	book	294	cut	319	direct	344	knew
270	letter	295	sure	320	pose	345	pass
271	until	296	watch	321	leave	346	farm
272	mile	297	colour	322	song	347	top
273	river	298	face	323	measure	348	whole
274	car	299	wood	324	state	349	king
275	feet	300	main	325	product	350	size

Vocabulary: unfamiliar words

The IDIOM for "finally making a decision at last" = "to bite the bullet". For instance: He *bit the bullet* and stopped procrastinating, for he decided to ask her to marry him! He had put off making a decision for two years, but now he was determined to ask her to be his wife, even though she might reject him!

Choose five new words or expressions from Chapter 2 and use a dictionary to explain their meanings.

1. _____
2. _____
3. _____
4. _____
5. _____

Synonyms

Pair the synonyms by matching each number with its correct letter. The words are found in *Chapter 2 Speak English Like Australians!*

1.	regarding	A.	bench
2.	counter	B.	settlement
3.	colony	C.	watching
4.	obliged	D.	reviving
5.	refreshing	E.	justice
6.	indoors	F.	compelled
7.	lodged	G.	wedding gift given by the family of the bride or groom to help their son or daughter marry
8.	consequently	H.	roomed
9.	fair play	I.	therefore
10.	dowry	J.	inside

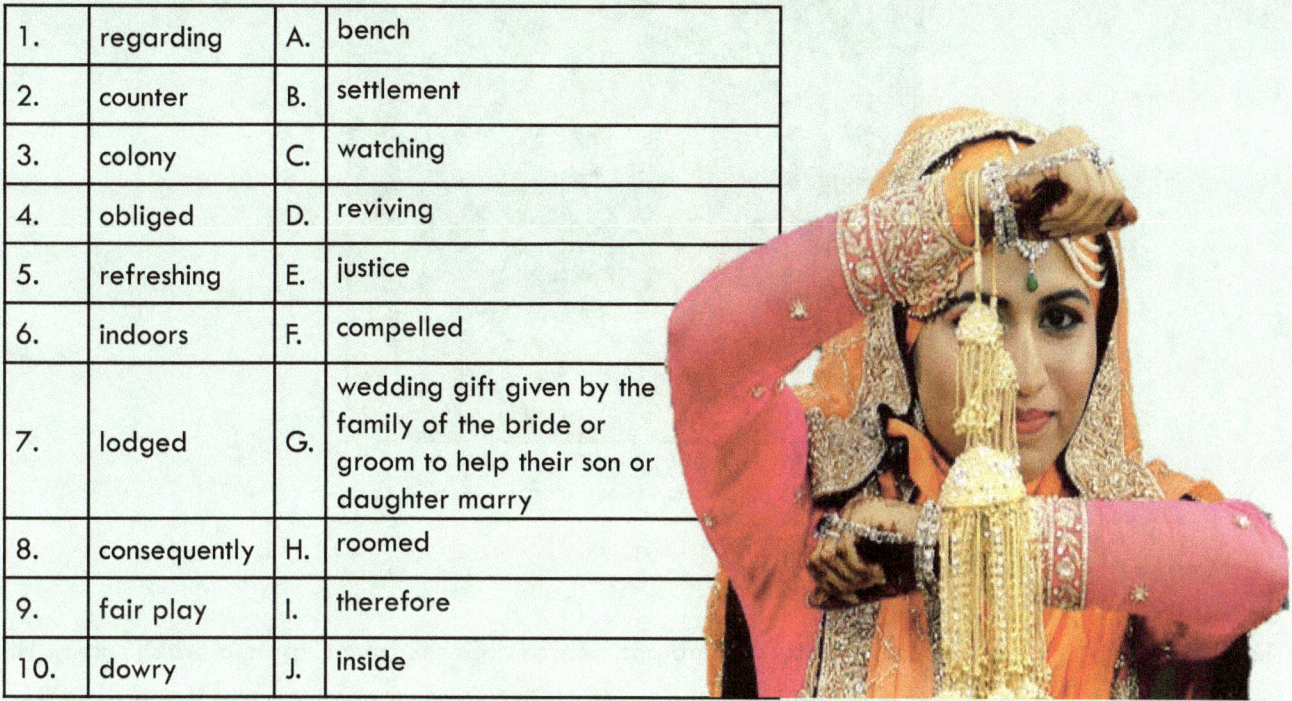

Answers: 1C 2A 3B 4F 5D 6J 7H 8I 9E 10G

Figures of Speech: allusion

An allusion is when you refer to something indirectly. It is a good writing technique because it develops different ideas and relationships using only a few words. Readers must be able to understand the allusions and be familiar with the hidden meanings behind the words or they will not know what is being alluded to!

Examples:

"My daughter's new husband is a real Romeo!"
By describing him as a "Romeo," it *alludes* to the passionate lover in the play called *Romeo and Juliet*, written by William Shakespeare in 1595. Therefore, the man being *alluded to* as a "Romeo" is a passionate lover.

William Shakespeare (1564–1616)

"My father-in-law earned a lot of money and was a Croesus."
Croesus was the king of Lydia from 560–547BC. Around this time the Lydians were the first people in Asia Minor to make gold and silver coins. Croesus was a very rich man.

Greek King of Lydia–King Croesus
https://en.wikipedia.org/

Underline the allusion.

The other man, Andy, was the owner of Lucas Café and he was a Greek from Cyprus, a British colony. His English was pretty good, because he had learnt the language in Cyprus as a young child. Anyway, to Theo Andy was a Shakespeare! While they talked, Theo told him he needed a job.

Answers: Andy was a Shakespeare!

Proverbs: know and do

Write an example from life to explain each proverb more clearly.

1. Customs are stronger than laws.
Traditional ways of doing things are so normal and so long-established that they are more important to follow and harder to break than laws.

2. Ignorance is bliss.
When you are unaware of something that is wrong, then you are at peace and feel untroubled and happy. It is more comfortable not to know some things.

3. Do not be wise in your own eyes; Fear the Lord [with reverent awe and obedience] **and turn** [entirely] **away from evil.** – The Bible, Proverbs 3:7

4. A wise son accepts his father's discipline, but a scoffer does not listen to rebuke. – The Bible, Proverbs 13:1

5. The person who says it cannot be done should not interrupt the person doing it. Chinese proverb

6. If a thing's worth doing, it's worth doing well.
If you are going to do something make sure you put all your effort into it and do as good a job as you can do!

Writing: a paragraph

A paragraph is made up of two or more sentences about **one** topic.

As shown below, a paragraph begins with a topic sentence (TS= a general sentence) to introduce the topic. After that, write sentences of examples, explanations or statistics (1-5): <u>to support the topic sentence</u>. Lastly, write a final sentence (FS) that concludes the paragraph. The final sentence can be written a different way to stress the topic. If you have information from a source in an *in text citation* (ITC), then a fuller mention of it must appear in a Reference (R), listed at the end of the essay of writing.

For example:

(TS) Smoking causes dangerous health problems. [1] One such common health problem related to smoking is cancer. [2] In 2010 lung cancer was the fifth most common cancer in Australia [ITC] (http://canceraustralia.gov.au). [3] Also it has been proven that smokers have an increased chance of having heart disease later in life. [4] In Australia, cigarette packets have warnings on them to show smokers the dangers. [5] Furthermore, many doctors say that passive smoking is even more harmful than smoking and can cause lung diseases and cancer too. (FS) It seems clear that smoking is a dangerous habit and should be avoided.

[R]Reference

< http://canceraustralia.gov.au/affected-cancer/cancer-types/lung-cancer/lung-cancer-statistics>

Of course, in your writing you would not include the "TS" and "FS" etc. These have been included in the example to help your understanding.

1. Please underline the linking words in the above paragraph. (The answers are below.)

2. Choose a topic from below and write a paragraph.

Melbourne's weather

Flooding and heavy storms

Our Prime Minister

They keep their dog inside their house

Hay fever

Building my dream-house

Australian laws

Dentists

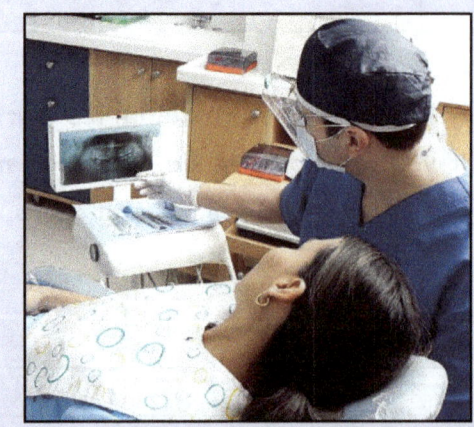

Answers: Smoking causes dangerous health problems. One such common health problem connected to smoking is cancer. In 2010 lung cancer was the fifth most common cancer in Australia. Also it has been proven that smokers have an increased chance of having heart disease later in life. In Australia, cigarette packets have warnings on them to show smokers the dangers. Furthermore, many doctors say that passive smoking is even more harmful than smoking and can cause lung diseases and cancer too. It seems clear that smoking is a dangerous habit and should be avoided.

Parts of Speech: nouns

Nouns are names of people, places and things. Nouns usually have "a/an/the" in front of them, except for uncount nouns, infinitive nouns and gerunds. Many nouns can be plurals. **Noun types include:**

- COMMON NOUNS – people, cities, books, doctor, pianos, street, country, rivers, mountains, suburbs, university, school, apple

- PROPER NOUNS – John, Melbourne, Melways, Dr Jim, Victoria, Stud Road, Thailand, the Yarra River, Mt Dandenong, Wantirna, Swinburne TAFE, Mt Fuji

- ABSTRACT NOUNS – hope, love, beauty, kindness, greed, opportunity, courage

- COLLECTIVE NOUNS – team, bunch, choir, herd, band, government, family, mob

- COMPOUND NOUNS (two or more words used together as one noun) – raindrop, can-opener, swimming pool, brothers-in-law, homework, carwash, playgroup, chopsticks, fingernail, address book, film star

- UNCOUNT/MASS NOUNS (take no plural "s") – hair, advice, knowledge, work

- GERUNDS (-ing words used for names of actions) – <u>Running</u> is good exercise. I enjoy <u>eating</u>. She is good at <u>dancing</u>.

- INFINITIVE NOUNS – <u>To swim</u> is fun. <u>To work</u> makes me tired. I like <u>to read</u>.

Can you underline the 29 nouns in the list?

books	the	kiosk	it
run	Sue	student	hair
running	am eating	will go	as
beauty	is	think	goes
pretty	Peter	went	flock
tall	doctor	household	but
biggest	street	with	lady
Swinburne	High Street	her	bus
to write	because	beach	boy
and	Mr Morrison	Sunday	door
carpet	vase	school	into
advice	knowledge	to dream	work

Individually (or in pairs) write down one object in the room for each letter of the alphabet. You may also use a person's name but it must be capitalised! The first to finish correctly wins.

Answers: books, running, beauty, Swinburne, to write, carpet, advice, Sue, Peter, doctor, street, High Street, Mr Turnbull, vase, knowledge, kiosk, student, household, beach, Sunday, school, to dream, hair, flock, lady, bus, boy, door, work

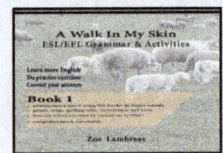

Grammar: word order in sentences

A) In English most sentences follow the pattern (SVO):
subject + verb + object
I like chocolate.
Does Mei like chocolate?

EXCEPTIONS: In many Yes-No questions; WH- questions and "or" questions the verb precedes the subject.
E.g. Are they coming?   When will you be twenty?   Did she have tea or coffee?

B) Usually the verb is followed by the place (where).
E.g. Peter drives to work.   They live in Dandenong.

C) Time (when) goes after place. Alternatively, time words can be at the beginning of a sentence.
E.g. I'll be going to school at 11 o'clock.   At 11 o'clock I'll be going to school.

D) **Frequency adverbs** (usually, generally, often, always, sometimes, occasionally, seldom, rarely, never) go in front of simple verbs (walks, walked). Also they go in front of "to have" verbs.
E.g. Amy never walks to school.   They always had an argument in the car.

E) **Frequency adverbs** go after a "to be" verb.
E.g. We are always happy to come to class.

F) **Frequency adverbs** go after the first verb in perfect tenses (has gone, had gone, will have gone) and continuous verbs (is going, had been going, will have been going).
E.g. Amy has rarely walked to school.   Fred will sometimes be shopping here for hours.
*But in negative sentences won't goes after the adverb: Fred sometimes won't cycle here.

G) "**Both**" and "**all**" follow the same rules as frequency adverbs. (D, E, F)
E.g. They all walk to school.   They are both here now.   We are both working at the shop tonight.

Also "**both**" and "**all**" can be first in a sentence when talking of nouns/pronouns.
E.g. All of them are coming.   Both girls are very clever.

H) Words like: **everyone, everybody, nobody, no one, someone, somebody, etc.** go in front of all verbs, even "to be" verbs & perfect/continuous verbs. They are treated like the third person (she/he/it).

E.g. **Nobody** was in the room.   **Everyone** loves Raymond.   **Everybody** has gone.

But it is different for questions when these words go *after* verbs → Where is **everyone**?
Is **anyone** coming?   Why isn't **anyone** here yet?

Rewrite each sentence and organise the words in the correct order.

1. He coming is later? _____
2. The dog the man bit on the leg. _____
3. Do drink lots of coffee they? _____
4. Martha along the beach walks. _____
5. We in the work city. _____
6. Our neighbours in enjoy jogging the park. _____
7. She for school will leave in the morning. _____
8. After the party went they home. _____
9. Apollo 11 in July 1969 landed on the moon. _____
10. My always grandparents eat early. _____
11. Sonia and Sally usually doughnuts have. _____
12. The school has a holiday on Cup Day rarely. _____
13. They often seen walking hand in hand were. _____
14. Has arrived anybody? _____
15. She is late for sometimes class. _____
16. We were reading in the often library. _____
17. Jenny already has left. _____
18. Why Jenny has already left? _____
19. Have come you ever here for dinner? _____
20. Both are coming over to your place of us. _____
21. We are feeling very happy about your all decision. _____
22. Wendy and Michael both are very tall. _____
23. How everyone is feeling today? _____
24. Saw them no one as they left the room. _____

Answers: 1. Is he coming later? 2. The dog bit the man on the leg. 3. Do they drink lots of coffee? 4. Martha walks along the beach. 5. We work in the city. 6. Our neighbours enjoy jogging in the park. 7. In the morning she will leave for school. or She will leave for school in the morning. 8. After the party they went home. or They went home after the party. 9. Apollo 11 landed on the moon in July 1969. or In July 1969, Apollo 11 landed on the moon. 10. My grandparents always eat early. 11. Sonia and Sally usually have doughnuts. 12. The school rarely has a holiday on Cup Day. or On Cup Day the school rarely has a holiday. 13. They were often seen walking hand in hand. 14. Has anybody arrived? 15. She is sometimes late for class. or Sometimes she is late for class. or She is late for class sometimes. 16. We were often reading in the library. 17. Jenny has already left. 18. Why has Jenny left already? 19. Have you ever come here for dinner? 20. Both of us are coming over to your place. 21. We are all feeling very happy about your decision. 22. Both Wendy and Michael are very tall. 23. How is everyone feeling today? 24. No one saw them as they left the room.

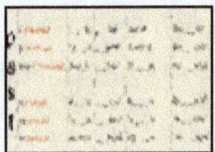

Verb Tenses: present simple tense

One of the most commonly used tenses is the present simple tense. It can be used for various situations.

Present Simple Tense

When is the present simple tense used?

(*Don't forget the third person "s" for she/he/it) E.g. She eats meat.

a) For the general present
E.g. I like science books. We are students.

b) For unchanging facts or truths
E.g. Lions eat meat. The sun sets in the west.

c) Personal planned future events
E.g. We leave next week. Thomas finishes class at 6pm tomorrow.

d) Public timetabled events (scheduled for now & the future)
E.g. The bus comes at 8:15am. Our plane departs at 21:15.

e) Regular habitual actions
E.g. Oscar eats fruit for breakfast every day.

But in most **questions and negatives** there is **no 3rd person "s"** because the base verb (to eat; to see) is used with:
   do/does/don't/doesn't/can/could/should/will/may/might etc.

Questions: Do you make dinner? Does she make dinner? Can he help? Also with the "to be" verb: Is she early? Am I correct? Are we late?

Negatives: No, I don't make dinner. No, she doesn't like him. No he won't help us!

Put the number of each sentence into the correct category.

1. I have a lesson at eight.   2. What can you see?   3. Hurry up!   4. The capital of Australia is Canberra.   5. The bus leaves soon.   6. I enjoy studying English.   7. Where is he?   8. Come in.   9. One human year is seven years for a dog.   10. Sally and Thomas are sick.   11. I collect stamps.   12. Next semester we finish our course.   13. The sun rises in the east.   14. He always eats fish on Friday.   15. Men are physically stronger than women.   16. Lions are carnivores (meat eaters).   17. I usually jog with my neighbour in the evenings.   18. I plan to arrive at your house at 7pm.   19. People are lazy.   20. My mother buys spoons from every new place she visits and displays them in a glass case.   21.   We fly out of Melbourne this Saturday.

a) For the general present	b) For unchanging facts/truth	c) Personal planned events (planned for the future)	d) Public timetabled events (scheduled for now & the future)	e) Regular and habitual actions

Answers: 1c 2a 3a 4b 5d 6e 7a 8a 9b 10a 11e 12c 13b 14e 15b 16b 17e 18c 19a 20e 21c

Verb Tenses: list of irregular verbs, bases & participles

Irregular Past Verbs

BASE FORM	PAST SIMPLE	PAST PARTICIPLE
Use **with** *do, does, did* – for questions *and* with modal words: *could, should, would, can, could, may, might, must, have to, ought to,* etc. Also, use <u>base verbs</u> for directions and commands too. Examples: *Did Mary <u>take</u> the car today?* *Could I <u>have</u> the car keys?* *I have to <u>go</u> there.* *"<u>Go</u>!" Sam shouted. "<u>Turn</u> left."* *"<u>Leave</u> now," he said, "before I lose my temper."*	Use the past simple verb **alone**—*without* an auxiliary verb. Examples: I <u>took</u> the car yesterday. She <u>left</u> me the car yesterday. We <u>watched</u> TV for three hours. In 2020 the world <u>experienced</u> Covid-19. We <u>went</u> to the park for an early morning jog. The teacher <u>began</u> our lesson by correcting last week's homework.	Use the past participle to form the Passive Voice **with**: *was, is, were, being, been.* Also its used to form the perfect tenses with: *has, have, had.* Examples: Today the car <u>was taken</u> by Mary. (past simple passive voice) Oh no! I think our wallets <u>have been stolen</u> by someone! (present perfect passive voice) Yesterday, when I went into the garage I saw she <u>had left</u> me the car. (past perfect tense)
arise	arose	arisen
awake	awoke	awoken
be	was/were	been
beat	beat	beaten
become	became	become
begin	began	begun
bend	bent	bent
bet	bet	bet
bid	bid	bid
bite	bit	bitten
blow	blew	blown
break	broke	broken
bring	brought	brought
broadcast	broadcast	broadcast
build	built	built
burst	burst	burst
buy	bought	bought
catch	caught	caught
choose	chose	chosen
come	came	come
cost	cost	cost
creep	crept	crept
cut	cut	cut
deal	dealt	dealt
dig	dug	dug
do	did	done
draw	drew	drawn

Verb Tenses: list of irregular verbs, base & participles

BASE VERB	PAST SIMPLE	PAST PARTICIPLE
drink	drank	drunk
drive	drove	driven
eat	ate	eaten
fall	fell	fallen
feed	fed	fed
feel	felt	felt
fight	fought	fought
find	found	found
flee	fled	fled
fly	flew	flown
forbid	forbade	forbidden
forget	forgot	forgotten
forgive	forgave	forgiven
freeze	froze	frozen
get	got	got
give	gave	given
go	went	gone
grow	grew	grown
hang	hung	hung
have	had	had
hear	heard	heard
hide	hid	hidden
hit	hit	hit
hold	held	held
hurt	hurt	hurt
keep	kept	kept
kneel	knelt	knelt
know	knew	known
lay	laid	laid
lead	led	led
leave	left	left
lend	lent	lent
let	let	let
lie	lay	lain
light	lit	lit
lose	lost	lost
make	made	made
mean	meant	meant
meet	met	met
mistake	mistook	mistaken
pay	paid	paid
put	put	put
quit	quit	quit

Verb Tenses: list of irregular verbs, base & participles

BASE VERB	PAST SIMPLE	PAST PARTICIPLE
read	read*	read*
ride	rode	ridden
ring	rang	rung
rise	rose	risen
run	ran	run
say	said	said
see	saw	seen
seek	sought	sought
sell	sold	sold
send	sent	sent
set	set	set
sew	sewed	sewn
shake	shook	shaken
shine	shone	shone
shoot	shot	shot
show	showed	shown
shrink	shrank	shrunk
shut	shut	shut
sing	sang	sung
sink	sank	sunk
sit	sat	sat
sleep	slept	slept
slide	slid	slid
speak	spoke	spoken
spend	spent	spent
spit	spat	spat
split	split	split
spread	spread	spread
spring	sprang	sprung
stand	stood	stood
steal	stole	stolen
stick	stuck	stuck
sting	stung	stung
stink	stank	stunk
strike	struck	struck
swear	swore	sworn
sweep	swept	swept
swim	swam	swum
swing	swung	swung
take	took	taken
teach	taught	taught
tear	tore	torn
tell	told	told

Verb Tenses: list of irregular verbs, base & participles

BASE VERB	PAST SIMPLE	PAST PARTICIPLE
think	thought	thought
throw	threw	thrown
understand	understood	understood
wake	woke	woken
wear	wore	worn
weep	wept	wept
win	won*	won*
write	wrote	written

Use the verb in the brackets to make sentences in the past simple tense.

1. Susan _____ (wake) up early because the wind was very loud during the night.
2. When her boyfriend proposed to her, she _____ (weep) with joy and excitement!
3. Harry _____ (quit) his job when he was didn't want to learn all the new policies and protocols.
4. Why did Denise _____ (write) such a long letter to her grandmother?
5. Could it be that they did not _____ (understand) his directions? Did they _____ (go) lost?

Answers: 1. woke 2. wept 3. quit 4. write 5. understand; get

Verb Tenses: list of irregular verbs, base & participles

Complete the general "it" statements to form past sentences using the verbs in the brackets.

1. It had been _____ (think) hundreds of years ago that the Earth was flat, and that one could _____ (fell) off the edge if you went too far!

2. It is _____ (think) the Black Death had _____ (sweep) through the world in the mid-1300s, when twelve ships from the Black Sea _____ (dock) at the Sicilian port of Messina.

3. It _____ (is) unseemly when a president put his arm on the Queen's back as they _____ (are) walking around outside Buckingham Palace.

4. It was _____ (consider) necessary to _____ (took) out "bad blood" when a patient had a fever and doctors _____ (use) leeches to do it. This was _____ (do) throughout the 19th century and was frequently _____ (practice) in Europe, America and Asia.

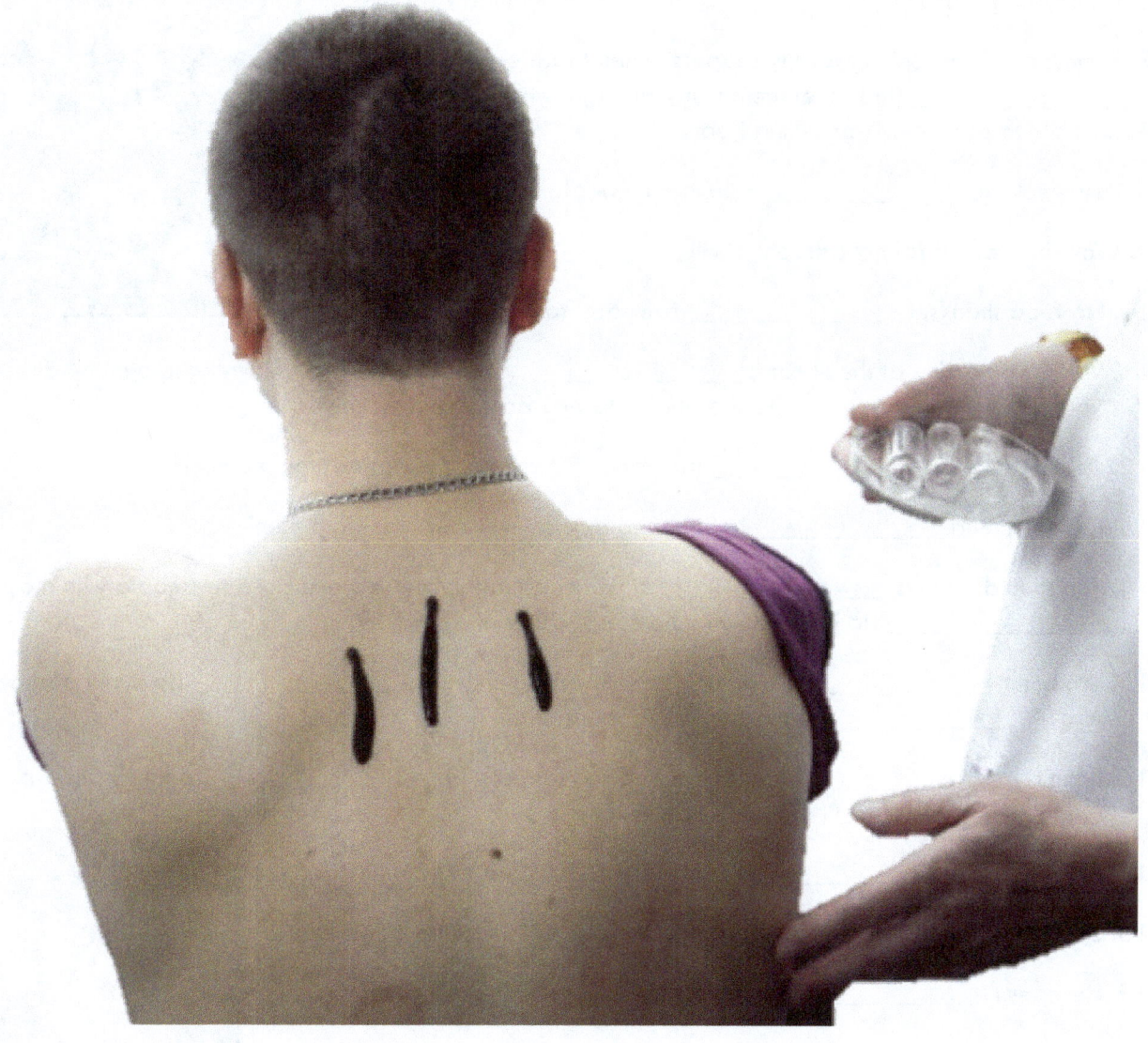

Answers: 1. thought; fall 2. thought; swept; docked 3. was; were 4. considered; take; used; done; practiced

Verb Tenses: list of irregular verbs, base & participles

Write the correct form of the infinitive verb suggested in the brackets. (Choose from the base form of the verb, the past simple tense or the past participle used for the passive voice and perfect tenses.)

1. _____ (to take) the shopping bags inside and put them on the kitchen bench.

2. The thieves _____ (to see) stealing a car at the shopping centre, so they _____ (to catch) by the police in the next half hour.

3. Last July Peter and Daniela _____ (to marry) by their pastor in their church.

4. Could I please _____ (to ask) you a question about my course of study?

5. _____ (to look) across the road! There _____ (to be) an accident and the police are there too.

6. Could you please _____ (to open) the window for me?

7. Yesterday I was looking for my slippers, when I suddenly realised I _____ (to leave) them in my garage, where I had taken them off to put on my gardening boots.

8. Last week we _____ (to meet) our old teacher in the park.

9. Wow, how great for my garden! It will _____ (to rain) soon!

10. No food thanks, I _____ (already to eat) my lunch.

11. When you arrive at the library, _____ (to turn) left after you walk through the doors and you will _____ (to see) the children's books on the shelves.

12. Doesn't Amelia _____ (to want) to play with her toys at the moment?

13. Didn't Amelia _____ (to want) to play with her toys right then?

14. You should always _____ (to wear) a mask when you are close to people who may _____ (to have) an infection, especially of Covid-19.

15. I couldn't _____ (to find) the box anywhere, so I _____ (to think) perhaps my wife _____ (to move) it somewhere.

16. I can't _____ (to find) the box anywhere, so I _____ (to think) perhaps my wife _____ (to move) it somewhere.

17. My niece _____ (to take) to school by her neighbour today.

18. Samantha _____ (to get) big blue eyes, just like her dad.

19. He doesn't _____ (to have) a clue what's going on!

Answers: 1. Take. 2. were seen; were caught. 3. were married. 4. ask. 5. Look; has been. 6. open. 7. had left. 8. met. 9. rain. 10. have already eaten. 11. turn; see. 12. want. 13. want. 14. wear; have. 15. find; thought; had moved. 16. find; think; has moved. 17. was taken. 18. has got. 19. have.

Page 68

Chapter 3 The Marriage Proposal
Reading Comprehension

After reading *Chapter 3 of Speak English Like Australians!*, answer the following questions in full sentences. That is, include the question as part of your written answer, so that the question is recognised by the person reading your answer.

1. Who did Theo ask to find Argyro and talk to her?

2. Why did Argyro take so long to reply to Theo's offer of marriage?

3. Why did Argyro's cabin mates on the ship feel sorry for her?

4. What was the first thing the women asked for when they got off the *Tasmania*, in Fremantle?

5. What was Theo really like in his appearance?

6. Why couldn't Theo and Argyro get married in a Greek church, in Melbourne?

7. Do you think Argyro made the right decision to leave Greece? Please write your opinion.

Answers: 1. Theo asked Ilias, his cousin, to find Argyro and talk to her. 2. Argyro took so long to reply to Theo's offer of marriage because she was enjoying her life in Athens and her studies too. 3. Argyro's cabin mates felt sorry for her because they thought she was going to marry an old man. 4. The first thing the women asked for when they got off the *Tasmania*, was water. 5. In his appearance Theo was really a very tall, good-looking man in his early thirties. 6. Theo and Argyro couldn't get married in a Greek church in Melbourne because they were booked out with so many couples wanting wedding ceremonies.

Speaking: arranged marriages ACSF 2.07

Group Work:
Board Game about Marriage

Take turns to express your opinions and to disagree politely. Don't forget to use good listening skills. (Refer to Chapter 2 Speaking)

---

share = all players speak about it
tell = tell others
ask = ask others

polite disagreement
I see what you mean but ...
That's a good idea but ...
I suppose so but have you thought about ...

opinion
In my opinion ...
As I see it ....
I honestly feel ....
Personally, I think ....

START

1 (share) Should Argyro have agreed to marry Theo?

2 (tell) Do you think arranged marriages are a good idea?

3 (ask) Absence makes the heart grow fonder. Is this proverb true for spouses?

4 (share) What is your opinion about boys getting a dowry from their wife's family?

5 (share) Should a wife change her family name and use her husband's family name?

6 (tell) Would you try to arrange a marriage for your son or daughter?

7 (ask) Why do so many married movie stars end up divorcing?

8 (share) How do you know you have found THE ONE?

9 (ask) What type of person would be your PERFECT spouse? If this is even possible!

FINISH

10 (share) What things make a marriage successful?

Speaking: reading about arranged marriages

Group Work

Take turns reading the article from The Age, (Melbourne) dated 27th Jan. 1958. Then discuss these questions together.

1. What is a proxy bride?
2. What are the benefits of being a proxy bride?
3. What are the negatives of being a proxy bride?
4. Why do you think the men become uncontrollable?
5. Given that Melbourne has the largest Greek population of any city in the World – outside of Greece, do you think these marriages benefitted Australian society? Explain using *Expressions for Opinion* (refer to Chapter 2 Speaking section).

Greek Migrants Rush "Bride Ship"

Thousands of Greek men demonstrated at Station Pier, Port Melbourne, on Saturday after the arrival of the "bride ship" Castel Felice.

They had waited impatiently nine and a half hours for the ship carrying 800 women —many of them proxy brides—to berth and then because of a mix-up over the storage of luggage, another two hours passed before the first girls disembarked.

Police were called to the pier to control the crowd which Customs officials described as "the biggest in memory."

As the ship berthed the men became uncontrollable.

Women on board opened lower portholes and many men struggled through these into the ship before police and Customs officials could get through the crowd to close the portholes.

Others climbed ropes hanging over the side, some scaled a giant crane on the wharf next to the ship.

Crates Smashed

Hundreds more trampled and smashed crates of food which had been stacked on the wharf to be loaded on the ship.

Crowds started to form early on Saturday morning, although the Castel Felice was not due until noon.

When the ship eventually berthed at 3:30 p.m., train and bus loads of people were still arriving at the pier.

One man, reaching for the hand of a girl on the ship, overbalanced and fell into the water. Friends quickly hoisted him back on to the wharf and drove him off in a private car.

Customs men were kept busy all afternoon seizing parcels and tins containing food and articles of clothing thrown by the girls to the wharf.

Two fire brigades from Port Melbourne and South Melbourne were called to Station Pier about 7 p.m. when a cigarette butt set fire to a section of the wharf near the entrance.

The Castel Felice was carrying 1400 migrants. All but 300 of the passengers were Greek. The rest were Hungarians, Yugoslavs and Italians.

- **THESE NEW AUSTRALIAN MEN** couldn't wait for the migrant vessel Castel Felice to properly berth on Saturday before they clambered through an open porthole to see their proxy wives. "The largest crowd in memory" jammed Station Pier to meet the ship which carried 800 women—about 500 of them proxy wives.

http://collections.museumvictoria.com.au/items/273363 (used by permission)

Chant: Proxy Marriage

Practise your pronunciation and intonation, by singing the song until you can say it easily and keep the rhythm going. Stress the bold text to get the rhythm right. Enjoy it!

Theo **wrote** to pop the **question**
an' **waited** with bated **breath**.
He **didn't** get her **answer**;
it **scared** him half to **death**!

He **asked** his cousin **Ilias**
to **travel** to Athens by **bus**,
and **speak** to Argyro **kindly**;
she **agreed** without any **fuss**.

On **board** she felt very **lonely**;
as to **'stralia** she went by **ship**.
She **didn't** feel like **talkin**g
and **cried** for most of the **trip**!

He **greeted** her with **flowers**;
Red **roses** clutched in his **hand**.
They **married** at the **registry**;
Then to **Hamilton**, as they **planned**!

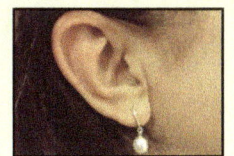

Listening: text cloze

Use the Internet to go to YouTube: Home and in the search bar type *Zoe Lambreas – Chapter 3.* Then find and click on *The Marriage Proposal–part 1. Or use the QR code on your phone for my website.*

Listen to the narration and write the missing words. Some gaps have two words missing.

Theo decided ¹_____ a letter to Argyro's father. He wrote that he wanted ²_____ his daughter. Theo respected her father and he knew he was a strict dad. Would he allow his daughter to go to Australia? Would Argyro be willing ³_____ her family? Theo did not know the Australian Government wanted to get more white people into Australia. The Government wanted the single migrant men who worked in Australia, ⁴_____ in Australia and to have families. So the Government paid, for single women from places like Greece and Italy, ⁵_____ to Australia to get married to these men. Theo didn't know about this government plan, so he sent money to Argyro's father, for a one-way ticket by ship. He hoped Argyro would take the money and come to Australia to be his wife.

But, during this time Argyro had left her village and moved to the capital city, Athens. She lived in a flat with her older brother, Nick, who was a student at the university there. Athens was a busy city and Argyro loved the city life and noise, as there was always something ⁶_____ and do. Because Argyro wanted to learn how to make clothes, she ⁷_____ very hard at a sewing school in Athens. She loved sewing and pattern-making. Everything the teacher showed her was easy for her, and she was the best student in her class.

When Argyro's father ⁸_____ her that Theo was asking to marry her, it was very difficult for her to make a decision. Argyro enjoyed her life in Athens and she didn't want to leave her country. She knew she would miss her family and she loved her studies and her new friends. Athens ⁹_____ an interesting city after the slow, boring farming life she had in her village.

Time moved on and she still didn't know what to do. She put it all in the "too hard basket", so she did not give an answer to Theo, who was waiting in Australia. Argyro ¹⁰_____ that delay is the thief of time! In Australia, after *six months* of waiting, Theo still had no answer from Argyro! What was going on? Theo needed to know. He ¹¹_____ to his cousin Ilias, who was also his best friend. Theo asked Ilias to go to Argyro and talk together with her, face-to-face, about going to Australia to marry Theo.

To speak to Argyro and ¹²_____ an answer for Theo as soon as he could, kind Ilias left for the city that same day. He ¹³_____ where Argyro was living because Argyro's brother was his friend and everyone knows each other's business in the small village where they ¹⁴_____.

Did you notice which *part of speech* the missing words belong to? Are they adjectives, nouns or verbs?

Answers: 1. to write 2. to marry 3. to leave 4. to stay 5. to come 6. to see 7. studied 8. told 9. was 10. forgot 11. wrote 12. get 13. knew 14. lived All the missing words are verbs.

Page 73

Dictation: running dictation

Pair Work: Learners work in pairs for this dictation.

Skills: speaking, listening, patience, writing and team work, good sportsmanship, pronunciation, spelling, reading

Learner A quickly goes to the written text which has been positioned in a strategic location on a wall. After reading some of the text, the learner returns to Learner B to dictate the text to Learner B who writes it down. Learner A may spell words, and also seek pronunciation help from the instructor, but may not actually write the text for Learner B.

When Learner A completes dictating their text, they swap places with Learner B, to hear and write the dictation underneath the writing of Learner A.

The paper with the completed written dictation, should have both names of the learners on it. Written work is handed to the instructor ,who removes the text from the wall and ensures points are allocated in order of completion for each pair. i.e. The first pair to complete gets 20 points, the next gets 18 points and so on. However, points are deducted for every error, including punctuation. The final winner is the pair with the highest score. They are invited to share their winning strategies with the other learners!

Learner A
Theo had sent Argyro a photo of himself too, but she hated how he looked in it. She thought he looked angry and harsh. She didn't like to look at it. For this reason, when her room mates had shown photos of their future husbands to each other, during their long voyage, Argyro had not.

Learner B
As girls usually do, they had asked Argyro, "Is he handsome? Is he tall or short?" Argyro had replied, "He is an old man." (He was nine years older than she was.) So they didn't talk to her about it again. The other girls felt sorry for her because they thought poor Argyro was going to marry a really old man.

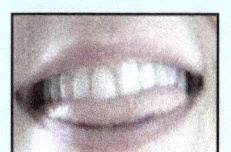

Pronunciation: reminder
Practise the pronunciations of the Aussie Sounds in Chapter 1 Pronunciation.

Pronunciation: stressing and grouping words together when you are reading

Focus: reading aloud and text "chunking"

One great benefit of reading aloud is that learners concentrate on *how* they're speaking, without thinking about *what* words to use. Reading aloud a "chunked" text is also helpful for learners who speak too fast, or incorrectly pause in the middle of a phrase. Of course there are different ways of chunking and more experienced learners can produce their own version. It is a good idea to write each chunk on a separate line as it is easier to pause between "chunks".

Ask learners to say each line after you. Make sure that they're stressing the right syllable of the highlighted words. E.g. the second syllable of "decided", the first syllable of "Theo". Learners can then practise in pairs, reading the first line, then the first two, then the first three, and so on, gradually building up to the full text, trying not to pause in the middle of a chunk.

Of course they may pause for as long as they need to between chunks. As they do this, they'll probably begin to learn some of it by heart and to reproduce it with less and less reference to the text.

Task 1

Silently read the text below and make sure you understand it.
Theo decided to write a letter to Argyro's father. He told him that he wanted to marry his daughter. Theo respected her father and he knew he was a strict dad. Would he allow his daughter to go to Australia? Would Argyro be willing to leave her family? Theo did not know the Australian Government wanted to get more white people into Australia. The Government wanted the single migrant men who worked in Australia, to stay in Australia and to have families. So the Government paid, for single women from places like Greece and Italy, to come to Australia to get married to these men.

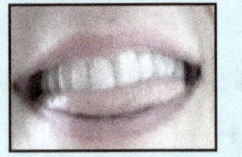

Task 2

Now practise reading the text bit by bit, "in chunks". Pause between the chunks, but not in the middle of a chunk, and pay attention to the stress at the places highlighted. Remember, stress the bold syllables and pause only after each chunk of text, at the end of each line. The dictation will make more sense to the listeners if you pause at the end of each chunk.

Th**eo** de**ci**ded to wr**i**te a **le**tter
to Argyr**o**'s **fa**ther.
He **told** him that he w**a**nted
to m**a**rry his d**au**ghter.
Th**eo** respected her **fa**ther
and he kn**ew**
he was a str**i**ct d**a**d.
Would he all**ow** his d**au**ghter
to go to Austr**a**lia?
W**ou**ld Argyr**o** be w**i**lling
to l**ea**ve her **fa**mily?
Th**eo** did not kn**ow**
the Austr**a**lian G**o**vernment
w**a**nted to g**e**t
more wh**i**te p**eo**ple **i**nto Austr**a**lia.
The G**o**vernment w**a**nted
the **si**ngle m**i**grant men
who w**or**ked in Austr**a**lia,
to st**ay** in Austr**a**lia
and to h**a**ve **fa**milies.
So the G**o**vernment p**ai**d,
for **si**ngle w**o**men
from pl**a**ces like Gr**ee**ce and **I**taly,
to c**o**me to Austr**a**lia
to get m**a**rried to these men.

Phonograms: "augh" and "ough"

The letters "augh" and "ough" have seven possible sounds. Look at the top of each column for the International Phonemic Alphabet symbol. Practise saying each column of words until you feel comfortable with the pronunciations.

International Phonemic Alphabet symbols for "augh" & "ough" pronunciation (Refer to page 16.)	/ɔː/ always followed by "t"	/ɑːf/ with "laugh"	/ʌf/	/ɒf/	/uː/	/əʊ/	/æʊ/
The phonograms using the letters **augh** or **ough** can have <u>seven</u> different sounds altogether.	bought	laugh	enough	cough	through	although	bough
	caught	laughable	rough	trough		dough	plough
	daughter	laughed	tough			though	
	draught	laughing					
	distraught	laughingly					
	fraught	laughter					
	thought						
	haughty						
	naught						
	naughty						
	ought						
	slaughter						
	taught						

Tongue Twisters: "f"

Say each tongue twister until you can say it easily and smoothly. Have some fun not getting your tongue confused!

1. Philip forgot to buy flowers for his wife Phyllis' forty-fifth birthday!
2. Four fabulous foods that are my favourites are: figs, fish, fruit and fennel.
3. Fe, Fi, Fo, Fum!
   I smell the blood of an Englishman,
   From the English fairy tale *Jack and the Beanstalk*
4. Friday is fun for Freda and Fred for they often fly to Florence from France.

Conversation Bits: What a coincidence/fluke! No way!

Repeat the conversation until your intonation is native-like. Say the expressions in one breath, without pausing between words. Practise the dialogue with a friend to make it more natural.

Denis	I went to the bank today and who do you think I met there?
Meryl	No idea, but I went to the shops and the bank today too!
Denis	I met my high school friend whom I haven't seen for ten years!
Meryl	No way! You were there together? What a fluke!
Denis	Yeah and we had lunch together. He is married and has a son and a daughter just like us!
Meryl	What a coincidence! Just wait till I tell you another one. I met my high school friend in the shopping centre, whom I haven't seen for a long time too!
Denis	That's amazing! That is such a coincidence!
Meryl	It sure is!
Explanations: No way! = expression of great surprise What a coincidence/fluke! = by chance similar things happen	

Spelling: adding suffixes to silent "e" words

1a. Some words end with a silent "e" like "stare" and "love". With these words you remove the *final e*, when adding a suffix (an ending) that starts with a *vowel* sound. For example suffixes like:
–ing, –er, –or, –est, –ist, –ed, –or, –ance, –ation, –ence, –ity, –al, –ise, –ish, –ion, –ism, etc. Notice these words:

care—caring, cared, carer   name—naming, named   donate—donation, donated, donator
ignore—ignorance, ignorant, ignoring   advance—advancing, advanced   orate—orator, oration
distribute—distributor   active—activity, activation, activated   responsible—responsibility

1b. Also remove the final e when you want to add a "y". Why do you think "'y" is a special case? It is because "y" is usually pronounced as the *vowel sound* /ɪ/ and is treated as a *vowel suffix*. Observe:

taste—tasty, tasted, taster, tasting   juice—juicy, juicer   haze—hazy, hazily   breeze—breezy
wheeze—wheezy, wheezing   mumble—mumbly, mumbling, mumbled   multiple—multiply, multiplied

2. However, do not remove the final "e", if adding a suffix starting with a *consonant*. Suffixes like: –ful, –ness, –ly, –liness, –most, –ward, –person, –less, –ment, –wise, etc.

care—careful, careless   middle—middlemost   sales—salesperson, salesman   love—loveliness, lovely
taste—tasteless, tastefully, tasteful   advance—advancement   home—homely, homeward   name—nameless

Add as many suffixes as possible to the words.

1. perspire—_____
2. marriage—_____
3. finalise—_____
4. encourage—_____
5. type—_____
6. white—_____
7. smoke—_____
8. store—_____
9. create—_____
10. complete—_____
11. craze—_____
12. fertilise—_____
13. lone—_____
14. same—_____
15. manage—_____
16. state—_____
17. fore—_____
18. surprise—_____

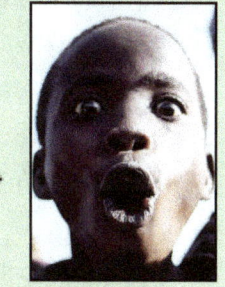

Answers: 1. perspiration, perspiring, perspired 2. marriageable, marrying, married, marries 3. finalisation, finalised, finalising 4. encourager, encouraging, encouraged 5. typing, typed 6. whiteness, whited, whiting, whitening 7. smoky, smoked, smoking, smoker 8. stored, storing, storer 9. creator, creation, created, creating, creative 10. completly, completed, completing, completion 11. cazy, crazily, crazed 12. fertilised, fertilising, fertilisation, fertiliser 13. lonely, loner 14. sameness 15. managed, managing, management, manager 16. stated, stating, statement, stately 17. foremost, foreward 18. surprised, surprising, surprisingly

Vocabulary: synonyms

Replace the underlined words with plausible alternatives that make sense in the text. Use a thesaurus if you need help.

Meanwhile Argyro had left her village and had moved to the capital city of Athens, where she shared a flat with her older brother, Nick, who was studying at university there. Athens was a thriving city and she loved the city <u>vibe</u> as there was always something to see and do.

Since she wanted to be a seamstress, she studied diligently. She loved sewing and pattern-making and had a natural <u>flair</u> for it. Everything she was taught was a <u>sinch</u> for her, so she was easily the best student in her class.

Consequently, when Argyro was told about Theo's <u>offer of marriage</u> by her father, she found it very difficult to make a decision, as she didn't have any <u>desire</u> to leave her country. She knew she would <u>miss</u> her family and besides, life was very <u>exciting</u> for her at this time and she loved her studies and new friends. Athens was an interesting, <u>bustling</u> city and it suited her after the farming life she had led in her village. Therefore, time moved on and she <u>dissembled</u> and pushed the thought aside, heedless of Theo's <u>agony</u>. Argyro quite forgot that <u>procrastination</u> is the thief of time!

<u>Meanwhile</u>, back in Australia, after six months of waiting, Theo had still received no answer from Argyro! What was going on? They say that necessity is the mother of <u>invention</u>, so in desperation he wrote to his cousin Ilias, who was also his best <u>friend</u>. Would Ilias talk with Argyro and ask her if she would <u>go</u> to Australia to <u>marry</u> Theo?

Answers: vibe=atmosphere, spirit, feeling flair=talent sinch=very easy offer of marriage=proposal desire=wish, longing, aspiration, yearning miss=pine for, yearn for, long for, be homesick exciting=exhilarating, thrilling, stimulating bustling=busy, lively, energetic dissembled=stalled, put off agony=pain, anguish procrastination=postponement, deferment, delay meanwhile=for now, for the time being, for the meantime invention=creativity, discovery, development friend=mate, buddy go=travel, move marry=wed, get hitched to, tie the knot with, join Theo in matrimony

Describing People

In Chapter 3 we read a description of Theo. "Argyro pointed to a very tall, good-looking man in his early thirties. He was dressed in a suit and he was holding a bunch of roses. He was a very handsome young man!"

Physical Attributes

There are physical attributes/characteristics/traits of a person that are the things you can <u>see</u> about them. For instance:
She has blue/**hazel**/dark/light/green/brown eyes.
They are small/large/huge/big/**almond-shaped** eyes.

He's/She's attractive/**stunning**/good-looking/ugly/unattractive. She's beautiful/pretty.
He's handsome/**a hunk**. She's gorgeous/lovely/beautiful.
She's slim/thin/**skinny**/fat/overweight. She has a slim build. She is of slim build. She is slimly built.
He's of average build. He's of medium/heavy/square/solid build. He is medium built. He has a big **build**.

Describing People

He has a small stature. He's tall. He's small/little. She's tallish/shortish/short. She's of average stature. She is of average/medium height.

He's **broad-shouldered**. She's slim-waisted. She's large-hipped. She's silver/grey-haired. He's one-legged. He's got wide/big shoulders. He's round-shouldered and **hunch-backed.** She's **narrow-hipped** and small-waisted. He's pot-bellied and big-footed. He's deep-voiced.

She's in her teens/twenties/thirties/forties. He's a senior man. She's a pensioner. She's an older person. She's in the wintertime of her life. He's in the **spring** of his life. He's a youth/teenager. He's in his **prime**. She's in her declining years/winter years.

She has beautiful, long/short, curly/straight hair. He's bald. He's got a moustache and a beard.
She has very thick hair. His hair is thin and **baldin**g. He's **a redhead/ranga!** She has red hair. She's got red/auburn hair. Her hair is red. She has brown hair. She's a brunette. He's got blonde hair with red **highlights.**

He's black-haired. He's fair-haired. He's dark-haired. He has **salt and pepper** hair. He's grey-haired.

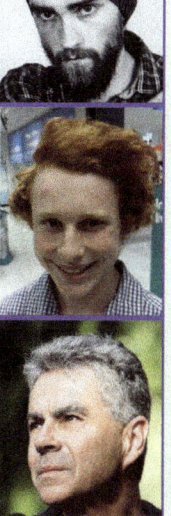

Character Attributes

There are also character attributes that <u>cannot be seen</u> by looking at someone but you find out about a person after you know them for a while. It is part of their inner personality. For example:

He's an honest/dishonest person. He's tactful. She's **tactless**.
She's kind/unkind. They are hard-working people. They are lazy people.
She's generous/thoughtful/considerate/loving and friendly.

He's greedy/ambitious. He's unambitious. He's a **complex**/simple person.
She's talkative/chatty/**garrulous**. He's quiet/shy.
He's interesting. She's boring. He's truthful. He's a liar/cheat.
She's a sensible lady. She has a lot of common sense. She's **down-to-earth**.

He's trustworthy. She got patience. She's patient. She's a patient person. He's impatient. She's faithful/loyal. He's adventurous. She's serious. She's confident and **self-motivated.** He's home-loving. She's fun-loving, cheeky and **out-going.** She's moody.
She's bad-tempered. He's easy-going. He's reserved/conservative.
She's an **extrovert** and an optimist. He's an introvert and a pessimist.

In Chapter 2 of the novel *Speak English Like Australians!*, there is a description of Argyro, a single Greek lady.

What was Argyro like? She was honest, hard-working and nine years younger than Theo. She was of average height and build. Her hair was shortish, wavy and dark brown. Her eyes were hazel.

The past tense is used because the story is set in the late 1940s and early 1950s. Notice the "ish" ending in the word "shortish" which means not short and not long: it is *sort-of-short*.

Read the description of the woman below. Please notice the use of the present tense because we are looking at her photo now and there is no story about her to tell us she is from the past. Also notice the <u>hyphenated adjectives</u>.

She is a <u>stockily-built</u> young woman of medium height and is probably in her twenties. She's got shortish, straight, <u>dark-brown</u> hair and <u>light-coloured</u> eyes. She's not wearing glasses and is dressed in a casual, grey jumper with a zip and a hoodie. She looks kind and caring.

Did you notice that both descriptions above use both physical and character attributes?

Let's practise using some of this new vocabulary in the correct order.

ORDER OF ADJECTIVES

opinion → size → physical quality → shape → age → colour → nationality → material → type
+ NOUN
(Usually a short word goes in front of a longer, hyphenated word.)

Look at the description below, and change the sentences in the same way.

E.g. a lady (noun) with a bad (adjective) temper (noun)

→ She's (pronoun) a bad-tempered (hyphenated adjective) lady (noun).

1. a woman with a heavy build → _____
2. a boy with long hair → _____
3. a lady who dresses well → _____
4. a man with round shoulders → _____
5. a boy with big feet → _____
6. a child with a soft voice → _____

Answers: 1. a heavy-built woman 2. a long-haired boy 3. a well-dressed lady 4. a round-shouldered man 5. a big-footed boy 6. a soft-voiced child

Describing People

Describing a person requires quite a bit of skill in order to draw a mental picture with words. Describe the people in the photos below by using the expressions for physical and character attributes.

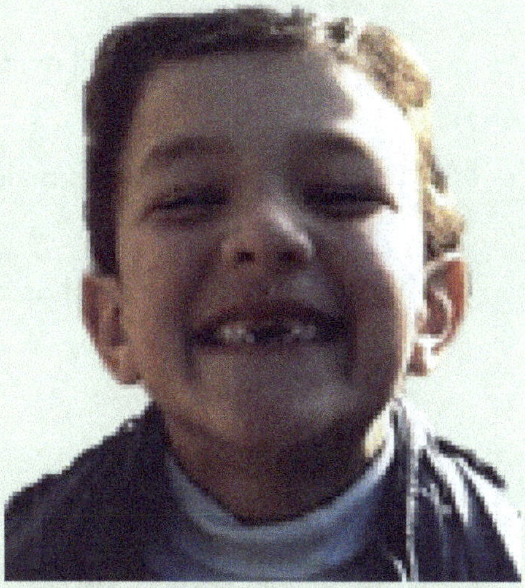

_____
_____
_____
_____
_____
_____
_____
_____
_____
_____

_____
_____
_____
_____
_____
_____
_____
_____

_____
_____
_____
_____
_____
_____
_____
_____

Figures of Speech: antithesis

Antithesis is a figure of speech that contrasts opposite ideas. Antitheses help to compare and stress two opposite thoughts. The two antitheses are usually, though not always, separated by the words "or", "yet" and "but", or by a comma. If they are complete sentences then you can separate them with a colon. Notice the examples:

"We must learn to live together as brothers **or** perish together as fools."
Martin Luther King, Jr.

Many are called, **but** few are chosen.
The Bible, Matthew 22:14

Give me liberty **or** give me death."
Patrick Henry, Virginia, 1775

"That's one small step for a man, one giant leap for mankind."
Neil Armstrong, first man to walk on the moon

Money is the root of all evil: poverty is the fruit of all goodness.

Love is an ideal thing, marriage a real thing.

Patience is bitter, but it has a sweet fruit.

Underline the two antitheses from the text of Chapter 3 *Speak English Like Australians!*

Argyro, being the second oldest, felt responsible to help them and she knew it would be easier for her mum and dad if she left for Australia to get married, even though she really didn't want to leave her country. She was very patriotic and loved Greece yet she was the one in her family doomed to leave it. Concern for her family constrained her to forsake her people and her country! Just as Theo had done before her, Argyro based her decision to migrate on her sense of duty and concern for what was best for her family.

Answers: She was very patriotic and loved Greece yet she was the one in her family doomed to leave it. Concern for her family constrained her to forsake her people and her country!

Proverbs: travel

Proverbs are short, pithy expressions of popular wisdom. Some would say proverbs are used to pass on wisdom to the next generation. Proverbs share life lessons in general and offer advice.

Write your opinion of the meanings of the following proverbs. Then compare your answers with those of the author, in the answers at the bottom of the page.

1. It is better to travel hopefully than to arrive.
_____
_____

2. He who would travel through the land, must go with open purse in hand. (Dutch)
_____
_____

3. Abroad to see wonders the traveller goes, and neglects the fine things which lie under his nose.
_____
_____

4. The world is a book, and those who do not travel only read a page. (Saint Augustine)
_____
_____

Underline the proverb and explain its meaning.

Argyro enjoyed her life in Athens and she didn't want to leave her country. She knew she would miss her family and she loved her studies and her new friends. Athens was an interesting city after the slow, boring farming life she had in her village. Time moved on and she still didn't know what to do. She put it all in the "too hard basket", so she did not give an answer to Theo, who was waiting in Australia. Argyro forgot that delay is the thief of time! In Australia, after *six months* of waiting, Theo still had no answer from Argyro!

What is the meaning of "too hard basket"?
_____

Answers: 1. The hope and anticipation of travelling are often better than the reality. 2. Your travelling will be more successful if you show generosity to the people you meet. 3. A traveller looks forward to seeing wonderful things away from home but does not notice the wonders of his own land. 4. If you never go anywhere, you have a very limited view of the world. The proverb in the text is: Delay is the thief of time! It means that time is wasted when people can't decide what to do and so they don't do anything at all. "Too hard basket" means something that should be done, but it is left undone as it is too difficult.

Page 85

Writing: two contrasting paragraphs (persuasive genre)

A paragraph comprises of a main topic sentence, followed by supporting sentences with examples, facts or a story from life. Here there are two contrasting paragraphs discussing nursing homes, each with its main topic/reason/argument, followed by sentences that strengthen the topic or try to prove it. To begin, there is an introduction paragraph.

When considering professional aged-care, there are both positives and negatives about nursing homes. Therefore, serious consideration needs to me taken before making a decision.

One of the nicest things is the care and devotion of staff who love to care for the elderly. They offer help to bathe and to dress them when it is necessary. Nutritious meals are provided and medicines are given at the correct times so the residents don't have to worry about forgetting to take their tablets.

On the other hand, nursing homes may be very noisy places so staff can't hear the residents' cries for help. Also, noise levels could prevent seniors from getting enough rest and tranquillity. Then some seniors may become very upset with other residents who play their radio or television too loudly, because it is difficult to be patient with others when you lose your sleep.

Do you agree with the writer's opinions?

A) Write your own two contrasting paragraphs about whether it is a good idea to give a driving licence to 14-year-olds.

_____ _____
_____ _____
_____ _____
_____ _____
_____ _____

B) Rewrite the sentences in the paragraphs below so they are in the correct order.

Because of this, many new housing areas are designed with gardens and parks for the locals to use. Most people enjoy nature. They like to see trees and greenery around them; not just concrete everywhere.

_____
_____
_____

Later, during the evening we all got around the BBQ for dinner and sang some songs. We slept very well that night. It was a great day and everyone enjoyed themselves. Some people decided to go swimming while others went for a walk along the beach.

_____
_____
_____

Answers: B) Most people enjoy nature. They like to see trees and greenery around them; not just concrete everywhere. Because of this, many new housing areas are designed with gardens and parks for the locals to use. It was a great day and everyone enjoyed themselves. Some people decided to go swimming while others went for a walk along the beach. Later, during the evening we all got around the BBQ for dinner and sang some songs. We slept very well that night.

Parts of Speech: infinitives & gerunds

Infinitive verbs all have "to" in front of them. E.g. to sing, to dance, to drive, to shop etc.

Read the information about infinitives and how they are used.

particular verb + object + infinitive

ask   tell   expect   teach   want   would like   invite

I asked her to come to my party.
Mum told me to open the window.
The boss expects Kevin to work a lot of overtime.
Jack teaches my son to play soccer.
They want Henley Homes to build their dream house.
My neighbour would like me to cut down my tree.
Did he invite her to meet his brother?

adjective + infinitive

important   nice   stupid   possible   difficult   expensive   easy   tall   expensive   wrong

It's important to practise driving before going for your licence.
I was stupid to eat so much food for dinner.
It isn't possible to have an appointment until next week.
Robyn thought the test was too difficult to pass.
The dress is very expensive to buy.
It's easy to see that they love each other.

particular verb + infinitive

want   afford   decide   expect   hope   learn   promise   would like   intend   agree

I want to leave early today.
We can't afford to buy a new car.
When will you decide to marry me?
I expect to see you here tomorrow.
Jenny hopes to be with us next week.
The students are learning to work hard.
Don't promise to help if you are not sure.
They would like to return to Australia next year.

By the way, did you notice that the first six missing words in the *Listening: test cloze* of this chapter, were all infinitives? Check it out.

Parts of Speech: infinitives & gerunds (continued)

Gerunds are nouns that *name actions* (sometimes called *verbal nouns*). All gerunds end with "ing". E.g. singing, dancing, driving, shopping etc.

Read the information about gerunds and how they are used.

particular verb + gerund

enjoy   finish   mind   dislike   can't stand   suggest   stop   practise   postpone   risk

They enjoy shopping together.   I finished writing my essay yesterday.   Sally doesn't mind waiting for the bus.

go + a sport gerund

jogging   running   swimming   golfing   boating   skating   fishing   cycling   surfing   sailing

Tom goes jogging every other day.
They are going swimming tomorrow.
Our friends went skiing last month.

preposition + gerund

in   at   inside   about   before   above   below   beside   next to   etc.

I'm very good at cooking.   How about walking with me?   Are you interested in gardening?
Thanks for helping us.   Let's eat before going out to the movies.   Mum is inside, ironing the shirts.

particular verb + gerund or infinitive

love   hate   like   begin   start   prefer   continue   can't stand

We like going to the shops. OR We like to go to the shops.
She loves making cakes. OR She loves to make cakes.
I hated visiting the dentist. OR I hated to visit the dentist.
They have begun studying at Swinburne. OR They have begun to study at Swinburne.
Thomas will start learning Italian tomorrow. OR Thomas will start to learn Italian tomorrow.

Use an infinitive or a gerund form of the verb in the brackets to complete the sentences.

1. Jenny hopes _____ with us next week. (be)
2. I finished _____ my essay yesterday. (write)
3. Thanks for _____ us. (help)
4. Sally doesn't mind _____ for the bus. (wait)
5. She loves _____ cakes. (make)
6. I was stupid _____ so much food for dinner. (eat)
7. I expect _____ you here tomorrow. (see)
8. Mum is inside, _____ the shirts. (iron)
9. I'm very good at _____. (bake)

Answers: 1. to be 2. writing 3. helping 4. waiting 5. to make/making 6. to eat 7. to see 8. ironing 9. baking

Grammar: gerunds & infinitives

Revision: Gerunds

Gerunds are words like reading, writing, singing and running. They are used as nouns: the names of actions and activities.

Gerunds are often called verbal nouns because they are made by adding –ing to a verb.
E.g. sing > singing
Usually gerunds are not plurals. E.g. I like ~~singings~~.

Commonly, gerunds are used after all prepositions:

preposition + gerund

E.g. Yesterday, I finished my day **by working** in my garden.

Complete the following sentences using gerunds.

1. This mechanic is very good at _____ (repair cars).
2. She is very fond of _____ (sing)
3. He won the prize by _____ (work hard).
4. I cannot stop him from _____ (go)
5. She learnt the recipes by _____ (cook) for her family.
6. His love of _____ (read) is evident from his large library.
7. They lost weight by _____ (jog) every morning.
8. They relax after dinner by _____ (watch) TV.
9. I improved my English by _____ (go) to language class.

Some verbs can be followed by either a gerund or an infinitive without changing meaning:
(love, like, hate, intend, prefer) + **gerund** or **infinitive**

E.g. Alice likes painting. Alice likes to paint.
John likes playing tennis. John likes to play tennis.
I like reading. I like to read.
I intend to visit my parents next week. I intend visiting my parents next week.
She prefers eating ice-cream to chocolate. She prefers to eat ice-cream to chocolate.

Some Practice for you

10. John prefers _____ (run) than _____ (swim). John prefers _____ (run) than _____ (swim).
11. We love _____ (go) out for dinner. We love _____ (go) out for dinner.
12. I hate _____ (watch) football! I hate _____ (watch) football!

Answers: 1. repairing cars 2. singing 3. working hard 4. going 5. cooking 6. reading 7. jogging 8. watching 9. going 10. to run, to swim OR running, swimming 11. going, OR to go 12. watching OR to watch

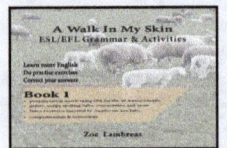

Grammar: gerunds & infinitives (continued)

Fill in the blanks below with the correct form of the verb in the brackets.

1. It appears that some car salesmen are only interested in (make) _____ money.
2. Michael couldn't get a taxi so I offered (drive) _____ him to the airport.
3. We managed (book) _____ three front row seats for the play.
4. She promised (send) _____ me her new phone number.
5. Sally was glad (meet) _____ an old friend at the market.
6. He avoids (take) _____ his car to work in the city, especially on weekdays.
7. I finished the job my boss wanted me to do by (work) _____ 16 hours a day.
8. Julie sent an SMS to her friend (say) _____ she would be (attend) _____ the party.
9. Many people enjoy (drive) _____ in the hills of Dandenong.
10. I intend (speak) _____ to my manager about a pay increase.

Gerunds and infinitives are used to begin interesting sentences.

E.g. She wanted to help her children. It meant giving them a good education.

infinitive phrase=to help her children   gerund phrase=helping her children

   new sentence=To help her children meant giving them a good education.
   new sentence=Helping her children meant giving them a good education.

E.g. We hoped to walk 20 km each day so we had to be fit.

infinitive phrase=to walk 20 km   gerund phrase=walking 20 km

   new sentence=To walk 20 km each day we had to be fit.
   new sentence=Walking 20 km each day, we had to be fit.

Use the sentences to construct new sentences beginning with gerunds and infinitives.

11. When someone drives a car it is a big responsibility.

gerund phrase= _____

new sentence= _____

infinitive phrase= _____

new sentence= _____

12. It is a good idea for everyone to have a yearly check-up with their doctor.

gerund phrase= _____

new sentence= _____

infinitive phrase= _____

new sentence= _____

Answers: 1) making 2) to drive 3) to book 4) to send 5) to meet 6) taking 7) working 8) attending 9) driving 10) to speak 11) driving a car; Driving a car is a big responsibility. to drive; To drive a car is a big responsibility. 12) having; Having a yearly check-up with your doctor is a good idea. to have; To have a yearly check-up with your doctor is a good idea.

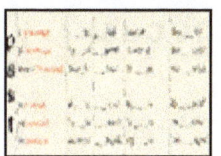

Verb Tenses: present participles

Continuous tenses use the present participle which always ends with "-ing". Of course these "-ing" ending words are verbs and not gerunds, which are nouns. Notice that when the **present participle** is acting as a verb in the continuous tenses there is a "to be" verb always included? Also, there are two, three or four words used in the continuous tenses. Look at the examples.

present continuous tense: I *am reading* my book at the moment.
past continuous tense: I *was reading* yesterday.
future continuous tense: I **will** *be reading* my book next week.
present perfect continuous tense: I **have** *been reading* my book all afternoon.
past perfect continuous: I **had** *been reading* my book when the phone had rung.
future perfect continuous: I **will have** *been reading* my book for two hours before you get home!
passive voice present continuous: My book *is being read* by his son at present.
passive voice past continuous: My book *was being read* by his son yesterday.

When a **present participle** is used as a gerund-noun, the "to be" verb is **not** present to form a verb tense.

E.g. Argyro hated *living* in a small village so she loved *studying* in Athens.
Sewing was fun for Argyro and she found it easy to do.

Furthermore, a **present participle** can be used as an adjective to provide more meaning to a noun. E.g. He bought her a *cooking* book for her birthday.

For each sentence, underline & name the "ing" ending words as an adjective (a), gerund (g) or present participle (pp) of a verb tense.

1. We are going out after washing our clothes.
2. Emilia believes that singing is good for your soul!
3. Julie is living in Toorak until renting there becomes unaffordable.
4. Jogging is a healthy pastime, so I am jogging this evening.
5. I am reading the writing in Simon's exercise book.
6. They were studying well into the night.
7. Most people are shy of public speaking.
8. We had been visiting Canberra many times over the years before we moved there.
9. Have you seen the cooking show called "My Kitchen Rules"?!
10. Knowing how to swim could save your life, so swimming lessons are a good idea as part of everyone's education.
11. My parents will have been dancing in competitions for twenty-five years next October.

Answers: 1. pp=going, g=washing 2. g=singing 3. pp=living, g=renting pp=jogging 4. g=jogging, pp=jogging 5. pp=reading 6. pp=studying 7. g=speaking 8. pp=visiting 9. a=cooking 10. g=knowing, a=swimming 11. pp=dancing

Verb Tenses: present simple & present continuous tenses

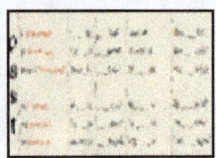

When and how are these two tenses used? Let's compare them.

Present Simple Tense	Present Continuous Tense
permanent situations E.g. I **live** in Wantirna, Melbourne.	temporary situations E.g. I **am living** with my friend until I find my own place to rent.
habits, regular actions E.g. They **catch** the train to work.	still happening actions E.g. Harry **is reading** the newspaper at the moment.
future public timetabled events E.g. The bus **leaves** in five minutes.	future personal plans and arrangements E.g. He **is going** fishing next month.
unchanging truth/facts E.g. Ice **melts** and **becomes** water.	talking about what is in photos E.g. She **is wearing** a lovely dress and he **is holding** their son on his shoulders.

Use the verb in the brackets to form the correct tense.

1. My neighbours _____ (plan) a holiday to Hawaii. They ^{2}_____ (leave) tomorrow with Qantas. When they ^{3}_____ (get) there, they _____ (stay) on an island. As you can see in the photo, they ^{4}_____ (hope) to learn some traditional hula dancing.

5. She _____ (read) her book in order to pass her test and _____ (get) a top mark.

6. Oh no! I _____ (see) a policeman _____ (write) me a ticket for parking in a clearway zone!

7. In the morning she _____ (get) out of bed and _____ (go) into the kitchen and _____ (make) a cup of coffee.

8. He _____ (run) to catch his friend so they can walk to school together.

9. They _____ (plan) to train in the gym together, because they can encourage each other.

10. She usually _____ (get) her daughter ready for school and then she _____ (take) a quick walk with her husband.

11. Usually, after finishing their work, they _____ (go) home.

12. The sun _____ (rise) in the east.

13. She _____ (stay) only until her husband comes to pick her up.

14. We _____ (love) one another!

Answers: 1. are planning 2. are leaving 3. get, are staying 4. are hoping 5. is reading, get 6. see, is writing 7. gets, goes, makes 8. is running 9. are planning 10. gets, takes 11. goes 12. rises 13. is staying 14. love

Some verbs are **not** used in the *continuous tenses*. E.g. I *am seeing* it now! These include the following verbs:

- Using your brain

know, understand, think, believe, remember, imagine, realise, recognise, mean

- Communication

mean, promise, surprise, deny, agree, disagree, satisfy

- Senses

taste, hear, sound, see, smell, appear, feel, seem

- States

be, concern, need, possess, own, owe, depend, matter, involve, belong

- Feelings

love, hate, like, wish, want, prefer

Complete the sentences using the correct form of the verb in brackets.

1. Look up there! I _____ (to see) the plane arriving.

2. Every Sunday we _____ (to go) to church.

3. She _____ (to believe) in God.

4. Rod _____ (to like) fruit and vegetables.

5. My cousins _____ (to plan) to go to Europe next year.

6. He _____ (to promise) to take her out this evening.

7. We _____ (to think) you are telling the truth.

8. They _____ (to know) what they are talking about!

9. She _____ (to work) at McDonalds and at Bunnings too.

10. It _____ (to seem) the right thing to do.

11. You know that I _____ (to love) you now and always!

12. I _____ (to owe) my parents a lot of money and gratitude too.

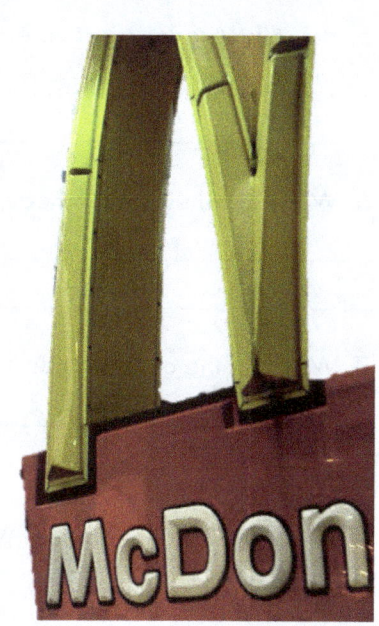

Answers: 1. see 2. go 3. believes 4. likes 5. are planning 6. promises 7. think 8. know 9. is working 10. seems 11. love 12. owe

Chapter 4 Family
Reading Comprehension

After reading Chapter 4 of *Speak English Like Australians!*, answer the following questions in full sentences. That is, include the question as part of your written answer, so that the question is recognised by the person reading your answer.

1. Why did Argyro feel ashamed when she went into hospital to have her first baby?
   _____
   _____

2. Why did Theo and Argyro hope to have a son?
   _____
   _____
   _____

3. What were Argyro's feelings about having a baby girl?
   _____
   _____
   _____

4. What were the names of their children and future grandson?
   _____
   _____

5. How did Argyro treat Peter's injured hand?
   _____
   _____

6. What did the children hear coming from over the fence?
   _____
   _____

7. Why did the children stand on chairs?
   _____
   _____

8. Who was John Landy and what did he do to win the hearts of the world?
   _____
   _____

Answers: 1. Argyro felt ashamed when she went into hospital to have her first baby because she couldn't understand English. 2. Theo and Argyro hoped to have a son to carry on the family name. 3. Argyro felt unhappy about having a baby girl as she remembered her brother-in-law's words about wanting to hear she had had a son. 4. The names of their children were: Voula, Peter and Jimmy. Later their grandson was named Theo. 5. Argyro treated Peter's injured hand by chopping up onions and garlic, adding oil and vinegar, putting it all on a tea-towel and then wrapping up the injured hand with the tea-towel for a bandage. 6. The children could hear a lot of interesting sounds coming from over the fence. 7. The children stood on chairs so they could see over the fence into the school yard. 8. John Landy was a famous Australian track athlete, who won the hearts of the world when he kindly stopped to help a young competitor, during a preliminary race for the Olympic Games.

Speaking: getting a listener's attention

What can you say to get someone's attention when you are trying to tell them something and they are not really listening to you? Here are some suggestions to practise using with a partner.

Pair Work

Discuss them and rate them together from 1 to 8.

Which expressions would you use only with people you know very well? _____

1 MOST polite ↓

a. Are you listening?   ....
b. Is something wrong?   ....
c. Do you agree?   ....
d. What do you think?   ....
e. Am I boring you?   ....
f. Did you hear what I said?   ....
g. Are you with me?   ....
h. Are you paying attention?   ....

8 LEAST polite

Take turns speaking the dialogue and pretend your listener is not paying attention. What do you say?

Learner A	When did you arrive in Australia?
Learner B	I arrived in 2020, in June.
Learner A	Really? Your English is very good.
Learner B	Thank you. I practise speaking every day and I listen to stories on YouTube.
Learner A	That's a good idea.
Learner B	What were your first impressions of Australia when you got here?
Learner A	I thought it was strange that the shops were closed!
Learner B	Yeah me too. We wanted to find a cafe that was open late at night. We couldn't find one!

Share your memories of your first day in Australia.

1. Where was the first place you landed in Australia?
2. Who was with you?
3. What were your first thoughts of Australia?
4. What did you notice first of all?
5. Have your ideas changed since then? Explain.

Group Work

a) Use your listening and speaking skills (refer to Chapter 2 Speaking) to share your opinions and discuss why you decided to migrate to Australia and if you intend to return to your country of birth/origin.

I came to Australia because ………   I would like to ………….

I don't intend to …………..   Eventually, I intend to ………….

Chants: Family

Practise your pronunciation as well as your intonation. Enjoy singing the three chants until you can say them easily and keep the rhythm going. Stress the bold text to get the correct rhythm.

Sure... a family is **good**
A family is **right**
Till you're **misunderstood**
And have a big **fi**ght!

Well... a **family** is **fine**
I **know** and under**stand**
It **is** like **wine**
And im**prove**s with **time**!

I've **got** a **wife**
The **delight** of my **life**
Got four **girls**
With **golden curls**
We've **got** a **dog**
That **caught** a **frog**!

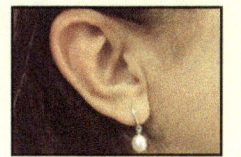

Listening: cloze activity

The text below should be read out load two or three times, at normal speed. This is a listening activity and missing words are to be written in the gaps. The educator should stress that spelling is not the focus as it is a listening activity and that spelling will be corrected at the end of it. Alternately the text may be heard on the Internet www.speaklikeaustralians.com , AUDIO & VIDEO – *Chapter 4.*

In March 1956 the Olympic Games came to Melbourne and Australians were [1]_____ about the fast runner, John Landy. When he ran his [2]_____ trial race, all of Australia wanted him to win. However during this race, at Olympic Park in Melbourne, he stopped to help a young runner, Ron Clarke, who had fallen. But John Landy did not give up and he started running the race again. He ran so fast that he won the race, even though he had stopped to [3]_____ someone else! Because of John Landy's kind behaviour, people started calling him Gentleman Landy. He had won the hearts, not only of all Australians, but of the rest of the world, because of his kind and respectful attitude!

Argyro didn't go to the Olympics. She stayed in Hamilton, trying hard to get used to living there after her life in Greece. It was a [4]_____ town so there were no English classes to help her. Anyway, everyone thought a migrant would somehow learn English by themselves, and would [5]_____ the Aussie way of doing things. Also, Australians were not interested in other cultures. Migrants had to become *New Australians* and had to change their "old" way of life. Furthermore, because most Australians did not [6]_____ other cultures, they were impatient with migrants. "Go back to where you came from!" they sometimes told migrants, or "speak English like Australians!"

In those days, [7]_____ culture was common and taught in schools. Australians loved everything about England, which was the "motherland". There was a [8]_____ called *The White Australia Policy* that encouraged white migrants, and especially British immigrants to migrate to [9]_____. From 1944 to 1949, a British citizen living in Australia, automatically became an Australian citizen! That is how important Britain was to Australia.

Hamilton Hospital

Anyway, Argyro became pregnant soon after her marriage. She went to hospital to have her first child. Sadly, it was a [10]_____ time for her because she didn't know much English. When the nurses tried to tell her things, poor Argyro did not understand at all! She was very scared! She also felt ashamed that she didn't [11]_____ English. Argyro wished she could understand what the nurses were telling her to do! To make things worse, men were not allowed to be with their wives during the birth, so Theo waited in [12]_____ room for news of his wife and baby.

Answers: 1. excited 2. famous 3. help 4. country 5. accept 6. understand 7. British 8. law 9. Australia 10. stressful 11. speak 12. another

Dictation: aural

The instructor, or a learner who wants to practise their pronunciation, dictates the texts in chunks and repeats them twice before continuing. Correct individually or as a class.

Because of the primary school next door, little Peter and Voula could hear a lot of interesting noises coming from over the fence. It was a mixture of yelling, laughing children at play. Peter and Voula sometimes stood on chairs, to look over the fence, at the primary school children playing in the school yard.

Dictation: in pairs

Pair up to give each other pronunciation, listening and writing practice. Repeat the text slowly and clearly so as not to confuse your listener.

Learner 1

After the birth, Theo was taken by a nurse to see his daughter in the nursery. He could not help feeling disappointed, but he was a practical man. He soon pushed away his negative thoughts.

Learner 2

When Theo was allowed to see his wife, Argyro thought she saw his disappointment. She started to cry and refused to take her newborn daughter from the nurse.

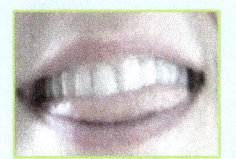

Pronunciation: linking sounds /w/ & /n/

Often, when we speak, we join one word to the next word with a sound: a "linking" sound. The linking sound is made longer to join with the next word. A common linking sound is: /w/ and is used after words ending with an /u:/ sound that are followed by a word beginning with a vowel sound.

Read the word pairs and practise saying them fast and joining them with the /w/ linking sound.

blue eggs

through all

too old

Sue opened

you asked

new umbrella

Another common linking sound is: /n/ and is used after words ending with /n/ and followed by a word starting with a vowel sound.

Read the word pairs and practise saying them fast and joining them with a strong /n/ linking sound. Have fun!

ten oranges

can open

can ask

fun audio

join up

win again

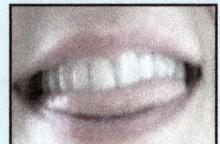

Pronunciation: linking sounds /r/ & /ə/

When a word ends with /r/ and is followed by a **vowel sound** (single, double or triple), then use /r/ as a strong linking sound between the two words. This is used in normal speech to improve speed and for more fluid speech.

For example: Would you like an orange or an apple?
/r/

Say the sentences, while making sure to use a strong /r/ linking sound in the correct places. Notice that if a word ends with /r/ and is followed by a word beginning with a /r/, then also use /r/ as a strong linking sound between the two words.

Their eyes are red from the smoke.   Your car roof rack looks sturdy.
/r/   /r/   /r/

Some of our eggs are broken.   I don't like competing or racing against you!
/r/   /r/

Where are all the flowers I planted last year in April?
/r/ /r/   /r/

Decide where to use the linking /r/ in the following sentences and practise saying them until you feel confident. Check your answers below.

1. Would you like some more ice-cream?
2. Where are they going for their August holidays?
3. They're on their way.
4. Do you like my new pair of shoes?
5. It's rude to stare at other people!

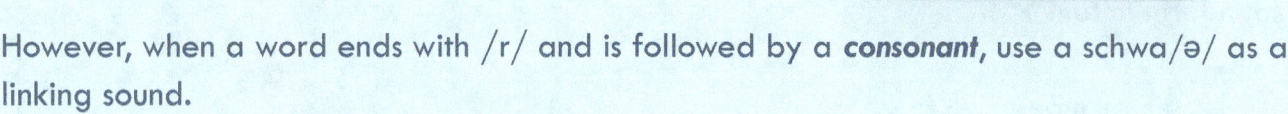

However, when a word ends with /r/ and is followed by a **consonant**, use a schwa /ə/ as a linking sound.

For example: Our dog is black.
/ə/

Practise saying the sentences after deciding where to use the linking schwa.

6. Sally and Martin love their computer games.
7. They're late for the class.
8. My son lives here with me.
9. Please sit on the chair next to me.
10. Your hair looks lovely today.

Answers: 1. /r/ between "more" & "ice-cream" 2. /r/ between "where" & "are"; "their" & "August" 3. /r/ between "they're" & "on" 4. /r/ between "pair" & "of" 5. /r/ between "stare" & "at" 6. /ə/ between "their" & "computer" 7. /ə/ between "they're" & "late" 8. /ə/ between "here" & "with" 9. /ə/ between "chair" & "next" 10. /ə/ between "hair" & "looks"

Phonograms: "aw", "ay", "c"

Both "aw" and "ay" have only one pronunciation, whereas, "c" has two possible pronunciations.

Read the examples in the tables.

IPA for "aw" pronunciation	/ɔː/
Spelling using the letters **aw**, has only one pronunciation and is most often at the ends of words.	saw
	flaw
	strawberry
	claw

IPA for "ay" pronunciation	/ʌɪ/
Spelling using the letters **ay**, has one pronunciation only. *Exceptions: quay, kayak*	today
	delay
	freeway

IPA for "c" pronunciation	/ k /	/ s /
Spellings using the letter "**c**" can have two different pronunciations /k/ and /s/. "C" is pronounced /s/ when **followed** by "e", "i" or "y". *Exceptions: Celts, soccer, sceptic* [US spelling: skeptic]	concentrate	concentrate
	clever	cylinder
	concert	concert
	computer	recent
	calculate	cygnets =young swans
	come	celery
	circus	circus
	comfort	decide
	clapping	cyclone

Tongue Twisters: "r"

Say each tongue twister until you can say it easily and smoothly.

1. Robyn and Robert Rory remembered a rainy Christmas in Rowville.
2. I really like rainbows, ribbons, red roses and raspberries.

Conversation Bits: what a stereotype; no surprises there

Repeat the conversation until your intonation is native-like. Say the expressions in one breath and don't pause between words. Practise with a partner to make it more like a role play.

Denis	My mate at work loves hunting and he asked me to hunt rabbits with him this Saturday.
Meryl	Really! And you accepted?
Denis	Sure, I've never been shooting before. I think it'll be fun, and you can make rabbit soup for dinner.
Meryl	**What a stereotype!** You hunt for food and I'll cook it!
Denis	Yeah. What's wrong with that? I'm the bloke after all. You don't want to go shooting, do you?
Meryl	No, of course I don't. I'd feel so sorry for the little bunnies.
Denis	**Well no surprises there!** You're a **stereotypical** woman!
Meryl	I know some women who would be happy to hunt - it's just not me!
Explanations:	
stereotype = to unfairly think the behaviour of a group of people is the same for all of them	
No surprises there = you are not surprised, you knew/expected it	

Spelling: when to use double "s"

When changing a verb to a noun as in part 1 or when spelling short verbs and nouns as in part 2, here are some spelling rules you may find helpful. The accents used are to show the stress and are not usual in spelling these words.

1. Use double "s" when the verb ending "mit" becomes "mission" (to form a noun).
   For example: submit-submission   commit-commission

2. Use double "s" after áccented short (single) vowel sounds.
   For example: máss, bléss, kíss, lóss, fúss

Carefully say each word below and note why there is a *double* "s" for each one. Is it reason 1 or reason 2 mentioned above?
(Accents have been used just to show the stress of each word after which *double* "s" is used.)

1. discúss
2. mássive
3. lósses
4. kísses
5. mísses
6. rússet
7. omíssion
8. blésses
9. góssip
10. posséss
11. impréss
12. clássic
13. véssel
14. permíssion
15. éssence
16. crósses
17. progréssion
18. conféss
19. impréssion
20. addréss
21. distréss
22. aggréssion
23. pássion
24. bléss
25. góssip
26. admíssion
27. transmíssion
28. blóssom

Answers: 1.2 2.2 3.2 4.2 5.2 6.2 7.1 8.2 9.2 10.2 11.2 12.2 13.2 14.1 15.2 16.2 17.2 18.2 19.2 20.2 21.2 22.2 23.2 24.2 25.2 26.1 27.1 28.2

Vocabulary: synonyms

Add interest and variety to your writing by using synonyms (different words with the same meanings).

Look for the synonyms of these words. They can be found in Chapter 4 of "Speak English Like Australians!"

1. the small baby _____
2. to cry quietly _____
3. country town _____
4. gulped _____
5. noticed, discovered, saw _____
6. uncertain what to do, don't know what decision to make _____
7. telling someone that all will be well, that it will be alright _____
8. baby _____
9. unmusical, noise that that sounds harsh _____
10. laughing that is loud and hard _____
11. fascinating and interesting _____
12. racial slang word for migrants, especially used for Italian and Greek migrants _____

Complete the expression by writing the missing word.

13. As it happened, Argyro _____ pregnant soon after her marriage.
14. She went to hospital to _____ her first child.
15. Theo wanted to name his future son "Peter" after his own father who had passed _____ when Theo was barely out of his teens.
16. Argyro _____ birth to a perfect, tiny infant.
17. It was _____ for the school children, who often teased them and were not very kind at all.
18. The primary school children regarded Peter and Voula as _____ , sticking their noses over the fence.

A pregnant lady is also called a "lady-in-waiting".

Answers: 1. the small bundle 2. weep 3. rural town 4. swallowed 5. detected 6. confused 7. reassuring 8. infant 9. cacophony 10 cachinnating 11. intriguing 12. wogs 13. fell 14. have 15. away 16. gave 17. opportunistic 18. busybodies

Figures of Speech: synecdoche

A synecdoche /sɪ nék tə hɪ/ is a figure of speech that describes a *part* of something or the *material* it is made of, as if it is the *whole* of that thing. It is used to "colour" writing and to make it more interesting.

Here are some examples of synecdoche.

Could I have a glass? (It's referring to the glass, for the whole of the glass with the beer inside it!)

He's got a new set of wheels. (This refers to his new car by describing a part of it, the wheels, for the whole the car.)

When the police found the criminal, he was full of lead. (This describes his body as having bullets in it. The synecdoche is using the material of lead to refer to bullets.)

They owned fifty head of cattle. (It refers to fifty cows and denotes part of the cow, the head, with the whole of the cow.)

The early navy had twenty sails. (It is referring to twenty ships. The synecdoche is applying part of a ship, the sails, for the whole of the ship.)

Find the synecdoche in the text.

Theo really did love his daughter, naming her Voula, after his mother. He thought that maybe the next child would be a son... In fact, there were soon more mouths to feed and the next two babies were both sons, Peter and Demetrius (Jimmy), so Theo and Argyro were happy that they had "done their duty", and the family name could continue. Later in life they would have a grandson named Theo born to their first son, Peter.

Answer: The synecdoche in the text is: mouths to feed (The synecdoche refers to "mouths" for a whole "person".)

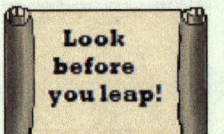

Proverbs: woman

Proverbs usually explain common sense or wisdom in a short sentence. Proverbs are well known and often repeated in a culture. In fact, the Bible has an entire book of Proverbs. Did you notice that the proverb, "The unexpected always happens," is used in Chapter 4 of the novel "Speak English Like Australians!"?

Write the *meaning* of each of the following proverbs.

1. A good woman is hard to find, and worth far more than diamonds.
   (The Bible, Book of Proverbs, chapter 31, verse 10)

2. Beauty is in the eye of the beholder.

3. Man is the head but woman turns it.

4. A man is as old as he feels, a woman as old as she looks.

Answers: Proverbs: 1. A good woman is priceless. 2. Everyone sees beauty differently. 3. Man may be the "boss" of the family but his wife can influence his thinking and guide him in his decisions. 4. As long as a man feels well and strong it does not matter how old he looks. With a woman, however, looks are more important, since a woman tends to be judged by them; if she looks old, people will think of her as old.

Writing: a childhood recount or an imaginary recount (narrative genre)

Argyro's children were curious to see what was going on over the fence. There is a proverb which says "curiosity killed the cat" and is used to warn of the dangers of unnecessary or too much inquiry. However, children are always very curious about their environment. For example:

Because of the primary school next door, little Peter and Voula could hear a lot of interesting sounds coming from over the fence. It was a mixture of yelling, laughing children at play. They sometimes stood on chairs, to look over the fence, at the primary school children playing in the school yard. But the school children teased them and were not very kind at all. They thought Peter and Voula were busybodies, sticking their noses over the fence and looking at them! Also Voula and Pete didn't seem very friendly, because they wouldn't speak to the Aussie school kids. There were two reasons why. Firstly, they were too shy and secondly, they couldn't speak much English!

Please write about an experience when you were a child and were curious about something going on around you. (Your recount can be factual or imaginative!)

_____
_____
_____
_____
_____
_____
_____
_____

The runner, John Landy, was expected to break the four-minute mile and thousands of Australians turned out to see him run his preliminary race leading-up to the Olympic Games. However, during the race he stopped to assist Ron Clarke who had fallen. He lost five seconds helping him up, but then went on to win the race! Mr Landy displayed great **sportsmanship** and was touted as a **gentleman.** He later became Victoria's Governor General.

Pretend you are part of the crowd watching the race. Express your feelings and explain the feelings of the crowd too. Tell what happened as you watched this amazing race.

_____
_____
_____
_____
_____
_____
_____

Writing: imaginary recount (narrative genre)

A RECOUNT shares memories of past experiences and events and is a way the writer can entertain and inform the reader.

- A RECOUNT tells about *past events*.
- It informs or entertains the reader.
- It can be about real or imaginary events.

some useful vocabulary

tell, happen, friends, last week, pack suitcases, bags, push down, holiday, ferry timetable, drive car, traffic, late, hurry to terminal, miss ferry, leave pier, disappoint, change plans

Write an imaginary recount. Start by writing some sentences for the photos about a ferry trip. Use your imagination.

Use pronouns like: I, we, they, she, he

Use mostly the past simple tense (I did...) and the past perfect tense (I had done...).

Make sure your events are in the correct time order (chronological).

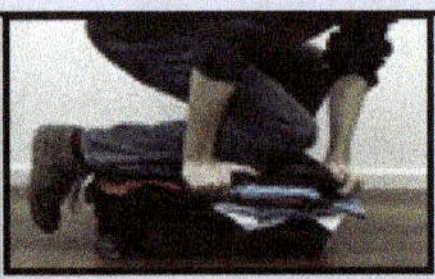

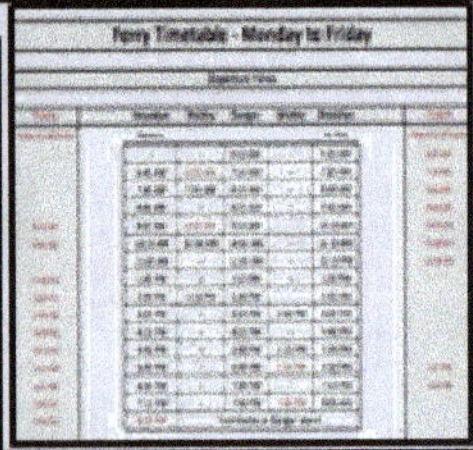

Read your photo sentences again. They could be part of a series of events for your *Recount Plan* (event A, event B, event C).

Think more carefully and write MORE information below, to plan your recount. Be brief, as it is only a guide for you to write your recount.

MY RECOUNT PLAN		
Introduction -paragraph 1	Who? _____ What? _____ Where? _____ When? _____ How? _____	
Events -paragraphs 2, 3, 4	event A _____ event B _____ event C _____	
Conclusion -paragraph 5	Use some of the same words and ideas from your introduction and share your thoughts and feelings. _____	

Now use your plan to write your recount of 5 paragraphs. Continue on the next page. Show your imaginary recount to an instructor or to a friend.

_____
_____
_____
_____
_____
_____
_____
_____
_____
_____
_____
_____
_____
_____
_____
_____
_____

Parts of Speech: determiners

Some determiners are quantifiers because they give information about the quantity of a noun/pronoun (refer to Chapter 1 Parts of Speech). In other words, quantifiers are used to explain about the number of something: how much or how many.

Sometimes we use a quantifier instead of "the".

For example: *The* children in my play group love fruit.   *Most* children in my play group love fruit.

We ate *the* bread you made.   *Some* bread is still uneaten.

These quantifiers are used with both **count** nouns (apples, jobs) and **uncount** nouns (rice, work, advice, furniture, luggage, information, knowledge, hair, sugar etc.):

| some | no/none of | any/not any | enough | less/least |
| a lot of | lots of | plenty of | more/most | all |

For instance: We ate *most* of the apples that were in the fridge.

We ate *more* of the rice as it was yummy!   He has lots of jobs to do around the house.   She has a lot of work to do before her guests arrive.

Some quantifiers can be used only with **count** nouns:

| a great/large/huge number of | a couple of | hundreds of |
| thousands of etc. | several | (a) few | fewer |

For instance: Yesterday I bought *a few* apples from the market.   Barry has got *a couple of* jobs at the moment: as a packer for Coles at night and as a furniture deliverer during the day.

Some quantifiers can be used only with **uncount** nouns:

| a little | (not) much | a great deal of | plenty of | a bit |
| of a large/a huge amount of | heaps of/tons of/loads of |

For instance: Would you give me *a little* rice on my plate please?   I have *a great deal* of work to do during the weekend.   My mother-in-law always gives me *heaps of* advice about housework!

Under each box, write your own sentences, using the quantifiers from the boxes. Use both count nouns and uncount nouns.

Parts of Speech: verb and preposition

A verb followed by a different preposition can change its meaning. Please look at the examples.

care to	Would you care to explain? (Would you like to explain?)
care for	She does not have a job as she cares for her children at home. (She looks after her kids.) Would you care for a cup of coffee? (Would you like a cup of coffee?)
care about	Do you care about climate change? (Does climate change concern you?)
listen to	Joe likes to listen to the news every day. (He likes the news on the radio.)
listen for	I heard a noise, so I listened for some more sounds! (Listen for some particular thing.)
listen with	My granddaughter loved my stories and listened with great interest.
look at	I looked at my hair in the mirror.
look for	They looked for their friend in the restaurant. They found him after a few minutes.
look forward to	I am looking forward to visiting you in your new house!
look into	The police looked into the bank robbery of last year and found some new information. (They investigated the old robbery.)
look up	If you ever go to Rome, please look up my auntie. (Go and visit my auntie.)
meet at	Do you want to meet at the cafe? How about we meet at 5pm?
meet for	Let's meet for one hour. They met for *old times sake*!
meet in	They met in the dark. He meets (clients) in his office.
meet over	Let's meet over lunch and catch up!
meet with	Could you meet with me to talk about it?
work at	I work at the old office building across the road. I work at McDonald's.
work by	She works by hand, knitting jumpers. He knows all the work by heart. (Remembers how to do it.)
work in	We work in a circus. They work in the evenings.
work for	Martha works for a very large company.
work with	Bruce works with Mark. I work with my hands.
work through	We can work through these problems. (Work to solve the problems.)

Write the missing preposition.

1. When I visited New York, I looked _____ my old high school friend and we met _____ a cup of coffee.
2. The students listened _____ attention, to what the teacher was telling them to look _____ on the Internet.
3. We must listen _____ the weather details, so we will know if we can work _____ the garden tomorrow.

Answers: 1. up, over. 2. with, up. 3. for, in.

Parts of Speech: verb and preposition

agree about/on	We should try to agree about/on where to go for a holiday. (Decide together.)
agree to	My friend and I agreed to meet for lunch at the cafe at 1pm. (We reached agreement.)
agree with	I agree with you that it is difficult to trust a politician! (We have the same idea.)
apply for	I want to apply for a job at the bank.
apply to	He will apply to the Bank of Melbourne for a loan.
apply with	You can apply with a click of a mouse. You can apply with your credit card.
arrive at	We arrived at the bus stop early. The bus will arrive at 3pm.
arrive in	Our neighbours had bought a new car and we saw them arrive in luxury!
arrive with	Susan arrived with her grandmother, holding her hand.
turn in	It is late so I want to turn in. (Go to bed.) The criminal turned in his partner and the police arrested him. (He informed the police about his partner.) My grandmother would turn in her grave to see women wearing such short dresses! (Grandmother would be shocked!)
turn over	Turn over the page; I want to read the next paragraph. Turn over so I can rub medicine on your back.
turn with	The child turned with joy on his face when he heard his mother's voice.
wait at	Wait at the train station for me.
wait for	Please wait for me!
wait in	He waited in his room until it was dark. She waited in vain for his apology. (He did not say sorry.)
wait with	Please wait with me at the cafe!

Write the correct prepositions for each verb.

1. Do you agree _____ the plan Peter has made?
2. I think you should turn _____ for the night as you're tired!
3. The children arrived _____ their parents during the morning.
4. You must apply _____ a photo of yourself.
5. The President arrived _____ the conference in style!
6. He arrived _____ style with his wife wearing a new dress!
7. Could you please turn _____ the box so I can paint the base?
8. Is he going to wait _____ us so we can go together?

Answers: 1. with 2. in 3. with 4. with 5. at 6. in 7. over 8. for

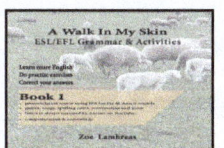

Grammar: determiners

ARTICLES are used in front of nouns or in front of the adjectives of the nouns. However, when speaking generally, we use the present simple tense and we **do not** use "the" or "a".

Write 'a,' 'an' or 'the' if needed.

The other day I saw [1]_____ woman coming out of [2]_____ lift near my office. She was wearing [3]_____ dark blue suit and she was carrying [4]_____ brief case. She looked lost so I asked her if I could help her. She told me she was looking for [5]_____ boss. I pointed to his office door. She walked to [6]_____ door and knocked. When [7]_____ boss answered she went in.

8. _____ Australians are famous for their surf lifeguard skills.
9. _____ English are cool, not hot-blooded like _____ Spanish.
10. Robin Hood used to steal ____ money from _____ rich to give it to _____ poor.
11. _____ people don't like _____ taxes.
12. _____ Romans ruled the world about 2000 years ago.
13. Does your daughter still go to _____ school? (generally speaking)
14. He is in _____ prison because he stole some money.
15. They will have their baby's christening in _____ church in High Street followed by ____ dinner in _____ restaurant in _____ Chapel Street.
16. I'm afraid of _____ spiders.
17. _____ doctors are paid more than _____ teachers.
18. Do you like _____ Chinese food?
19. Did you like _____ Chinese food we ate for lunch yesterday?
20. _____ children at my son's school are very scholastic.

Use the quantifiers in the box to rewrite the sentences below.

> a few, some, most, a little, much, many, a lot of, lots of, enough, any

21. ____ Australians are famous for their surf lifeguard skills.
22. _____ English are cool, not hot-blooded like _____ Spanish people.
23. Robin Hood used to steal ____ money from _____ rich people to give it to _____ poor people.
24. _____ people don't like _____ taxes.
25. Do you drink _____ water during the day?

Answers: 1.a 2.the 3.a 4.a 5.the 6.the 7.the 8.- 9.The, the 10.-, the, the 11.-, - 12.The 13.- 14.- 15.the, a, a, - 16.- 17.-, - 18.- 19.the 20.The 21.Some 22.Many/most, Most/many 23. lots of/a lot of/much, many, any/many 24. most, much/a lot of 25. enough/much/any/a lot of/lots of

Page 115

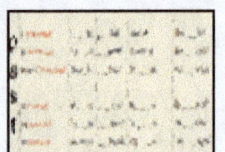

Verb Tenses: have got/gotta

When *speaking* or using *informal writing*, "have/has got" can be used *instead of* "have" and has exactly the same meaning. "Have" is a present simple tense and so is "have/has got". Although "have/has got" looks like the present perfect tense it is not! There are four times you can use the two words "have/has got" rather than using "have". But don't use "have/has got" when "do/does/did" is in the sentence, use "have/has" without "got".

1. **Physical characteristics**

    I have/have got blue eyes and brown hair.   He's got brown eyes.   Has he got blond hair?
    They've got very short hair.   Do they have moustaches.   She doesn't have long legs.

2. **Sickness or feeling out of sorts**

    I have a headache.   She's got a backache.   Hasn't he got asthma?   I've got the measles!
    Do you have a cold?   Has he got the flu?   He doesn't have the flu.   Doesn't he have allergies?
    No he hasn't got any allergies.   Does he have a fever?   He has got bad breath!

3. **Possessions or things that are ours**

    They have got a two-storey house.   They've got a single-storey flat.   We've got a new car.
    Our neighbours have got a new dog.   Haven't they got a cat too?   They don't have a cat.
    We've got fantastic news to tell you!   I've got a great idea!   I don't have the time to listen right now.
    I've got information to share.   She has got a lot of knowledge.   He's got a plan.
    Have you got a minute?   Do you have any time?   I've got time.   I have got only a moment.

4. **Relationships with people**

    My parents have got two sons and a daughter.   They've got three kids.
    I haven't got kids.   Do you have grandchildren?   Yes, I've got three of them.
    I don't have any.   We haven't got any either.   Well we don't have uncles or aunties.
    No you don't, but I haven't got a brother and you do!

*The expression "have got to" or "gotta" (informal spoken) means "must/have to"

   I've *gotta* go before it gets too dark!   She's *got to* go to the bank.   He *has got to* go!

Complete the sentences.

a) Do you _____ time?

b) I've _____ to leave before it gets dark!

c) They don't _____ their books.

d) We haven't _____ our car with us.

e) I've _____ pick up my three kids from school.

f) He's _____ tinnitus and hay fever.

g) I've _____ time to help you with your homework.

h) Doesn't he _____ a blocked nose?

i) She _____ got her award yet.

j) I don't _____ any idea about that.

k) Has he _____ a mobile phone?

l) They haven't _____ the skills to perform CPR.

Answers: a. have b. got c. have d. got e. got to/gotta f. got g. got h. have i. hasn't j. have k) got l) got

Verb Tenses: making questions with the simple tenses—conjugation

Making Questions using the Simple Tenses

Complete the sentences in the empty boxes.

present simple tense (with 'to be' negative verb)

statement	question	'why/how'	tag question
Sally isn't late.	Isn't Sally late?	Why isn't Sally late?	Sally isn't late, is she?
They			
We aren't late.			
You			
I			

past simple tense (with 'to be' verb)

statement	question	'why/how'	tag question
Sally was late.	Was Sally late?	Why was Sally late?	Sally was late, wasn't she?
They			
We			
You			
I			

To ask a question using present & past simple verbs, other than 'to be', you must use the helping verbs do, does, did.

present simple tense (with 'do/does' + base verb i.e. to watch)

statement	question	'why/how'	tag question
Tom			
They			
We			
You			
I watch movies.	Do I watch movies?	Why do I watch movies?	I watch movies, don't I?

past simple tense (with 'did' negative + base verb i.e. to like)

statement	question	'why/how'	tag question
Tom didn't like the movie.	Didn't Tom like the movie?	Why didn't Tom like the movie?	Tom didn't like the movie, did he?
They			
We			
You			
I			

Answers: *present simple tense (with 'to be' negative verb)* They aren't late. Aren't they late? Why aren't they late? They aren't late, are they? Aren't we late? Why aren't we late? We aren't late, are we? You aren't late. Aren't you late? Why aren't you late? You aren't late, are you? I am late. Am I late? Why am I late? I am late, aren't I? *past simple tense (with 'to be' verb)* They were late. Were they late? Why were they late? They were late, weren't they? We were late. Were we late? Why were we late? We were late, weren't we? You were late. Were you late? Why were you late? You were late, weren't you? I was late. Was I late? Why was I late? I was late, wasn't I? *present simple tense (with do/does + base verb i.e. to watch)* Tom watches movies. Does Tom watch movies? Why does Tom watch movies? Tom watches movies, doesn't he? They watch movies. Do they watch movies? Why do they watch movies? They watch movies, don't they? We watch movies. Do we watch movies? Why do we watch movies? We watch movies, don't we? You watch movies. Do you watch movies? Why do you watch movies? You watch movies, don't you? *past simple tense (with did negative + base verb i.e. to like)* They didn't like the movie. Didn't they like the movie. Why didn't they like the movie? They didn't like the movie, did they? We didn't like the movie. Didn't we like the movie? Why didn't we like the movie? We didn't like the movie, did we? You didn't like the movie. Didn't you like the movie? Why didn't you like the movie? You didn't like the movie, did you? I didn't like the movie. Didn't I like the movie? Why didn't I like the movie? I didn't like the movie, did I?

Chapter 5   School

Reading Comprehension

After reading Chapter 5 of *Speak English Like Australians!*, answer the following questions in full sentences. In other words, include the question as part of your written answer, so that the question is recognised by the person reading your answer. This way your answers are much more understandable and less tiring for the reader to interpret.

1. What were the initial problems for Voula when she started primary school?

2. What did Argyro decide to do to Voula and why?

3. What was Voula's understanding of the expression "boss around"?

4. How did the kids bully little Voula at school?

5. Why was Voula often late back to school after lunch?

6. What do you think is the meaning of "busybodies"?

7. What was the reader, *John and Betty*, focussed on?

8. In your opinion, does shaving hair make it grow back thicker and stronger? (Start with "I think that ...")

Answers: 1. The initial problem for Voula when she started primary school was that it was all a strange new world because she didn't understand English and she felt different from the other kids. 2. Argyro decided to shave off all of Voula's hair to make it thicker. 3. By the term "boss around" Voula thought that it meant to make someone or to boss someone to go around in a circle. 4. The kids bullied little Voula at school by teasing her and laughing at her. 5. Voula was often late back to school after lunch because it was her job to take little Jimmy to kinder during her lunch-break and he couldn't walk very fast. 6. The meaning of busybody is someone who is interested in other people's business and shouldn't be: it is a negative thing. 7. The reader *John and Betty* was focussed on the traditional middle-class roles of girls and boys in Britain. 8. Opinions will vary.

Speaking: learning and school

Pair Work

Voula learnt English when she started primary school. She copied everything and she was *immersed* in English.

Discuss together what you think.

a) Do you think being immersed is the best way to learn a language?

b) What would you recommend?

c) What have you done to help yourself learn another language?

Take turns to be speaker A and B to practise this conversation together.

Situation Dialogue

A: Could you help me please?

B: Sure!

A: I don't know where my English class is.

B: Do you have your timetable?

A: Yes here it is.

B: Well if you look here, the letters are for the building and the numbers show the room.

A: Oh I see! It's in building WG. Do you know where that is?

B: Yes, just walk through the double glass doors; you'll see WG building ahead of you.

A: My class is in room number 106.

B: I have a class near there. I'll show you where it is.

A: Thanks a lot!

Group Work

Voula was just eight years old when she walked her little brother, Jimmy aged four, to his kindergarten. In those days children often walked to and from school alone.

1. Compare your opinions about whether you would allow your child to walk to school nowadays where you live. Give your reasons and use different expressions for opinion. (Refer to Chapter 2 Speaking section for *opinion expressions* and making *encouraging noises while listening*.)

2. Take turns to answer the questions on the board game *My Primary School Memories*. Please ask each other questions, look at each speaker, smile and make encouraging noises.

Speaking: board game

Take turns to answer and to ask the questions on the board game.

My Primary School Memories

1. Did you enjoy your primary school days?	2. What is your first primary school memory?	3. What is a good thing about going to school?
4. Why are some kids unhappy at primary school?	5. Do you think primary school days the best days of your life?	6. What is your best memory of primary school?
7. What is the worst memory of your primary school days?	8. What would you change about primary school, if you could go back in time?	9. Did you have a school uniform? Is it a good idea? Explain.
10. What is the most important thing you learnt in primary school?	11. Who was your best friend in primary school? Describe them.	12. Where was your primary school? Describe it.
13. At what age do you want your kids to start primary school?	14. Who was your favourite primary school teacher? Why?	15. What was your favourite subject at school?

Chant: Going to School

Practise your pronunciation, and sing the song until you can say it easily and keep the rhythm going. Stress the bold text.

I **sang** a song
As I **skipped** along
And **watched** for the birds
As they **nested** in the trees.

It **felt** really good
To be **going** to school
Until I tripped
An' **fell** on my knees.

I **bled** on my socks
And **into** my shoes
But I **tried** to be brave
And **not** to cry.

It took **all** my effort
'Cause I **felt** I really bad!
Time **seemed** so slow
As I **walked** with pain.

But I **strugg**led along
Till I **got** to my class.
My **tea**cher cleaned me up
An' **gave** me spare socks.

And to **my** surprise
I **got** better fast!

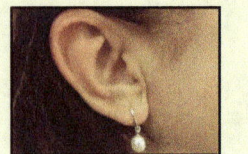

Listening: follow the text along

Go to YouTube:Home on the Internet. Search for "Zoe Lambreas – Chapter 5: School". Listen to the audio as you read along. You can pause and replay it any time you need to. Enjoy the Aussie accent! Corrections are at the bottom of the page.

You can change the speed of the audio by clicking on the settings icon and selecting a new speed.

Listening Cloze from page 41, of the novel *Speak English Like Australians!*
Fill in the blanks with the missing words that you hear.

Finally, the day arrived when Voula reached the ¹_____ of five and started preps. She found that primary school was a ²_____ new world of blah, blah, blah! Voula learnt that she had to be quiet and not speak until the teacher asked her a question. That was not a problem ³_____ she couldn't speak much English at all! Everything she learned was by copying what the other kids did in class. If they stood up behind their little chairs, so did Voula. If they walked to the front of the class and sat on little mats, so did Voula too. Everything seemed very different. She thought the teachers ⁴_____ very tall and strict. Especially when they stood on the platform in front of the blackboard. Voula felt different from her classmates, even though she ⁵_____ a school uniform like them. She was still ⁶_____ the other kids ⁷_____ of her ⁸_____ skin and she had no freckles like a lot of the sun-burnt English kids.

Things got ⁹_____. One day, Argyro decided to ¹⁰_____ off *all* of Voula's hair with a razor, to ¹¹_____ it thicker. She thought it was too thin and that it was ¹²_____ for girls to have lots of lovely, thick hair! Well! Voula had an even more difficult time at school, ¹³_____ at ¹⁴_____ the children pulled off her little ¹⁵_____ to laugh at her bald, shiny head. All of ¹⁶_____ differences separated Voula from her ¹⁷_____. ¹⁸_____ of the other kids wanted to be friends with such a ¹⁹_____ girl!

What do all the missing words have in common? _____

Answers: They are all words that end with silent "e". 1. age 2. strange 3. since 4. were 5. wore 6. unlike 7. because 8. olive 9. worse 10. shave 11. make 12. nice 13. because 14. playtime 15. beanie 16. these 17. classmates 18. None 19. strange All the missing words have a silent "e".

Page 122

Dictation: a different running dictation

Group Work

Skills: speaking, listening, patience, writing and team work, good sportsmanship, pronunciation, spelling, reading

Three learners work in a group together as denoted by A, B and C.

Each Learner C is positioned outside the room at a predetermined location but fairly close together. The instructor spends time with them to practise their pronunciation of the words. They then memorise chunks of the text so they are able to tell it to their group members, with only a bit of reading. (A volunteer tutor could remain with these learners to assist them at intervals, if necessary.)

Learner A quickly goes to Learner C, who tells Learner A some of the text. Learner A returns to Learner B to dictate the text while Learner B writes it down. Learner A may spell words and seek pronunciation help from Learner C or the instructor, but may not write the text for Learner B.

When Learner A completes dictating their text, he/she swaps places with Learner B who meets with Learner C while Learner A writes this time.

As each group finishes they give their written dictation, along with their names, to the instructor. Learner Cs must remain out of the room until all groups have finished.

When they re-enter the room, the instructor ensures points are allocated to each group in order of completion. However, points are deducted by the instructor for every error, even punctuation. The final winner is the group with the highest score. They may share their winning strategies with the other learners and give them hints for future improvement!

Learner A

The children learnt to read from a "reader" called *John and Betty*. Everyone had their own book and took it home to practise reading. During class, Voula took her turn going to the teacher's desk, to read *John and Betty* out loud to her.

Learner B

She read one or two pages per day and when she got to the end she read it again until she could read it quickly. (Then she received her next reader, which was more difficult.)

Learner C

The children learnt to read from a "reader" called *John and Betty*. Everyone had their own book and took it home to practise reading. During class, Voula took her turn going to the teacher's desk, to read *John and Betty* out loud to her. She read one or two pages per day and when she got to the end she read it again until she could read it quickly. (Then she got her next reader, which was more difficult.)

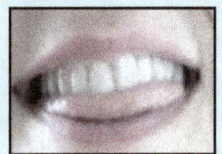

Pronunciation: plural "s"

(Revision of Chapter 2 Pronunciation: plural nouns & present simple verbs)
Plural "s" can have three different pronunciations.

1. /əz/ if it is after the letters s, z, ss, ge, dge, sh and ch

2. /s/ if preceded by an unvoiced sound. For example (c, f, h, k, p, t)

3. /z/ if preceded by a voiced sound. For example (l, b, g, j, m, n, r, v, w)

Decide if the final s in the following words has an /əz/, /s/ or a /z/ sound.

1. kisses _____
2. struggles _____
3. judges _____
4. pleases _____
5. flaps _____
6. watches _____
7. assemblies _____
8. lasts _____
9. fabrics _____
10. pleases _____
11. claims _____
12. classes _____
13. teachers _____
14. metres _____
15. roles _____
16. words _____
17. steaks _____
18. computers _____

Answers: 1. /əz/ 2. /z/ 3. /əz/ 4. /əz/ 5. /s/ 6. /əz/ 7. /z/ 8. /s/ 9. /s/ 10. /əz/ 11. /z/ 12. /əz/ 13. /z/ 14. /z/ 15. /z/ 16. /z/ 17. /s/ 18. /z/

Phonogram: "ch"

The letters "ch" have three possible sounds. Practise saying each column of words until you feel confident. Can you think of some words to add?

IPA for "ch" pronunciation	/tʃ/	/k/	/ʃ/
Words using the letters **ch** have three possible pronunciations. *Exception:* **choir** sounds like "kwire"	champion	Christmas	chef
	cheese	monarch	chute
	children	chemical	chandelier
	bachelor	patriarch	champagne
	manchester= things made of linen or cotton cloth that are used in the home, for example sheets	stomach	crochet
	attach	orchestra	machete
	peach	ache	creche
	mulch	archeology	quiche
			chassis=the base frame of a car

Tongue Twisters: "s" & "ch"

Say each tongue twister until you can say it easily and smoothly without getting tongue-tied!

1. Sixty-six snakes slithered smoothly across the snowy stones.

2. Children chat in Chinese and chew cashews and chips dipped in chilly.

3. Six thick thistle sticks stay sturdy and strong.

a thistle plant

Conversation Bits: dilly-dally! lift my game! I was mortified!

Repeat the conversation until your intonation is native-like and you feel confident with your pronunciation, stress and intonation.

Say all the expressions smoothly in one breath, so you don't pause between words.

In Chapter 5 of *Speak English Like Australians!*, Jimmy dilly-dallied on the way to kindergarten and Voula felt mortified. Do you understand the context? Look at the explanations below.

Denis	Is something wrong?
Meryl	Yes actually. I had a horrible day at work.
Denis	What happened?
Meryl	My boss told me that I was taking too long to do my work! He thinks I **dilly-dally**!
Denis	I'm sure you work hard. Can't he see that?
Meryl	He knows I work overtime to catch up but he told me I had to **lift my game**.
Denis	Well try to work faster even if you don't do so good a job.
Meryl	I think that's good advice! I'll do that. But **I was really mortified**, especially because he talked to me in front of two of my workmates!

Explanations:
dilly-dally = waste time through not making a decision, slow to finish
lift your game = do better, get better results, work harder to improve
feel mortified = feel very ashamed/ embarrassed

Page 126

Spelling: silent "e" rules

There are 5 kinds of silent final "e" at the ends of words.

Silent e – Spelling Rule 1

The last three letters of some words are a vowel, a consonant and a final "e".

The silent "e" often makes the single vowel sound into a double vowel sound. For example: "i" can have the short /ɪ/ sound but when a silent "e" is added to the end of a word, it becomes the double vowel sound, /aɪ/ (or we may say that it becomes a long sound like its alphabet name). This happens whenever there is a single vowel followed by a single consonant and then the final "e". Such words follow the pattern v+c+ "e".

Here are some examples:

late, here, file, rose, tune, file, cute, refute, astute, state, plate, complete, graduate, assimilate, alone, bloke, rope, became, shake, stake, mistake, write, mate, dictate, debate

Sometimes there is a silent "e" even after **two** consonants, instead of just one consonant, as in *bathe* and *paste,* because without the final "e" these words would be *bath* and *past,* which have different meanings and only have single vowel sounds. These words are rare exceptions to *rule 1* as they follow the pattern v+c+c+ "e". Other examples are *purse* and *dense.*

Silent e – Spelling Rule 2

In English, we cannot end a word with a "v" or a single "u" so we add a silent "e" to avoid this happening.

Examples of these words are:

groove, move, prove, leave, love, nerve, clue, glue, issue, continue, dove

Some notable exceptions are abbreviations like "flu" which is short for "influenza" and foreign words like "impromptu" which is French.

Silent e – Spelling Rule 3

The silent "e" follows "c" and "g" to make them say /s/ and /dz/ respectively. Without the final "e" these sounds would be /k/ and /g/.

Examples of these words are: change, chance, lounge, mortgage, engage, advantage, assistance, advance, grimace, interference

Spelling: silent e rules (continued)

Silent e – Spelling Rule 4

There is a rule that every **syllable** in English must have at least one vowel. ble, cle, dle, fle, gle, kle, ple, sle, tle, zle are all syllables which would not have a vowel if there were no final "e".

Examples of this kind of words are: capable, cubicle, cradle, duffle, goggle, little, simple, title, battle, bottle, cattle, rattle, sizzle, dazzle, muzzle, puzzle, apple, ripple, ample, hassle, beetle

Silent e – Spelling Rule 5

Sometimes the final "e" is not needed. Perhaps in the past the silent "e" had a purpose but now it has outlived its usefulness in today's English and only hangs around from habit. Maybe in years to come the "e" letters will disappear from them. Anyway, for these words, rules 1–4 do not apply. We call this type of "e" the *no job* e.

Examples are: house, come, are, aware, compare, promise, some, rare, spouse, awe, rye

Use the silent "e" words listed below and for each one write the "silent e" spelling rule that it follows.

1. age
2. strange
3. since
4. were
5. wore
6. hide
7. unlike
8. because
9. olive
10. make
11. playtime
12. nice
13. have
14. shave
15. creature
16. ostracise
17. more
18. none
19. associate
20. strange
21. beanie

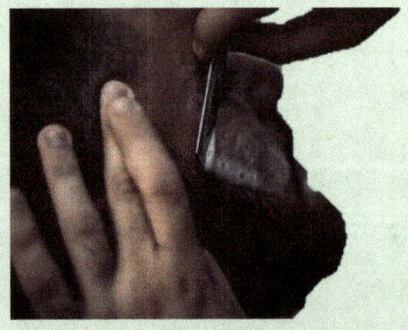

Answers: 1=rule 1 2=rule 1 3=rule 3 4=rule 5 5=rule 1 6=rule 1 7=rule 1 8=rule 5 9=rule 5 10=rule 2 11=rule 1 12=rule 1 13=rule 5 14=rule 1 15=rule 5 16=rule 1 17=rule 1 18=rule 5 19=rule 5 20=rule 3 21=rule 5

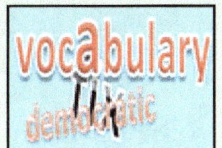

Vocabulary: crossword

Words from Chapter 5 of *Speak English Like Australians!* are used for the crossword. For 2 words do not leave any spaces in the crossword.

CLUES

Across

3. being unkind, unfriendly and hurtful to others with your words or by using force

4. small, brown spots on the skin because of being out in the sun

6. (2 words) to force or order someone else to do what you say

8. these days now

9. a knitted head covering worn as a hat

10. the name of the first book children learnt to read from in primary school was called "John and _____"

11. (2 words, slang) very busy working and have no time for anything else (starts with "f")

Down

1. after kindergarten in Victoria, children start in _____ school

2. different and not normal

5. (2 words) to cut with a razor so there is no more hair on the skin

7. the general name of a book children learn to read from

Answers: Across: 3. bullying 4. freckles 6. boss around 8. nowadays 9. beanie 10. Betty 11. flat out Down: 1. primary 2. strange 5. shave off 7. reader

Page 129

Figures of Speech: simile revised

Revision (Chapter 1, Figures of Speech)

A simile /sɪ məlɪ/ is a figure of speech comparing two unlike things, often introduced with the word "like" or "as."

Similes can follow these patterns:

X is (not) <u>like</u> Y

X is (not) <u>as</u> Y

X is (not) <u>similar to</u> Y

Examples of similes:

1. The lake did not look <u>as smooth as</u> glass as it was windy.
2. During the exam he was as cool as a cucumber.
3. My kite soared similar to an eagle.
4. The old soldier is as gentle as a lamb at home.
5. The puzzle wasn't as clear as crystal.
6. Beating my younger sister in basketball is like taking candy from a baby.
7. This room is as clean as a whistle-you can eat off the floor it's so clean!
8. These clothes are like warm toast.

1. Underline the words that make the similarity of the similes above. The first one has been done for you.

2. Underline the similes in the text.

Her impressions of the teachers were that they were very tall like giraffes and strict. Even the school uniform she wore did not protect her or hide her differences: she was still unlike the other kids because of her olive skin and she had no freckles like a lot of the sun-burnt Anglo-Saxon kids. She felt like an alien and was often left out of their games.

Proverbs: relationships

It is often difficult to "belong" in another society, and even at school. Write the meanings of these *wise sayings* about relationships which are very useful to know and to adopt.

1. No man is an island.
_____
_____
_____

2. When in Rome, do as the Romans.
_____
_____
_____

3. A soft answer turns away wrath.
_____
_____
_____

Answers: 1. People need each other and should not be isolated. 2. When you are away from home respect the tradition and culture of those around you and do like they do. 3. Don't say angry words when someone is upset with you, but use gentle, friendly words to defuse their anger.

Writing: Two Supporting paragraphs (persuasive genre)

Often we have strong *opinions* about a topic and want to explain it clearly and convincingly to others. A good way to do this is to think of two good reasons for why you think as you do. Each reason is written in its own paragraph with a topic sentence and supporting sentences.

Read the two supporting paragraphs below about nursing homes. Notice how the topic sentences are followed by their supporting sentences. They are clearly organised in each paragraph.

Nursing homes are often seen as terrible places to put your loved ones but the truth is that nursing homes provide a more stable and secure environment. Nursing homes employ professional carers who know how to look after the elderly; especially the frail or sick ones. Moreover, these professionals provide healthy meals, daily care and medication at the right times.

Furthermore, there are other senior people living in nursing homes, so there are many opportunities to make new friends and to socialise. They can play games together to pass the time and they can do craft activities they enjoy or make gifts for family and friends. Having other people around helps residents not to feel lonely and forgotten. They can ask for help whenever they need it or they can go into their rooms to be alone or to rest.

When would this idea be a good one: that children should not speak near adults unless they are spoken to first by them? "When Voula reached the age of five and started preps she started primary school... Voula learnt that she had to be quiet and not speak until the teachers asked her a question."

from *Speak English Like Australians!*, page 41

_____
_____
_____
_____
_____

Did you ever have this experience as a child: of being told not to speak near adults until they spoke to you first? Please explain.

_____
_____
_____
_____
_____
_____

What is your opinion about children not speaking, when there are adults around, until an adult speaks to them first? Please express your views by writing two supporting paragraphs with reasons and examples. Don't forget to leave an empty line between the two paragraphs! Show your instructor.

Writing: application for a course (persuasive genre)

If you enrol at a private institution, it is a good idea to check that it is an RTO. i.e. a Registered Training Organisation with the Department of Education. Apply for admission directly to the institution of your choice and complete the institution's application form, online. Submit the application form, and any necessary supporting documentation, to the institution. Or, after you submit your application, you may be requested for additional supporting documentation by email.

Your application should show you are motivated and committed to study. Also, write down any relevant work experience and knowledge of the course you are applying for. A typical *Statement of Application* aims to persuade the reader that you will be a successful and valuable student.

Here is **a model application** for someone wanting to be accepted into a nursing degree.

Be direct!	My parents are business people and have been running a successful restaurant for 31 years. Over the years they have encouraged me to join the family business but I have always had a different dream: I want to be a nurse. It is not that I don't admire my parents because I do, it's just that I
Show interest.	feel happiest when I care for people in times of need! I thrive on challenges and as a nurse I know that every day I will have new goals to achieve. The learning opportunities and the diversity of nursing makes it the ideal field
Show academic reasons.	for me to be a part of. I have studied biology and chemistry in my final secondary years and achieved my highest scores in these subjects, because I found them so interesting.
Share relevant experience.	As a volunteer in an aged care facility for three years, I found it satisfying and not as stressful as some people think. The interactions with people and the loving memories I have, provided me with a passion to impact the lives of people under my care. There is nothing so impacting as hearing first hand
Be modest.	how my small efforts as a volunteer have been appreciated and valued by those needing my help.
Show a willingness to learn and to be taught.	I have been very lucky over the years to speak with several nurses and they all love their work because of the good they are doing. One particular family friend advises me to "do what you love and love what you do!" I hope that with time, my own skills and understanding of nursing will equate to these marvellous, hard-working nursing professionals. I have a deep desire
Don't be too proud.	to make a positive difference in the lives of others. My volunteer experience encourages me that nursing and not business is my vocation. I hope that with diligence and much effort I can succeed in this course.

309 words

Guided Writing

Write an application for a primary teaching degree.

Explain why you want to do this course.

further reasons: interested in children

you like socialising

Feelings of fulfillment and reward

Some relevant experience as volunteer, interests and hobbies.

Polite conclusion

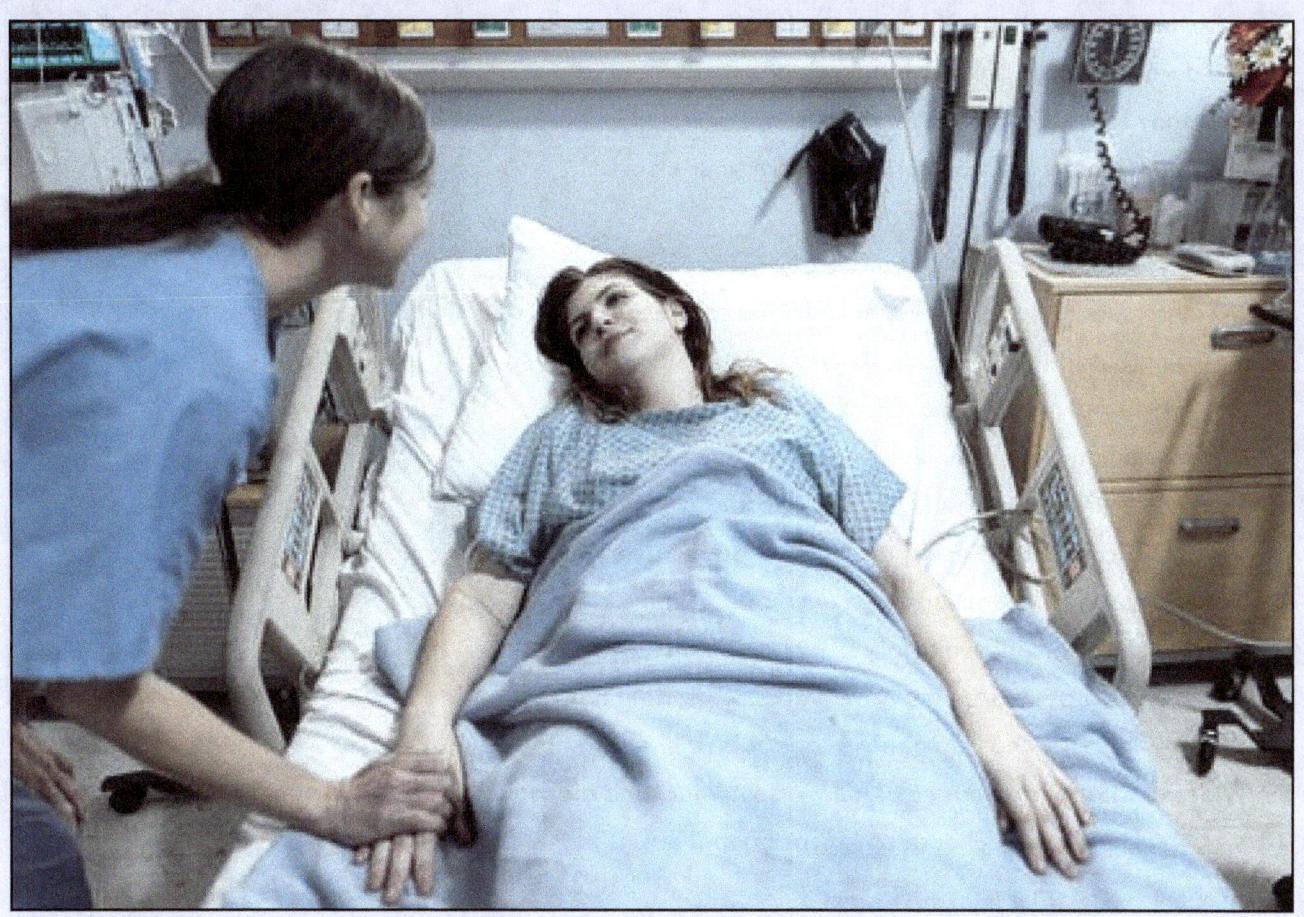

Parts of Speech: count and uncount nouns revision

Nouns are names of places, people and things. When we want to talk about more than one of something, we use the plural form of the noun by adding "s" "es" or "ies" to the end of it. However, some nouns cannot take a plural "s" and are considered as uncount nouns (non-count or a mass nouns). This type of noun is thought of as *one unit*. Some other differentiating qualities between count and uncount nouns are listed on the table on the next page. Please compare them.

Compare the words listed in the table.

Uncount Nouns	Count Nouns
water cheese sugar coffee butter milk bread *news furniture knowledge work advice information advice luggage music accommodation homework housework money traffic equipment ice electricity power gas scenery	apples toys tables bags cats dogs cities streets desks books ideas jobs cups fingers pianos violins cakes views teachers ladies

Cross-out the wrong count or uncount noun for each sentence.

1 Could you please give me advices/advice. I don't know what to do!
2 How many houses/house do you own?
3 He is working very hard. He has three jobs/job.
4 Would you like milks/milk in your coffee?
5 How many cities/city have you visited?
6 Can I please have the apples/apple from your tree?
7 I eat breads/bread for lunch every day.
8 Do you use butters/butter on your bread?
9 How much sugars/sugar do you take in your coffee?
10 I'm going outside to get fresh airs/air.
11 Our teacher gives us homeworks/homework.
12 Do you do houseworks/housework on the weekends?
13 There are fruit trees/tree in our back yard.
14 My husband reads the newspapers/newspaper every morning.
15 When I travel I take my luggages/luggage with me.
16 Do you have memories/memory of your parents?
17 We are not busy and do not have works/work right now.
18 We are not busy and do not have jobs/job right now.
19 I was very happy to hear news/new about your son's marriage.
20 My son likes cheeses/cheese on his spaghetti.

Answers: correct nouns are: 1. advice 2. houses 3. jobs 4. milk 5. cities 6. apples 7. bread 8. butter 9. sugar 10. air 11. homework 12. housework 13. trees 14. newspaper 15. luggage 16. memories 17. work 18. jobs 19. news 20. cheese

Uncount Nouns	Count Nouns
No – PLURAL "S" furnitures advices	Yes – PLURAL "S" apples students
No – A, AN furniture=Did you buy a new furniture? advice=I would like an advice from you please.	Yes – A, AN apple=Did you buy **an** apple? student=**A** student in our class works part-time.
yes – THE, THAT, THIS furniture=Did you buy the new furniture? advice=I would like that advice you promised me.	yes – THE, THAT, THIS, THESE, THOSE apple=Did you buy **the** ripe apple? student=**Those** students are in our class.
Yes – SOME furniture=Did you buy some new furniture? advice=I would like some advice from you please.	Yes – SOME apples=Did you buy **some** ripe apples? students=**Some** students work very hard.
Yes – A LOT OF, LOTS OF, A LITTLE furniture=Did you buy a lot of new furniture? advice=I would like a little advice from you please.	Yes- A LOT OF, LOTS OF apples=Did you buy **a lot of** ripe apples? students=**Lots of** students work hard.
Yes – MUCH, LESS, AMOUNT OF furniture=Did you buy much new furniture? advice=I would like less advice from you please. money=He earns a large amount of money now because he has completed his studies.	No – MUCH, LESS, AMOUNT OF apples=Did you buy much ripe apples? students=Less students in our class work. coins=She has a small amount of coins in her collection as she lost some.
No – MANY, FEWER, A NUMBER OF furniture=Did you buy many new furniture? advice=I would like fewer advice from you please. money=I have a large number of money in the bank.	Yes – MANY, FEWER, NUMBER OF apples=Did you buy **fewer** apples than I did? students=**Many** students work hard. coins=She has a small **number of** coins.
No – NUMBERS (1, 2, 3, 4 ....) furniture=Did you buy 2 new furniture? advice=I would like two advice from you please.	Yes – NUMBERS (1, 2, 3, 4 ....) apple=Did you buy **3** ripe apples? students=**Thirty** students are in our class.
Yes – QUANTITY WORDS (partitive words) advice=I got **two bits of** advice from my dad. bread=She'd like **3 slices of** bread for her sandwiches. furniture=Did you buy **2 pieces of** new furniture?	Yes – QUANTITY WORDS (partitive words) apples=Did you buy **3 whole** ripe apples? flowers=I bought **eight bunches of** flowers.

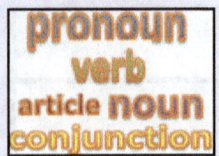

This time, write a suitable word that can be used with each count or uncount noun. Refer to the table on the previous page for extra help.

For example: Please give me <u>less</u> sugar than my husband.

1. Could you please give me _____ advice. I don't know what to do!

2. How _____ houses do you own?

3. He is working very hard. He has _____ jobs.

4. We are not busy and have very _____ work at the moment.

5. How _____ countries have you visited?

6. Can I please have _____ apples?

7. I eat _____ bread for lunch every day.

8. Do you use _____ butter on your bread?

9. How _____ sugar do you take in your coffee?

10. I'm going outside to get _____ fresh air.

11. Our teacher gives us _____ homework.

12. Do you do _____ housework on the weekends?

13. My son likes _____ cheese on his spaghetti.

14. There are _____ fruit trees in our back yard.

15. My husband reads _____ newspaper every morning.

16. Would you like _____ milk in your coffee?

17. I was very happy to hear _____ news about your son's marriage

18. Do you have _____ memories of your parents?

19. When I travel I only take _____ luggage with me.

20. If I had _____ worries it would reduce my blood pressure!

Answer: 1. some/a bit of/a little/lots of/a lot of 2. many 3. two/three/four 4. little 5. many 6. some/two, three etc. / a few/a lot of/ lots of/many fewer/a large number of 7. a slice of/two slices of/a piece of/some/a bit of 8. any/much/some/a little/a bit of/a small amount of 9. much 10. some/a bit of/a little 11. a little/a lot of/lots of/some/much 12. any/some/much/a bit of/a little/a lot of/lots of 13. some/a little/a bit of/lots of/a lot of/much/a large amount of 14. many/a large number of/some/a few/two, three etc. 15. a/the 16. any/some/a bit of some 17. the 18. any/some/many/a few/a lot of/lots of 19. a little/a bit of/some 20. no/fewer/a smaller number of

Page 138

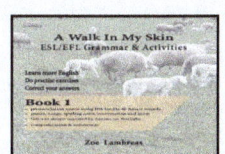

Grammar: the patterns of sentences

To better understand sentence structure it is not only helpful to study *part of speech* **word order** as explained on page 52, but also to look at the same idea from a slightly different perspective; by thinking about the *phrases* and *clauses* within a sentence.

Groups of words with a verb are called "clauses" and groups of words without a verb are known as "phrases".

E.g. clauses- I ran away.   The young girls were laughing all the way home.
E.g. phrases- very quietly (how)   ...next year (when/time)   .... along the road (where/place)
 ...because of the mud (why/reason)

Sentences can have many different patterns. To look at some of the patterns we will use:
S (subject): the doer of the action/verb, in the active voice
V (verb): the action
O (object): The action happens to the object^{direct}, which is a noun/pronoun.
   object^{indirect} = usually precedes the object^{direct} and refers to who or what received the direct object
C (complement): it adds more meaning to the subject or the object an is used with the verbs "to be", "to seem", "to feel" etc. It answers the question "what/who".
A (adverbial): answers the question "how", "when", "where" and "why".

Consider the following sentence patterns.

1. S+V   The boy is singing.   Mary cried.

2. S+V+O^{direct} The boy is singing a song.

3. S+V+C   The boy is ready. (The boy is what?)   That is him/he.$^{more\ formal}$ (That is who?)

4. S+V+A   The boy is singing at the concert. (The boy is singing where?)

5. S+V+O^{indirect}+O^{direct} The boy gave me a book.

6. S+V+O^{direct}+O^{indirect} The boy gave a book to me.

7. S+V+O^{direct}+C   The boy called Mary clever. (The boy called Mary what?)

Notice that adverbials are special because they can be used more than once in a sentence and in different positions too. For example compare 8a and 8b.

8a. S+V+O^{direct}+A^{when} The boy saw Mary in the afternoon. (The boy saw Mary when?)

8b. A^{when}+S+V+O^{direct} In the afternoon, the boy saw Mary. (When did the boy see Mary?)

Notice that usually A^{where} goes before A^{when}.

8c. A^{why}+S+V+A^{how}+A^{where}+ A^{where}+A^{when}
   Because the boy felt confident, he sang loudly ^{Ahow} in the choir ^{Awhere} beside his friend ^{Awhere} during the concert ^{Awhen}.

Page 139

8d. A^{why} + A^{where-1} + S+V+A^{how} + A^{where-2} + A^{when}

Because the boy felt confident ^{Awhy} beside his friend, ^{Awhere-1} he sang loudly ^{Ahow} in the choir ^{Awhere-2} during the concert ^{Awhen}.

8e. S+V+A^{how} + A^{where-1} + A^{where-2} + A^{when} + A^{why}

The boy sang loudly ^{Ahow} in the choir ^{Awhere-1} beside his friend ^{Awhere-2} during the concert ^{Awhen} because he felt confident ^{Awhy}.

8f. A^{when} + S+V+A^{how} + A^{where-1} + A^{where-2} + A^{why}

During the concert ^{Awhen}, the boy sang loudly ^{Ahow} in the choir ^{Awhere-1} beside his friend ^{Awhere-2} because he felt confident ^{Awhy}.

As mentioned in 8a & 8b, *when* phrases are also possible at the **end** of a sentence and we can also switch the order of the **where adverbials**.

8g. S+V+A^{how} + A^{why} + A^{where-2} + A^{where-1} + A^{when}

The boy sang loudly ^{Ahow} because he felt confident ^{Awhy} beside his friend ^{Awhere-2} in the choir ^{Awhere-1} during the concert ^{Awhen}.

Rewrite each *incorrect* sentence in two different ways. (Place and time adverbials practice.)

For example: Sofia jogs every day to work. (incorrect order of words)

Sofia jogs to work everyday. Everyday Sofia jogs to work. (correct: The time adverbials have two possible positions in the sentence.)

1. I want now a sandwich because I am hungry.
   _____

2. To the bank every Monday go I.
   _____

3. The wedding very much everyone really enjoyed last weekend.
   _____

4. Did you late go to bed last night?
   _____

5. I drink every weekend two cups of coffee with some cake.
   _____

6. They danced at the party only once yesterday because they were shy.
   _____

7. Some very interesting books found we last week at the library.
   _____

8. Lilly speaks quite well German as she learnt for five years.
   _____

Answers: 1. I want a sandwich now because I am hungry. Because I am hungry, I want a sandwich now. 2. I go to the bank every Monday. Every Monday I go to the bank. 3. Everyone really enjoyed the wedding very much last weekend. Last weekend, everyone really enjoyed the wedding very much. 4. Did you go to bed late last night? Last night, did you go to bed late? 5. I drink two cups of coffee with some cake every weekend. Every weekend I drink two cups of coffee with some cake. 6. Yesterday they only danced once at the party because they were shy. At the party yesterday, they only danced once because they were shy. 7. We found some very interesting books at the library yesterday. Yesterday we found some very interesting books at the library. 8. Lilly speaks German quite well as she learnt for five years. As she learnt for five years, Lilly speaks German quite well.

Verb Tenses: present simple & present continuous

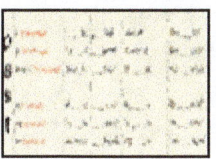

Change the verbs to the correct present tense. Some words are incorrect and need altering too.

Hello. My name am Rani and I came from Sri Lanka. Are you knowing where that was? Australia seemed like a very nice place to me and I was telling everyone how much I will enjoy living here. At present I was take English classes to improving my English speaking.

You should believing me when I told you that it is very, very nice to get away from my home duties and family responsibilities for a little times and just be with my classmate? I was surprise about that because at first it be a bit scaring. The teacher she understanding me and I am understanding everybody in my class too. I am listening all the times to learning something new every day. I really likes reading too but my favourites are the conversation.

Abbreviate the verbs.

For example: We are leaving soon. We're leaving soon.

1. I am early.
2. You are late.
3. He is coming later.
4. She is thinking about it.
5. We are visiting tomorrow.
6. They have an exam.
7. I am not coming.
8. She has not arrived yet.
9. You have not finished your work.
10. Have not you had enough to eat?
11. You would be happy with me.
12. Harry has been here many times.
13. She should not have told you that!
14. Our teacher has given us new books to write in.

Answers: Hello. My name **is** Rani and I **come** from Sri Lanka. **Do** you **know** where that **is**? Australia **seems** like a very nice place to me and I **tell** everyone how much I **enjoy** living here. At present **I'm taking** English classes to **improve** my English speaking. You should **believe** me when I **tell** you that it is very, very nice to get away from my home duties and family responsibilities for a little **time** and just be with my **classmates**? I **am surprised** about that because at first it **is** a bit **scary**. The teacher **she understands** me and I **understand** everybody in my class too. I **listen** all the **time** to **learn** something new every day. I really **like** reading too but my **favourite is the** conversation.

1. I'm early. 2. You're late. 3. He's coming later. 4. She's thinking about it. 5. We're visiting tomorrow. 6. They've an exam. 7. I'm not coming. 8. She's not arrived yet. 9. You haven't finished your work. 10. Haven't you had enough to eat yet? 11. You'd be happy with me. 12. He's been here many times. 13. She shouldn't have told you that! 14. Our teacher's given us new books to write in.

Practise using the present simple tense for *regular actions*.
Jan is a carpenter. What does she do *every* day?

Read about what she does and underline the present simple tense.
Jan: I get up at six every morning. I shower and have breakfast at 6:30am so I can start work at 7am. At four o'clock I finish work and pack up my tools. I drive to my mum's place and have dinner with her. I usually get home by 8 and go to bed at about 10.

What do you do every day? Write about Jan and yourself and make sure to use the third person "s" on the verbs when required.

Jan _____ at six. She _____ and _____ breakfast at 6:30am so she can _____ work at 7am. At 4pm Jan _____ her work and _____ to her mother's place and _____ dinner with her. She _____ usually in bed by _____.	I _____ at _____ and _____ to the bathroom. Then I _____ and _____ breakfast at _____ so I can be in class at _____. By _____ my class _____ and I _____ home.

The present simple tense, is also used, to ask about what jobs people do.
Questions: What does he do for a living? What do you do for a crust? (slang)
Answer: He's <u>an</u> electrician.

Write the questions and answers for each picture.

1. _____
   _____
   _____

2. _____
   _____
   _____

3. _____
   _____
   _____

Answers: Jan gets up at six. She showers and has breakfast at 6:30am so she can start work at 7am. At 4pm Jan finishes her work and drives to her mother's place and has dinner with her. She is usually in bed by 10. I get up at 7am and go to the bathroom. Then I shower and have breakfast at 7:30 so I can be in class at 8:30am. By 1pm my class finishes and I drive home.
1. What does she do for a crust/a living? She's a dentist. 2. What does he do for a crust/a living? He's a plumber. 3. What do they do for a living? They're musicians.

Chapter 6 School Ceremonies and Rituals
Reading Comprehension

After reading Chapter 6 of *Speak English Like Australians!*, answer the following questions in full sentences. Use some words from the questions as part of your answers.

1. When was Assembly Day?
_____
_____

2. What happened on this day?
_____
_____
_____

3. Why were all the other kids jealous of the drum boy?
_____
_____

4. Why do you think Voula fainted during assembly? (Start your sentence of opinion with: "As far as I can tell,…")
_____
_____
_____
_____
_____

5. What type of music has 4/4 time?
_____
_____

6. What was the job of the Milk Monitors?
_____
_____

Answers: 1. Assembly Day was every Monday morning. 2. On this day the entire school, except for the Infant Department, assembled to raise the Australian flag and to sing the National Anthem. 3. All the other kids were jealous of the boy who played the drum as he had the second best job in the school. 4. As far as I can tell, Voula fainted because she had been running and later standing in the hot sun, which made her dizzy, so that she fainted. 5. The type of music that has 4/4 time is marching music. 6. The job of the Milk Monitors was to go to a designated area and collect a crate of milk bottles for their grade. Next they used a pointy wooden stick to put holes in all the aluminium lids and then to put straws through the holes.

Page 143

Speaking: modals express possibility

Modals are used to express possibility.
Here are some modals: may be, could be, might be, probably, possibly

For example:
Fainting may be due to ……..
It could be because of ……..
Someone might faint if …….

Pair Work: feeling faint
Speak with a classmate regarding a time you or someone you know felt faint.
What was the cause? Why do you think people faint? Have you ever fainted?

Group Work: opinions

1. **In groups of four,** *share your views* **about why people these days seem to have more allergies than in the past.**

2. Together, complete the survey below by writing each person's name and opinion.
Use expressions of opinion like:

I reckon that allergies could be …   Personally I think that ..

I believe that …   From my point of view, it may be …

NAME	SENTENCES OF OPINION

3. Did you each have a different opinion or did some of you agree with one another? Explain.
_____
_____

4. Ask one person from your group to share the general views of your group with the class.

Page 144

Speaking: indirect questions—to ask politely

Modals (could, can, would, might...) and expressions like "I wonder if..., Do you know...?, Is it possible to...?" are used to ask for/offer help, or to get information/permission from people who are strangers, because we can form very polite indirect questions with them. For a normal question, the word order changes. However, notice the verb position, in the indirect question, is the same as for the declarative statement and is NOT like the direct question.

For example:

Verb Tense	Direct Question	Indirect Question	Declarative Statement
present simple	What is the time?	Could you tell me the time? *Could you tell me what the time is? *Do you know what the time is?	The time is 11am.
present continuous	When is she arriving?	I wonder if you can tell me when she is arriving?	She is arriving in the evening.
past simple	Why did he leave at 1pm?	Is it possible to tell me why he left at 1pm?	He left at 1pm.
past perfect	Where had he lived before moving next door?	I wonder if you know where he had lived before moving next door?	He had lived in Sunshine before moving next door.

*Would you know where the post office is?

Don't get confused. It is not... ~~Would you know where is the post office?~~

Pair Work: using polite indirect questions

Write 4 of your own indirect questions and ask your instructor to check the grammar.

In pairs practise asking each other your indirect questions and answering them.

Group Work: Speaking—speed dating

In this game learners get practice and more confidence, to say and answer indirect questions.

1. Arrange learners to sit opposite each other in two rows, so that they are almost touching knees.

2. Learners take turns to ask each other their questions and wait for their friend to answer.

3. After several minutes, at an appointed time, the instructor calls out, "Change!" Then, one row of learners moves one seat to the right, so that now each student will be facing someone else.

4. The questions are asked again and answers given.

Chant: School Rituals

Practise your pronunciation, singing the four verses until you can say them easily. Keep the rhythm going by stressing the bold text.

We have assem**bly**;
the Aussie Anthem **sing**.
We have assem**bly**:
hear the school bell **ring**!

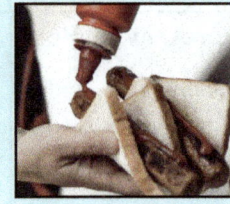

(sanga=slang for sandwich)
(snag=slang for sausage)
(dead horse=slang for tomato sauce)
(on'em=abbreviation for "on them")

We have **lunch** time:
a snag-sanga **please**.
We have **lunch** time;
dead horse on'em **squeeze**!

Raise the flag up **high**.
Stand straight and **salute**.
Raise the flag up **high**.
Play the merry **flute**!

The Southern Cross is a star consellation visible in the Southern Hemisphere and is shown on the Australian flag.

See the Southern **Cross**
flying in blue **skies**!
See the Southern **Cross**:
on our flag it **flies**!

Page 146

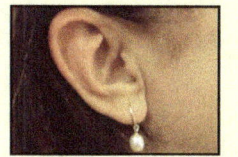

Listening: text cloze

Listen to your instructor read the text at normal speed and write the missing words taken from Chapter 6 of *Speak English Like Australians!* Part 1. Alternatively you may listen to it on YouTube:Home. Search for *Zoe Lambreas – chapter 6* (The cloze begins at 3:31 minutes.)

Singing the anthem was a very important ¹_____ of school life. It was an honour and a duty to show respect to your country. Children and adults stood up whenever the National Anthem was played at any public event. Voula certainly ²_____ proud to be part of this ceremony. It was taken very seriously and the children had to show respect by standing straight, ³_____ feet together, and looking forward ⁴_____ the flag. No speaking or moving around was allowed, or the children would be punished.

Furthermore, to make ⁵_____ the students sang very well together, the school recorder band played the music for the National Anthem. Just before the recorder band started, a boy ⁶_____ stood next to the flagpole, played his drum to introduce the singing. All the other kids were jealous of the drum boy! Everyone felt he ⁷_____ the best job in the school,... except for the boy who pulled the flag ⁸_____ to the top of the flagpole! That boy had the best job of all! Immediately ⁹_____ the anthem, the boys saluted the flag and the girls curtsied, holding their skirts.

A General Assembly was sometimes held after lunchtime. The children assembled in their ¹⁰_____ again, on the netball court, to listen to important information that the ¹¹_____ wanted to tell them. Also it was a time to announce the names of hard-working and good students. When these students went out to the front, the Head Master ¹²_____ their hands, congratulated and thanked them and then everyone clapped for them. It was for these assemblies that Voula was often late, because of taking Jimmy to kindergarten during her lunchtime. One summer day, poor Voula had just run all the way ¹³_____ to school from kinder, without being too late. As she stood under the hot sun, she started feeling dizzy, her knees started to feel wobbly and she heard ringing in her ¹⁴_____: that was the first time in her life that she fainted! Luckily she didn't hurt herself as she fell over the children near her before she ¹⁵_____ the ground.

Answers: 1 part 2 felt 3 with 4 at 5 sure 6 who 7 had 8 up 9 after 10. grades 11. teachers 12. shook 13. back 14. ears 15. hit

Dictations: aural & running dictation

Aural

The instructor reads the dictation, repeating as necessary, while the learners write what they hear. The instructor should say entire chunks of text when reiterating for the learners. This will assist them to understand about phrases belonging together, and of the natural pauses between chunks. Refer to page 47.

At Hamilton's Gray Street State School, every Monday morning was Monday Assembly Day. The whole school got together to hear what the Head Master had to say to them. However, the preps, grades 1 and grades 2 did not have the patience or the strength to stand up for a long time, so they had their own assemblies. They sat together in a big room, on little mats, and learnt songs and nursery rhymes with actions. It was fun!

Pair Work
Dictation Alternative: running dictation (refer to page 74 for instructions)

Part 1
Assembly seemed quite long to the older pupils, as they gathered in their grades and waited in a big U-shape, on the netball court, in front of the school.

Part 2
On the left side of the school was a flagpole and every year a sixth-grade boy had the pleasure of slowly raising the Australian flag while the school sang the Australian National Anthem.

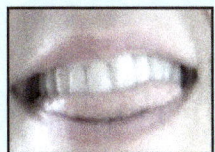

Pronunciation: reminder
Practise the pronunciations of the Aussie Sounds in Chapter 1 Pronunciation.

Pronunciation: minimal pairs /ʃ/ and /tʃ/

Learners take turns to say one word thrice from each pair. The listener tells the speaker which word was said, either the first or the second word in the pair. If the pronunciation was clear and the hearer could discern the sounds, the correct word is chosen. The instructor can help learners with pronunciation and distinguishing the sounds if necessary.

Learner A to say and learner B to listen

a) shin   chin
b) shop   chop
c) ship   chip
d) mash   match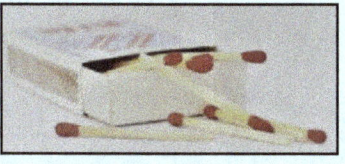
e) swish   switch
f) cash   catch
g) bash   batch
h) lash   latch

Learner B to say and learner A to listen

a) marsh   march
b) wash   watch
c) leash   leech
d) she's   cheese
e) shoes   choose
f) shook   chook (hen)
g) crush   crutch
h) wish   which

Say the sentences as smoothly as you can.

A. Does this shop sell washing machines?

B. Yes. This is our special washing machine.

A. Is it Swedish?

B. No. It's English.

A. Please show me how it washes.

B. Here, I shall put these shirts and sheets into the machine, shut the door and push this button.

A. The machine shouldn't shake like that, should it?

B. Washing machines always shake. Do you wish to buy it?

A. I'm not sure!

Phonogram: "ci"

The letters "ci" have six possible sounds. Read the explanations and then practise saying each column of words until you feel confident and it is easy for your tongue to make the sounds. Can you think of some words to add to the lists?

International Phonemic Alphabet	/sɪ/ if "ci" is followed by a consonant	/ʃɪ/ if "ci" is followed by a vowel
When the spelling of "ci" is **alone in a syllable**, it can have 2 different pronunciations: *si* and *shi*.	ac-**ci**-dent	app-re-**ci**-ate
	ci-gars	ass-o-**ci**-ate
	ci-nders	as-so-**ci**-a-ting
	ci-ne-mas	dep-re-**ci**-ate
	ci-vi-li-sa-tion	dis-ass-o-**ci**-ate
	de-**ci**-mal	e-ma-**ci**-a-ting
	el-ec-tri-**ci**-ty	ex-cru-**ci**-at-ing
	ha-llu-**ci**-nate	of-fi-**ci**-ate
	pre-**ci**-pi-ta-tion	
	spe-**ci**-fic	

IPA	/ʃə/	/sə/	/sɪ/	/s əɪ/
When "ci" is **not in a syllable by itself** there are 4 possible pronunciations.	an-**ci**ent	cir-cum-fer-ence	ann-oun-**ci**ng	cri-ti-**ci**se
	di-e-ti-**ci**an	di-s**ci**-pline	di-**ci**ng	de-**ci**de
	el-ec-tri-**ci**an	el-i-**ci**t	fan-at-i-**ci**sm	do-**ci**le
	gra-**ci**ous	med-i-**ci**ne	leg-a-**ci**es	ex-er-**ci**se
	ma-li-**ci**ous	ni-a-**ci**n	pier-**ci**ng	ho-mi-**ci**de
	math-em-a-ti-**ci**an	pen-**ci**l	poun-**ci**ng	pe-sti-**ci**de
	op-ti-**ci**an	pla-**ci**d	ra-**ci**sm	pre-**ci**se
	so-**ci**al	ran-**ci**d	skep-ti-**ci**sm	re-**ci**te

Tongue Twisters: "ci"

Practise saying these tongue twisters until you can say them easily in one breath. It's not easy!

1. Cinemas sell cigarettes and show short trailers to excite the public.

2. To become a mathematician, optician or dietitian requires discipline.

3. I appreciate that you want to participate and associate with ancient cultures.

Conversation Bits: it's up to you!

Repeat the conversation until your intonation is native-like and you feel confident with your pronunciation, stress and intonation. Say the expressions in one breath. Even better, practise the dialogue with a friend.

Denis	**Would you like to go out to dinner or to a movie?**
Glenys	Either one, it's up to you.
Denis	What would you prefer ?
Glenys	I really don't care. I just want to get out of the house.
Denis	Well, then how about dinner and a movie?
Glenys	That's a great idea!
Explanation: If you say that it is "up to you" to do something, you mean that it is their responsibility or decision to do it. *Example: The choice was up to Paula.*	

Spelling: "c" spelling rules and pronunciation

There are different pronunciations of "c". The pronunciation depends on the spelling and whether or not an "e", "i" or "y" come after the "c".

Learn the spelling and pronunciation of the words below. Say the words several times.

At the start of a word, "c" always says "s" when followed by *e*, *i*, or *y*.

cent   cement   ceremony   certificate   certain   cereal
city   citizen   circulation   circle   cinema   cigarette
cyclone   cyst   cycle   cylinder   cyclist   cymbals

At the start of a word, if the "c" is not followed by *e*, *i*, or *y*, then its sound is "k".

case   consider   cover   cream   cucumber   cushion

If there is a double "c", then the first "c" at the end of the syllable might say /k/ and the next "c" at the start of the next syllable can say /s/.   Otherwise the "cc" says /k/.

ac/cept   coc/cyx   ac/cede   hic/cup   ac/count   Mor/oc/co

Place the following words in the correct column. (crab, vaccinate, traffic, calm, accent, dice, calculate, civil, calendar, acid, cake, icy, pencil, access, procedure, coin, citizen, success)

words that have "c" sound like /s/	words that have "c" sound like /k/	words that have "cc" sound might sound like /ks/

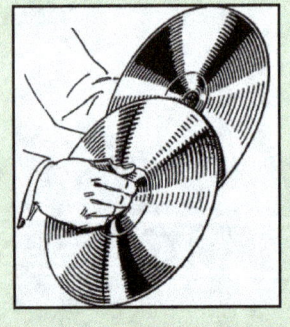

Answers: /s/=dice, civil, acid, icy, pencil, procedure, citizen   /k/=crab, traffic, calm, calculate, calendar, cake, coin   /ks/=vaccinate, accent, access, success

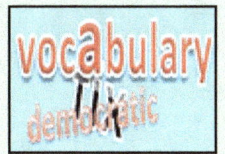

Vocabulary: crossword

Some words from Chapter 6 of *Speak English Like Australians!* are used to answer the clues for the crossword. For 2 words, don't leave a space.

Clues

Across

2. a conjunction meaning 'because'
4. and
6. to show respect, to give privilege to someone
8. (2 words) the song of a nation is its ____
11. strength, endurance
13. not humble
14. (2 words) in harmony, in melody

Down

1. level, uniform, straight
2. feelings, moods, life forces E.g. one's ___ are down when they are depressed
3. judged as (legal term), viewed as, believed to be
5. excellent and better than others
7. to perform or carry out an action
9. people who succeed and reach their goals
10. (past tense) soldiers do this to greet an officer
12. opposite of "out"

Answers: Across: 2. so 4. also 6. honour 8. national anthem 11. stamina 13. proud 14. in tune Down: 1. even 2. spirits 3. deemed 5. outstanding 7. do 9. achievers 10. saluted 12. in

Vocabulary: word families

Extend your vocabulary by completing the Word Families table.

Word Families			
Noun	Infinitive Verb	Adjective	Adverb
1. co-operation	2.	3.	4.
5.	6. to designate	7.	8.
9.	10.	11. contentious	12.

READ MORE

Choose four words from your completed table to write in sentences. Do this in order to increase your confidence and understanding. Ask your instructor to check your writing.

1. _____

2. _____

3. _____

4. _____

Answers: 2. to co-operate 3. co-operative 4. co-operatively 5. designation/designator 7. designated 8. — 9. contention 10. to contend 12. contentiously

Figures of Speech: merisms

A merism is a phrase referring to something by using several of its characteristics. It emphasises completeness and totality.

Examples of merisms:

- Hook, line, and sinker.

To swallow something hook, line, and sinker means to believe it completely. My little girl believes in the Tooth Fairy, hook, line and sinker!

- High and low.

To search high and low means to look for something everywhere. I looked for my bag high and low and still couldn't find it!

- Lock, stock, and barrel.

This refers to the different parts of a gun and, as a merism, it refers to the whole of any object. They moved all their belongings, lock, stock and barrel, to their new house.

- Flesh and bone.

Refers to the body. Maria is my daughter and is my own flesh and bones.

- Search every nook and cranny.

To search everywhere. It refers to unusual small places. I couldn't find my keys even though I searched every nook and cranny.

- Sun, sea and sand.

Refers to a seaside holiday destination. Our family had lots of fun in the sun, sand and sea.

Underline the two merisms in the text and explain their meanings.

Singing the anthem was a very integral part of school life and it was also considered an honour and a duty to show respect to your country. Young and old stood whenever the National Anthem was played at any public events. Voula certainly felt proud to be part of this ceremony. It was taken very seriously and the children had to show respect by standing straight with feet together and looking straight forward at the flag.

Answers: an an honour and a duty=it was a privilege as well as something that you were obliged to do; young and old=people of all ages

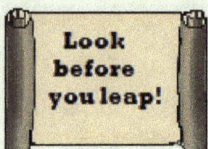

Proverbs: learning

Think about the meanings of these proverbs. Write your ideas and then check your answers. Do you get the *gist* of them?

1. By learning you will teach and by teaching you will learn.
___
___

2. The pen is mightier than the sword.
___
___

3. In a group of three people, there will always be one person I can learn from.
___
___

4. The more you learn, the more you want to know.
___
___

5. Learn from the mistakes of others. You can't live long enough to make them all yourself.
___
___

Answers: Proverbs: 1. As you learn things you can teach others too. Also, as you teach others you learn more about it. 2. You can persuade people more effectively with written ideas and words than by trying to force people to do what you want. 3. You have 2 others with you, so at least one person will show you something you don't know. 4. Learning becomes addictive and rewarding as you realise the benefits. 5. You can save time and trouble for yourself if you can learn a lesson from others mistakes.

Writing: a personal letter (transactional genre) ACSF 1.05 & 1.06

All writing has its own particular format, depending on its genre. (The kind or type of writing it is.) Letters belong to the transactional genre because there is communication of ideas and information *between individuals*.

Read the semi-formal letter and notice the format or layout. (the spaces, the address, the date, the opening salutation, the body, the complimentary close and the signature).

127 Smith St.,
Ferntree Gully, 3156

14th February 20_ _

Dear Learner,

Let me tell you a little about myself. I love my work and I've been teaching since 1979 but specifically English as a Second Language since 1994. Before that I was teaching maths and science in a secondary school in Sydney and before that, I was teaching primary school in the inner city area of Melbourne.

On a personal note, I was married in 1980 and we have raised four sons. Three are married and we have six grandchildren, so my family keeps me busy these days, but I am very contented with my lot.

My hobbies are: reading, walking, cycling, boating sometimes, watching movies, gardening, having people over for dinner and visiting friends. When I have more time I would like to paint portraits using watercolours, because I tried it years ago and I really enjoyed it.

My future plans are to continue working part-time. At some point, I would also love to travel and see more of Australia and the world.

I would like you to tell me, what you want to learn, so I can help you to improve your English. Therefore, please be specific. The harder you work, the quicker you will learn. Try to study at home. Use the Internet, YouTube and borrow CDs and books from the library. Listen to songs. Speak to people as much as you can. Record some programmes from the telly and then listen to them and say what you hear. Furthermore, do all your homework and ask for help if you don't understand. Try not to miss classes or be late. All the best!

Yours sincerely,
Zelambras
Zoe Lambreas

Please write your own personal letter explaining a little about yourself and about your future plans. Use the correct layout, beginning with your address and the date.

Parts of Speech: collective nouns

Collective nouns are used for groups of things, places and people. For example a group of players is a team; a group of flowers is a bunch or a bouquet; a group of singers is a choir.

Replace the underlined words with collective nouns from the box & correct any proper nouns.

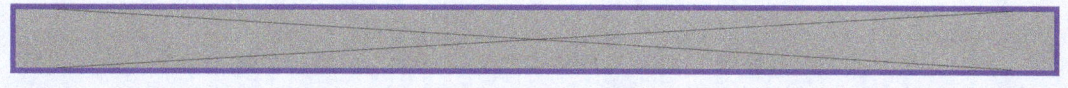

Last week my <u>husband, son and daughter</u> went for a drive to canberra to see parliament house. While we were there we watched a parliamentary debate between <u>prime minister turnball and his ministers</u> and <u>bill shorten, of the australian labor party, and his ministers</u>. They were arguing about the carbon tax. While we were sitting in the gallery we saw some <u>people who didn't like the tax</u>, holding placards and yelling slogans. <u>Some newspaper reporters</u> were also present taking notes and looking very busy.

With collective nouns you can use a **singular verb** if you are *thinking* of the noun as one unit or you can use a **plural verb** if you are *thinking* of the noun as having several members. It is really up to you and what you are thinking.

Use the correct verb for the collective nouns in the sentences.

1. The flock of warbling magpies was/were flying overhead.
2. Our family is/are leaving for Adelaide to visit our grandmother, next week.
3. The government is/are looking to increase our taxes to build a new freeway.

Many organisations and teams are collective nouns too and are used with a singular or a plural verb.

Choose the correct form of the verb for each sentence.

4. Sadly for Australian cricket fans, England is/are leading 121 for 4 and their captain is batting next.
5. The ABC was/were planning a new cooking program, hoping to improve their TV ratings.
6. Last week the choir was/were tired, for most of them were jet-lagged after their European performances.
7. The church always celebrate/celebrates the resurrection of Christ at Easter.

Answers: Last week my family went for a drive to Canberra to see Parliament House. While we were there we watched a parliamentary debate between the government and the opposition. They were arguing about the carbon tax. While we were sitting in the gallery we saw some protesters, holding placards and yelling slogans. The press were also present taking notes and looking very busy. 1-7 either form of the verbs may be used

Parts of Speech: collective nouns & male/female/young animals

Some collective nouns, words for groups of, are commonly known and used while others are rarely used at all, especially those of animals.

Complete the missing nouns.

collective noun	animal	male	female	young
1. clowder/clutter/glaring/pounce	2. cat	3. tomcat	4. molly	5.
6.	7. cattle	8. bull	9. cow	10. calf
11. brood	12. chickens	13. rooster	14.	15. chick/biddy
16. pack/kennel	17. dog	18. dog	19. bitch	20.
21. flock/brace	22. ducks	23. drake	24.	25. duckling
26. school/shoal	27. fish	28.	29. fish	30. fry/fingerlings
team/troop/mob	31. horse	32. stallion	33.	34. colt(mas.) 35. filly(fem.)
36. pride	37. lion	38. lion	39. lioness	40.
41. drove	42. pig	43. boar	44.	45. piglet
46. flock	47. sheep	48.	49. ewe	50. lamb

Answers: 5. kitten 6. herd 14. hen 20. puppy 24. gander 28. fish 34. mare 41. cub 45. sow 49. ram

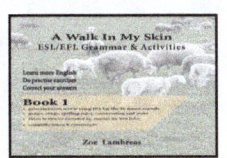

Grammar: indirect questions—polite questions

Indirect questions are formal and polite and do not always have a question mark, whereas direct questions are casual and always have a question mark. In indirect questions the subject and verb are inverted, so that the direct question, "Where can she go shopping?" looks like an affirmative statement when used in an indirect question, "Do you know where she can go shopping?"

Compare the position of the subject and verb in these questions:

direct question: What were those things? (V + S)

indirect question: Can you tell me what those things were? (S + V)

incorrect: ~~Can you tell me what were those things?~~

direct question: Where can I go shopping? (V + S)

indirect question: Would you please tell me where I can go shopping? (S

incorrect: ~~Can you please tell me where can I go shopping?~~

direct question: How can I get home by bus? (V + S)

indirect question: Do you know how I can get home by bus? (S + V)

incorrect: ~~Do you know how can I get home by bus?~~

direct question: What colour is her hair? (V + S)

indirect *statement*: I wonder what colour her hair is. (S + V) no question mark

incorrect: ~~I wonder what colour is her hair.~~

direct question (thinking to yourself): What time will my wife be home? (V

indirect *statement*: I wonder what time my wife will be home. (S + V)

incorrect: ~~I wonder what time will my wife be home.~~

direct question: What's the time please? (V + S)

indirect question 1: Do you know what the time is? (S + V)

indirect question 2: Could you tell me what the time is? (S + V)

~~incorrect 2: Could you tell me what's the time please?~~

direct question: Where are your children? (V + S)

indirect question 1: Would you tell me where your children are? (S + V)

indirect *statement* 2: I wonder where your children are. (S + V)

indirect question 3: Won't you tell me where your children are? (S + V)

~~incorrect 3: Won't you tell me where are your children?~~

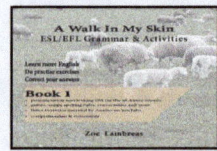

Omit the "to do" verb in the indirect question.

direct question: Does she live here? (S + V)

indirect question 1: Could you please tell me if she lives here? (S + V)

indirect question 2: Is it possible that she lives here? (S + V)

incorrect 1: ~~Could you please tell me does she live here?~~

incorrect 2: ~~Is it possible __ she live here?~~

direct question: Where do you live? (V + S)

Indirect *statement*: I wonder where you live. (S + V)

~~incorrect: I wonder where do you live?~~

Also please notice when using indirect questions for:
a) **reporting (to inform someone in reported/indirect speech) there is no question mark and**
b) **for yes/no questions**
c) **for "whether" and "if"**

... the subject is before the verb as in all indirect questions.

a) in reported/indirect speech: He asked me why she was late. (S + V) *no question mark
~~incorrect: He asked me why was she late.~~
But in direct question & direct speech: Why was she late? (V + S)

a) in reported/indirect speech: They wondered when the plane would leave. (S + V) *no question mark
incorrect: ~~They wondered when does the plane leave.~~
But for direct question & direct speech: When does the plane leave? (V + S)

b) yes/no indirect question: I suppose you are waiting for me? (S + V) No, I'm not!
incorrect: ~~I suppose are you waiting for me?~~
direct question & direct speech: Are you waiting for me? (V + S) No I'm not!

b) yes/no indirect question: Do you suppose it's going to rain? Yes, I do. (S + V)
incorrect: ~~Do you suppose is it going to rain?~~
direct question & direct speech: Is it going to rain? Yes it is. (V + S)

c) if indirect question: Do you know if it has rained? (S + V) Yes it has.
incorrect: ~~Do you know if has it rained?~~
direct question: Has it rained? (V + S) Yes it has.

c) whether indirect question: I wondered whether her hair was a different colour. (S + V)
incorrect: ~~I wondered whether what colour was her hair.~~
direct question: What colour was her hair? (V + S)

When using the "to be" verb for indirect questions, remember the word order is **S + V**, like all indirect questions. So, sometimes, the verbs "is", "are", "was" and "were" are at the end of an indirect question.

indirect question: Could you tell me where the toy was? (S + V)

incorrect: ~~Could you tell me where was the toy?~~

direct question: Where was the toy? (V + S)

Indirect question: Can you tell me what your name is? (S + V)

Indirect question: Can you tell me if your name is Sarah? (S + V)

~~incorrect: I wonder what is your name.~~

direct question: What is your name? (V + S)

Make correct indirect questions.

1. I wonder **if** is she waiting for me.
2. Might we know what is your name?
3. Could you tell me **if** lives Samantha here?
4. Do you know how can I get the bus?
5. He asked me why was I late.
6. I wonder where is your house.
7. She wondered **whether** it would rain.
8. When does the train depart?
9. Won't you tell me where are your children?
10. Can you tell me who was that boy?

Answers: 1. I wonder if she is waiting for me. (statement) 2. Might we know what your name is? 3. Could you tell me if Samantha lives here? 4. Would you know how I can get the bus? (omit the "do") 5. He asked me why I was late. (reported) 6. I wonder where your house is. (statement) 7. She wondered whether it would rain. (no question mark for reported speech) 8. Could/Can/Would you tell me when the train departs? 9. Won't you tell me where your children are? 10. Can you tell me who that boy was?

Grammar: determiners (articles and specific & non-specific determiners)

When we *know the thing* we are writing about and we can identify it, we use "the". It is called the definite article because we definitely know what it is we are discussing. When speaking *generally* do *not use any article*. E.g. I like ~~the~~ chocolate.

When we are writing about *any* of something, then we use "a". This is called the indefinite article. We use "an" before words beginning with a vowel **sound**. E.g. I want an apple.

Do you know the pronunciation of "the" (at normal speed) depends on the sound coming after it?

- In front of consonant sounds /ðə/   E.g. the barking dog; the school; double-storey house

To emphasise a noun or in front of vowel sounds "the" becomes /ðiː/. For example:

the umbrella   Yes, it's true that I saw **the** ex-Prime Minister!
the apple   I talked with the Aldi manager about a job.

Besides the definite article "the", we can use *specific determiners* when we can identify who or what we are talking about. These include: *this, that, these, those, my, your, his, her, its, our, their* (demonstratives & possessives – refer to *Chapter 1 Parts of Speech*)
E.g. Her dog ran towards my cat. These flowers are his gift to our mum.

Instead of "a" and "an", when we speak about *any* of something and *no particular* person or thing, then we use *non-specific determiners*. These are: *all, another, any, both, every, little, much, other, each, few, fewer, many, neither, several, either, more, most, no, some, enough, less, other*
E.g. You can come at any time you like. They have other ideas. I have several black shoes.

Write the correct article in the spaces of the sentences.

1. When I went to the shops I saw _____ very tall man.
2. When I went to the shops I saw _____ man I sit next to in class.
3. Would you like to eat _____ apple? I have _____ here for you.
4. Do you like _____ bananas?
5. Susan is _____ person you met yesterday.
6. Who is _____ lady you met at the cafe? I saw _____ men there too.
7. I need to buy _____ dress. Do you prefer _____ dresses or _____ pants?
8. I bought _____ red dress I tried on yesterday.
9. There is _____ fly in my soup.

Answers: 1. a 2. the 3. an, some 4. — 5. the 6. the; some/several/a few 7. a, —, — 8. the 9. a

Verb Tenses: revision present continuous tense

Use this tense for actions that are **still happening now** because the action is not yet completed. It is formed with **to be + "ing" word** (the present participle). E.g. He **is thinking** about it.

> sleep   sing   pray   hug   jog   concentrate   paint

Complete the sentences using the correct verb form of the words in the above box.

1. The girls _____ _____.
2. He _____ _____.
3. The old woman _____ _____.
4. The baby _____ _____.
5. Maria _____ _____.
6. He _____ _____ while he _____ _____.

The Present Continuous tense is often used for **personal future arrangements** and for **temporary situations**.

> E.g. What **are** you **doing** this weekend? We **are leaving** for Sydney this weekend.
> Sally **is living** in the flat until her contract ends. He **isn't staying** here for long.

> leave   go   come   plan   supervise   help   stay   cook

Use the correct form of the verbs in the box to complete the sentences.

7. She _____ next door for a coffee.
8. I _____ tomorrow.
9. I _____ my friend's surprise birthday party.
10. Oh, I _____ something delicious for them!
11. My friend is coming to my house and she _____ me cook dinner.
12. She ___ only _____ until her husband comes to pick her up.
13. He ___ _____ night shift for two weeks.
14. She ___ _____ us while our boss is on holidays.

Answers: 1. are hugging 2. is jogging 3. is praying 4. is sleeping 5. is singing 6. is concentrating, is painting 7. is going 8. am leaving 9. am planning 10. am cooking 11. is helping 12. is only staying 13. is working 13. is supervising

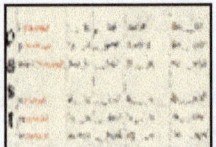

Verb Tenses: use the correct forms of the verbs

When we are **looking at photos and talking** about what is in them, we use the present simple tense.

Look at the picture and complete the sentences using the correct form of the verbs in the box.

smile
wear
fish
lie
look
be

There ¹____ a small boy ²_____. He ³____ ⁴_____ at the orange fish on his hook. Behind him there is a green bucket which ⁵___ ⁶_____ on the ground. He ⁷___ ⁸_____ a blue and white vest, some shorts and black shoes. He looks happy and maybe he ⁹___ ¹⁰_____.

Conjugate the verb "to do" by completing the table.

TENSES	Present Simple	Present Continuous	Present Continuous "wh" Questions	Present Continuous "to be" Questions	Present Continuous Contracted Negatives
1ˢᵗ person singular **I**	I do				
2ⁿᵈ person singular **you**		you are doing			
3ʳᵈ person singular **she/he/it**			What is she doing?		
1ˢᵗ person plural **we**				Are we doing well?	
2ⁿᵈ person plural **you**					You aren't doing well.
3ʳᵈ person plural **they**					

Answers: 1st column: you do; she/he/it does; we do; you do; they do
2nd column: I am doing; she/he/it is doing; we are doing; you are doing; they are doing
3rd column: What am I doing? What are you doing? What is she/he/it doing? What are we doing? What are you doing? What are they doing?
4th column: Am I doing well? Are you doing well? Is she/he/it doing well? Are we doing well? Are you doing well? Are they doing well?
5th column: I'm not doing well OR I aren't doing well. You aren't doing well. She/he/it isn't doing well. We aren't doing well. You aren't doing well. They aren't doing well.
1. is 2. fishing 3. is 4. looking 5. is 6. lying 7. is 8. wearing 9. is 10. smiling

Chapter 7 Imperial Australia
Reading Comprehension Chapter 7 ACSF 2.03 & 2.04

After reading Chapter 7 of *Speak English Like Australians!*, answer the following questions in full sentences, in order to improve your writing skills. It means that for each answer you must repeat some of the words in the question. This type of thorough answer will give you confidence with sentence structures and help to improve your writing skills.

1. What were the children waiting for at the window?

2. What were the shopping hours in Hamilton?

3. What was the very first fast food chain to open in Australia and in Hamilton?

4. Where and when did the tradition of Hot Cross Buns begin?

5. Which was easier to learn, the British money or the metric measurements and why?

6. Who were Australians **not** prepared to "give up"?

7. Why did Argyro collect *The Australian Women's Weekly* magazines?

Answers: 1. The children were waiting for the bakery van to deliver their Hot Cross Buns. 2. The shopping hours in Hamilton were: Monday to Friday 9-5:30, Saturday from 9-noon and closed on Sundays. 3. The first fast food store to open in Australia was KFC and it was also the first fast food store to open in Hamilton. 4. The tradition of Hot Cross Buns began in England in the nineteenth century when they were sold in the streets. 5. The easier to learn measurements were the metric measurements as they were based on the 10 times tables, whereas the imperial measurements were based on the 12 times tables. 6. Australians were not prepared to give up the royal family. 7. Argyro collected the Australian Women's Weekly magazines as she loved the many colourful photos of the queen wearing gloves, hats and often holding a matching handbag.

Speaking: class debate – monarchy or republic?
ACSF 3.07 & 3.08

Speaking in front of others can be daunting but it can be enjoyable too. Usually there are 3 members in a debating team but we can vary this. In a debate, each speaker has a particular role to play as part of a team effort involving argument, and not necessarily three good public speakers. What will the debate be about? Australians have an issue that is often debated periodically. Should Australia keep the Queen as Head of State or should we "ditch" her and become a republic? So far Australians have voted to keep the royal family, although they do not influence our politics.

Australia is a constitutional monarchy. Technically, Queen Elizabeth II is Australia's head of state. The head of state is the figurehead of a state, who represents the unity of the state. But, as Australia has its own constitution, the Queen doesn't really have any power and she is more "for show". She also appears on the "heads" or obverse side of our coins, and on our smallest note, which at the moment is the five dollar note.

Pair Work

Share your own ideas about kings and queens. Is it a good idea?
Does or did your country of birth ever have a monarchy?
Does or did it work well for the country?

Group Work:
Class Debate
In groups of 3, 4 or 5 people, discuss the pros and cons for a monarchy and for a republic. Below are some ideas.

Use the expressions for opinion suggested in "Chapter 2: Speaking" and also some "Expressions for Polite Disagreement" (see next page).

Reasons for supporting the Monarchy

Pro monarchists claim that by staying as a monarchy…

- countries have a focus for a national identity, unity and pride.
- there is stability and continuity, whereas politicians and governments change
- it is a safe system and has been good for us. It works well so why change it?
- there is support for voluntary service and excellence.

Reasons for opposing the monarchy

- The concept of a monarchy is undemocratic.
- A monarchy is not egalitarian. Why should someone inherit power because of their birth?
- Typically monarchs and their immediate family receive subsidies and are paid with our taxes.
- Monarchs do not have a **divine right** to rule. For centuries this was the main reason for royal authority.

"For" a republic – the affirmative team
Republicans argue that a republic...

- would give Australia greater independence.
- would be good for business and the economy.
- would allow an Australian-born citizen to be Australia's head of state instead of a queen/king.

"Against" a republic – the opposing team
Anti-republicans represent the majority of Australians

In 1999, Australia held a national referendum on the question.....'Should Australia alter the Constitution to establish the Commonwealth of Australia as a republic with the Queen/King and Governor-General being replaced by a President appointed by a two-thirds majority of the members of the Commonwealth Parliament?'

Result: 54% no, 46% yes.

viewed 2016 <http://debatewise.org/debates/2526-republic-or-monarchy/>

Debating is an excellent forum to improve your quick thinking, listening, speaking, pronunciation as well as helping reduce your fear of public speaking. Furthermore, team members can help each other by offering advise as they consult between speakers for 60 seconds and there is wisdom in many heads!

Have a class debate following strict rules of timing and debating etiquette. Use expressions for polite disagreement while debating with the opposition.

Read the debate rules on the following page and don't forget to review your performance after the debate, so you can keep improving with each experience.

Expressions for Polite Disagreement

I take your point but …	I beg to differ …
I see what you mean, but have you considered…	I'm afraid I disagree because …
I understand what you mean but …	I'm sorry, but I don't agree …
Sure/Yeah ……but on the other hand …	Sorry but I don't see it that way …
There's some truth in what you say, but still …	I hear what you're saying, but…
You're right about… but there is a problem with…	I get your point but it's not actually true/correct…
To a certain extent yes, but …	I see what you mean but…
That would be great except …	I see where you are coming from, however,…
Perhaps not as bad/good/difficult as that …	I appreciate why you think that, but…

Speaking: public speaking in a debate

Class Debating Rules

The **Affirmative Team** begins the debate. The first speakers have 3 minutes to introduce their team and very simply state what each speaker will argue about before beginning their own argument. The last speakers also have 3 minutes to make their arguments and then to summarise their teams' arguments and generally say they have proven their points, which are better than the opposing team's reasons. However, the remaining team speakers only have 2 minutes each to make their points.

Each speaker introduces themselves and politely rebuts the opposing speaker. Then they state their own argument very clearly. Next they give an example to solidify their position. All in 2 minutes! Speakers must stop when their time is up and not speak again.

Each team has 60 seconds consultation time, between speakers, to help their next speaker with ideas and suggestions.

Points are awarded for:

- clear speaking
- persuasive argument/reason
- rebutting the opposing speaker
- use of polite disagreement expression
- good use of time
- first speaker introducing their team and their main points
- last speaker summarising their teams points

Here is an **Instructor Rating Sheet** to help provide feedback to debate participants.

Debating Outcomes for: _____ *(participant's name)*

Topic: Should Australia remain a constitutional monarchy?

PRONUNCIATION
- Clear and easily understood
- Some pronunciation mistakes
- Often incomprehensible

AUDIENCE ENGAGEMENT
- Establishes rapport & eye contact
- Sometimes established eye contact
- No eye contact

BODY LANGUAGE
- Relaxed
- Closed and unrelaxed
- Somewhat fidgety

ARGUING SKILLS
- key argument rebutted
- logical key argument presented
- illogical- argument unclear
- supporting evidence/examples given
- no examples given

- uses conventions of debating (introduced the team, summarised team's points, polite disagreement etc.)

- clarifies misunderstandings & ambiguous points

- distinguishes fact as opposed to opinion of opposing speakers

TIME ALLOCATION (write: yes or no)
- achieved
- not achieved

(continued on next page)

Speaking: public speaking in a debate

Instructor Rating Sheet (continued from previous page)

CO-OPERATION WITH TEAM MEMBERS
- Collaborative and supportive during team discussions and organising
- Own & team members' roles established
- Did not collaborate and was unsupportive

GENERAL SKILLS
- Used appropriate register, style and tone
- Used/identified introduction, development and conclusions
- Used discourse markers: E.g. Firstly, In conclusion,

OUTCOMES
- Learner achieved overall outcomes
- Learner did not achieve overall outcomes

ANY OTHER COMMENTS or SUGGESTIONS:
_____
_____
_____

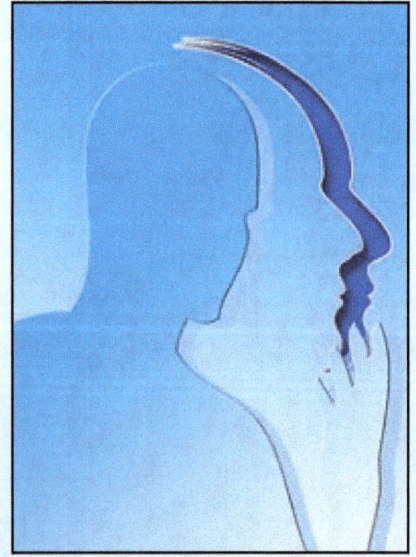

Speaking: public speaking in a debate

Those listening to the debate can offer their feedback to debaters. Here is a **peer rating sheet** to help learners provide feedback to debate participants.

Peer Checklist for the debate

Date _____   My name is _____

I am listening and giving feedback to (debater's name) _____

The topic is "Should Australia remain a constitutional monarchy?"

1 The speaker is *for* or *against* the topic? _____

2 Write the *main argument* of the speaker _____
_____

3 What *example*/s did she/he give to support their argument? _____
_____

4 Is the example a *fact* or an *opinion*? _____

5 Did the speaker *rebut* the other opposition? (circle) YES / NO

6 Write the rebuttal very briefly. _____
_____

7 Was the speaker 1st or last to speak for their team? (circle) YES / NO
   If yes, then did he/she *summarise* the team's arguments and /or *introduce* the team members?
_____

8 What was the *tone* (the sound of the voice) of the speaker? (sad, humorous, angry, worried, serious)
_____

9 Describe the *attitude* of the speaker? (interested, confident, tired, scared, positive, negative)
_____

10 Did she/he speak *well/convincingly* or *not*? _____
   Explain. _____
_____

11 What was her/his **best quality** during their turn in the debate? Please **underline at least 2 things**.

   passionate   knowledge   vocabulary   clear speech   tone   good volume   polite
   persuasive   confident   excellent eye contact   easy to understand   good example given
   He/She used words to organise their talk E.g. Firstly, Next, Then, After that, Finally, In conclusion, etc.

Speaking: sharing points of view
Board Game Monarchy or Republic?

Group Work:

Take turns to play! (Agree or disagree politely and express your opinion.)

polite disagreement
I see what you mean but ...
That's a good idea but ...
I suppose so but have you thought about ...

share= all speak about it
tell=the person speaks
ask= the person asks the others

opinion
In my opinion ...
As I see it ....
I honestly feel ....
Personally, I think ....

TAKE TURNS TO PLAY [Agree or disagree politely and express your opinion.]

START

1 (share) Should Australia remain a monarchy?

2 (tell) What is a good reason to have a queen or a king?

3 (ask) What is a negative thing about having a monarchy?

6 (tell) What is a good reason for Australia to become a republic?

5 (share) Should Australia get rid of the Queen and the royal family and become a republic?

4 (share) What is your opinion about the Governor General having the power to sack the Prime Minister if there is a 'hung parliament'?

7 (ask) What is a negative reason about a republic?

9 (share) Australian laws are based on the English Westminster system and the Ten Commandments. Do you think this is a good idea?

8 (ask) Would you like to change the Australian way of voting for a political party instead of for a leader?

FINISH

Page 174

Chants: old English nursery rhymes

Practise your pronunciation, singing each chant until you can sing it easily and keep the rhythm going. It is helpful to stress the bold text.

The **Queen** of Hearts, **made** some tarts,
All on a summer's **day**.
The **Knave** of Hearts, **stole** the tarts,
And **took** them clean **away**.

The **King** of Hearts called **for** the tarts,
And **beat** the Knave quite **sore**.
The **Knave** of Hearts brought **back** the tarts,
And **vowed** he'd steal no **more**.

From an English nursery rhyme based on a deck of cards, by an anonymous author

Pussy cat, **pu**ssy cat, **where** have you **been**?
I've **been** to **Lon**don to **look** at the **Queen**.
Pussy cat, **pu**ssy cat, **what** did you **there**?
I **frigh**tened a **little** mouse **under** her **chair**!

From a popular old English nursery rhyme by an anonymous author

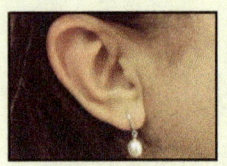

Listening: text cloze

Use The Internet to go to YouTube and open *Speak English Like Australians! – Chapter 7: Imperial Australia*

Listening: shadow reading in chunks

Listen to your instructor read the text in "chunks" of phrases, at normal speed. Chunks are groups of words that normally make sense and belong together. Repeat the words with the same intonation as your instructor.

Most magazines
were in boring black and white,
because colour
cost too much money.
They only used colour
for the front cover.
But, when the queen
came to Australia,
the women's magazines
also used colour
inside their magazines,
showing the queen's
lovely dresses,
hats, bags and shoes.
Everybody,
especially the ladies,
wanted to see
what the Queen was wearing!

Listening: on the Internet watch and listen to a YouTube video

On the Internet, find this video "1963 Royal visit to Queensland, Australia, Part 4 of 6"
It is 3:23 minutes in length. Notice the cultivated accent of the narrator, which was common on broadcasts and on television news in those days.

Please write the missing words of the video report.

And here on the ¹_____ side of the city are assembled the school children of the southern ²_____ at the Brisbane Cricket Ground, watching with fascination as the ³_____ couple enters the arena.

Her Majesty and Prince Philip are welcomed by the Treasurer and Minister for Housing, the Honourable T. A. Hiley and Mrs. Hiley. And a rousing ⁴_____ is given as Her Majesty and her husband walk onto the royal dais in the centre of the ⁵_____ oval.

The honour of presenting Her Majesty a bouquet of flowers goes to Yvonne Burke, a tall, graceful ⁶_____ lady, who at this moment must find it so hard to ⁷_____ that its really she who's been chosen to undertake this ⁸_____ courtesy.

Well even at the cricket ground the queen hasn't a chance of retiring from the incredible ⁹_____ these children are making. Listening to them is a ¹⁰_____ and a very moving experience. And by the looks of it, the royal couple ¹¹_____ to be delighted at this wonderful ¹²_____.

And for the second time today the royal couple prepares to ¹³_____ round the mass of children thrilled to see a close up of their queen and for ¹⁴_____ of them their first glimpse of this really wonderful lady.

The excitement is almost over and Her Majesty and His Royal Highness now ¹⁵_____ to the entrance of the oval amid great cheers, as they leave the children at the Brisbane Cricket Ground.

Answers: 1 south 2 suburbs 3 royal 4 cheer 5 cricket 6 young 7 believe 8 delightful 9 noise 10 fantastic 11 seem 12 welcome 13 circle 14 many 15 proceed

Dictation: dictogloss

As language learners continue their journey to acquire and approach native-like English, they reach incremental stages of competence. This activity is invaluable in showing learners that indeed their English exhibits **common** "flaws" and patterns of "error". Therefore, it may be argued that each recognisable stage of learner English is identifiable and may be considered a bona fide language in its own right!

1. Read the sentences to the class as learners listen without writing.
2. Give learners time to individually reconstruct the sentences in the correct order. Emphasise that key words and meaning is more important than exactness.
3. Pair learners so they can help each other.
4. Read the sentences one last time, as the students listen without writing. The pairs continue writing and adjusting their writing.
5. Finally, students group into fours, so they can brainstorm and help each other.
6. Ask the groups to decide on a scribe to write their sentences, on butcher's paper.
7. Tack each group's sentences at the front of the room, and ask the class to suggest grammar corrections. The instructor can give clues by underlines errors etc. and waiting for student suggestions for corrections.

Sentences for the dictogloss

<u>Introduce each sentence. (Read slowly and at a steady rate. Read all four sentences through and don't repeat each one. Pause between sentences.)</u>

1. Most magazines were in boring black and white, because colour cost too much money.

2. They only used colour for the front cover.

3. But, when the queen came to Australia, the women's magazines also used colour inside their magazines, showing the queen's lovely dresses, hats, bags and shoes.

4. Everybody, especially the ladies, wanted to see what the Queen was wearing!

Alternative sentences for the dictogloss

1. On the Saturday that the children waited for the bakery van, the shops closed at noon.

2. So, the bakery truck driver wanted to deliver all his buns before noon too.

3. The three kids knew their buns would come some time in the morning.

4. Their noses were on the lounge window, as they looked for the van.

5. They only got one Hot Cross Bun every year, for Easter.

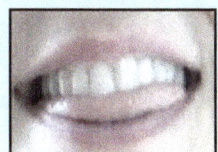

Pronunciation: reminder

Practise the pronunciations of the Aussie Sounds in Chapter 1 Pronunciation. Or use the QR code to hear the sounds and say them.

Pronunciation: minimal pairs /iː/ and /ɪ/

Learners take turns to say one word twice from each pair. The listener tells the speaker which word was said, either the first or the second word in the pair. If the pronunciation was clear and the hearer could discern the sounds, the correct word is chosen. The instructor can help with pronunciation and discerning of sounds as required by learners.

Learner A to say learner B to listen

1. peat   pit
2. seat   sit
3. neat   knit
4. beat   bit
5. meal   mill
6. field   filled
7. steal   still
8. peel   pill

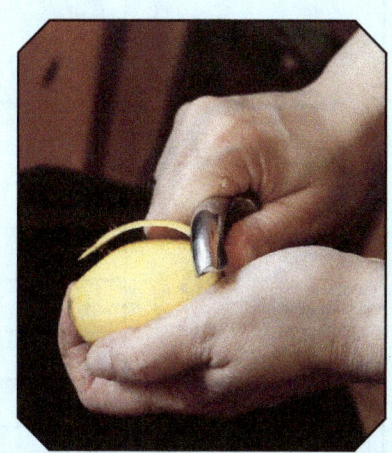

Learner B to say learner A to listen

A) feel   fill
B) deep   dip
C) seep   sip
D) weep   whip
E) sheep   ship
F) keeper   kipper
G) leave   live
H) peeler   pillar

Spelling rule for "ei" & "ie"

Here is a very good spelling rule for the long /iː/ which can either be spelt with "ie" or "ei". If the proceeding letter is "c" use "ei" after it so that the letters "cei" sound like "see". For example: c**ei**ling, re**cei**ve, de**cei**ve' re**cei**pt. Otherwise use "ie" as in bel**ie**ve, ach**ie**ve, retr**ie**ve, n**ie**ce.

Phonogram: "i"

The letters "i" have seven possible sounds. Read the explanations and then practise saying each column of words until you feel confident.

IPA PRONUNCIATIONS OF THE LETTER "i"	/ɪ/	/ə/	/j/	/i:/	/aɪ/	
With the letter "i" there are 5 possible pronunciations.	when followed by a single consonant sound in the same syllable	when in an unstressed syllable- especially as "ci, si, ti"	sounds like /j/ between "l", "n", "v" and a vowel	French "ee" sound in foreign words	at the end of a stressed syllable	stressed and word ends with "gn", "gh", "st", "ld", "nd", "nt"	when followed by a consonant and silent "e"
	En/glish	sus/pi/cion	brilliant	machine	ri/val	design	alive
	wil/ling	trad/i/cion	billiards	chlorine	i/dol	align	wide
	ig/loo	med/i/cine	familiar	margarine	di/al	sign	quite
	fin/ish	de/si/cion	rebellion	ski	fi/nal	high	time
	rib/bon	vi/sion	million	intrigue	pri/or/i/ty	fight	file
	lis/ten	col/li/sion	peculiar	visa	spi/ky	mild	like
	fin/ish	pos/si/ble	onion	litre	mi/nor	child	dice
	rich	im/pre/ssion	union	kilo	Mi/chael	mind	arrive
	miss	con/di/tion	companion	boutique	pi/ning	find	knife
	dis/tance	pos/i/tion	behaviour	police	si/lent	kind	hide
	lick	in/ves/ti/gate	oblivion	oblique	siren	grind	nine
	stick	in/di/cate	previous	fatigue	di/cing	behind	crime
	inch	bi/ki/ni	saviour	petite	di/gest	pint	wine
	twist	a/ni/mal	view	mosquito	li/bel	Christ	ripe

Tongue Twisters: "i"

Say each tongue twister until you can say it easily and smoothly.

1. Isabel idly inquired of Ian if the Immigration officer was interviewing Irish immigrants.

2. Isn't it important to listen and be familiar with friends' issues and interests?

3. Iris 's eyes easily widened with interest while listening to information on the Internet.

4. Christians believe Christ died for the sins of humanity: to justify God's sense of justice.

Conversation Bits: photobombed! some random!

Repeat the conversation until your intonation is native-like. Say the English expressions in one breath.

Denis	We had a really nice time at the beach last week.
Meryl	Yeah. It was lovely catching up with Tom, Julie and their boys.
Denis	Well I just had a look at the photos we took and I saw something unexpected.
Meryl	What was that?
Denis	The shot they took of us in our stinger suits was **photobombed**!
Meryl	Really? By whom?
Denis	An old lady. Just by **some random**.
Meryl	What a pity!
Explanations: photobombed = to get into a photo where you don't belong some random (person) = someone not known, any unknown person	

This lady got into the photo, even though the person taking the photo did not want her in it! She *photo-bombed* the photo!

Spelling: "er", "en", "est" and "y" suffixes (word endings)

1. For words ending with a single vowel and single consonant (E.g. b**ig**), double the consonant before adding the suffix (E.g. bi**gg**er, bi**gg**est)

For example:

sad → sadder/saddest
wet → wetter/wettest
slop → sloppy
skip → skippy
glad → gladder/gladden/gladdest
fat → fattest/fatter/fatten
flat → flatter/flatten/flattest
tall → taller, tallest

2. For words ending with "e" → remove the "e" and add "er" or "est"

For example:

large → larger/largest
fine → finer/finest

3. For words ending with "y" → remove the "y" and add "ier" or "iest"

For example:

lovely → lovelier/loveliest
tidy → tidier/tidiest

<u>Practice for you.</u>
Choose two words from each section and write each one in a sentence.

_____
_____
_____
_____
_____
_____
_____
_____
_____
_____

Vocabulary: crossword

Solve the crossword using vocabulary from *Speak English Like Australians!*, Chapter 7 Imperial Australia.

CLUES:

Across

3. the name of a small city in western Victoria that Queen Elizabeth visited in 1954.

4. The Australian Prime Minister was Robert _____ in 1963, when Queen Elizabeth visited Australia.

6. Queen Elizabeth's husband was named _____ Philip

9. Sunday is traditionally known as the Day of _____

10. these days now

Down

1. Magazines used to be mostly in black and white because _____ was too expensive.

2. King _____ VI was the father of Queen Elizabeth II.

5. The first fast food store to open in Australia was Kentucky Fried Chicken, in _____ in 1968.

6. famous poem: I did only see her _____ by, And yet I will love her till I die

7. In 1965, the money used in Australia was the same as the British money: pennies, shillings and _____.

8. a famous bridge in Sydney is "Sydney _____ Bridge"

Answer Key: Across: 3. Hamilton 4. Menzies 6. Prince 9. Rest 10. nowadays Down: 1. colour 2. George 5. Sydney 6. passing 7. pounds 8. Harbour

Figures of Speech: tautology

Tautology is an expression that uses *two words* of *similar meaning* to say the same thing, so it **emphasises something**. It is an unnecessary repetition of more than one word to say the same thing. Also, logical tautology can be a statement that is true in every possible interpretation by the way it is expressed, so there can be no argument against it. An example is "x=y or x≠y".

Examples:
- From my point of view, babies are a lot of <u>work and effort</u>! (This is indeed the person's opinion and so must be accepted as such.)
- It's a <u>free</u> democracy. (Democracies are free.)
- <u>Future planning</u> is needed for our school. (Planning is always for the future.)
- I can see the <u>frozen ice</u>. (Ice is always frozen.)
- That is <u>totally and completely</u> true. (Totally IS completely.)
- The meal you provided is adequate enough. (Adequate IS enough.)
- <u>Necessary essentials</u> are water and food. (Essentials are always necessary!)
- "With malice toward none, and with charity for all."—Abraham Lincoln
- "You can observe a lot by watching."—Yogi Berra
- You've got to do what you've got to do.

"There once was a fellow from Perth
Who was born on the day of his birth.
He got married, they say
On his wife's wedding day,
And died when he quitted the earth."

en.wikipedia.org

Examples of logical tautologies that cannot be argued about:
- The dog is either brown, or the dog is not brown.
- Trevor was lying through his teeth or he was not lying at all!

Underline the four tautologies in the text.
The Kings Bakery, in Brown Street, is still there opposite and facing Melville Oval in Hamilton. The honest truth is that back then in Australia, there were no fast food chains to go to whenever you felt like it, or late night shopping hours. When the shops closed at 5:30pm, you had to wait till the next day to buy and pay for what you wanted. Of course it was more restful for shop keepers and their employees not to work long hours and to have time off.

Answers: opposite and facing   honest truth   buy and pay   not to work long hours and to have time off.

Proverbs: birds

Proverbs always make us think! That is their purpose: to make us reflect about truths and how to apply them to enrich our lives.

Write the meanings of these wise sayings.

1. Birds of a feather flock together.
_____
_____
_____

2. Hope for the best, but prepare for the worst.
_____
_____
_____

3. A bird in the hand is worth two in the bush.
_____
_____
_____

4. The early bird catches the worm.
_____
_____
_____

Answers: 1. People who are similar like to spend time together. 2. Be ready for negative situations and problems but live your life thinking positively. 3. Something that you already have is better than the gain of losing it for the gain of more uncertain things. 4. Be early to get what you want before others compete with you and you lose it.

Writing: a letter to a friend (transactional genre) ACSF
2.05 & 2.06

Pretend you were in the crowd, waving a Union Jack flag as Queen Elizabeth was driven past, during her Royal Tour of 1963. Pretend you are the same age as you are now. Describe your feelings, what you heard, what you saw and what you were thinking as the Queen went by. Use lots of adjectives to bring your *word picture* to life. Use the present tenses.

Writing: comparing & contrasting (persuasive genre) ACSF 3.05 & 3.06

Here is an example of two paragraphs that compare (or look for similarities) and contrast (find differences between) cats and dogs. The first paragraph begins with a general introduction of the topic, and then gives a topic sentence about cats followed by supporting sentences. The second paragraph starts with a topic sentence about dogs and then it too is supported with examples.

Regarding household pets like cats and dogs, most people are either cat or dog lovers, but of course some like them both. Cats are very easy to care for as they clean themselves and generally consume less food being smaller animals than most dogs. They usually feel soft and sleek when patted and sit lightly on one's lap. However, they are not very patient with much handling and like their own space and privacy too. Cats do not enjoy going for walks around the neighbourhood with a leash around their necks, so there is a limit to their exercise and fitness value.

On the other hand dogs enjoy going for walks and don't mind a leash either. They can be trained to fetch, bring in the newspaper from the yard where is has been thrown by a newspaper deliverer, and they can bark and growl when they sense danger. Guide dogs help the blind and police dogs track down criminals and drugs. They are indeed very useful and like exercise too. Although dogs offer many benefits to people, they are pricey to feed and require time and energy to maintain, unlike their feline counterparts who are more independent.

Compare the positive and negative points of a monarchy and for a republic. Write two paragraphs, one for each system of government. Use words like: Looking at a monarchy,.... On the other hand.... However,... Comparing a monarchy with a republic..... Although there are benefits, there are also some negative points like......

_____
_____
_____
_____
_____
_____
_____
_____
_____
_____
_____
_____
_____

Writing: genres—six types

There are various ways to classify the different genres/types of **writing**. The classification used in this series of *Grammar & Activities* books is according to the purpose of the texts.

GENRES	TYPES/KINDS of TEXTS
POETIC	Poetry is a form of self-expression that uses words in an imaginative way to arouse emotions. It includes: free verse, rhymed, Haiku, sonnet, epics, blank verse, form, narrative, satirical, prose and couplets.
TRANSACTIONAL	This genre involves direct communication BETWEEN people: personal speeches, blogs, SMS texts, emails, tweets, letters, postcards, invitations and interviews.
PROCEDURAL	The purpose of this genre is to give instructions about how to do something. For example: recipes, directions to go somewhere, experiments, game rules, meeting agendas and manuals for machines/work processes.
EXPOSITORY	The reason for this genre is to inform, explain, describe or to expose and clarify. Texts types include: biographies, autobiographies, meeting minutes, descriptive essays, cause and effect essays, compare and contrast essays, informational reports and media articles, texts-books, encyclopedias, scientific reports.
PERSUASIVE	These kinds of texts try to convince readers to accept the writer's views and opinions and comprise of: argumentative essays, advertisements, letters to the editor, editorials, reviews, pro and con essays, political cartoons & political speeches and cover letters.
NARRATIVE	The texts of this genre tell a story in a series of chronological events and are for readers who want to relax or be entertained. Texts kinds include: science fiction, romances, fiction, fantasy, historical fiction, fairy tales & fables, adventure, recounts, personal essays, screenplays, plays, short stories and novels.

For each text, define its *text kind* and its *genre*.

A.

17th April 2025

Dear Mr. Wetherby,

I am most appreciative of your offer of employment. It is unfortunate that your offer arrived when it did, as I have just started my own franchise business. The opportunity was presented to me a week after our interview. Should my situation change, I will be in prompt contact with you. However, I believe the franchise business, which I have chosen to associate with, holds great promise.

Thank you for your time and consideration.

Yours sincerely,
Will Smith

B.

Builder of fine homes

Buy now before the end of the month and save on GST.

We construct quality homes to your plans.

We deliver on time and use the best trades..

List your hours or the time and date of your event.

Located in the heart of Melbourne's CBD

Awarded by MBA last

Tel: 043 789 3341

C.

Thank you God for mothers,
(And special thanks for mine)
She cooks and cleans and drives the car
And loves me all the time.

I thank you Mum for everything
That you so gladly do,
This love-heart shows I bought this gift
Especially for you.

So have a happy Mother's Day,
I know that you'll agree
You're very blessed- because you've got
A kid as great as me!

D.

Although not proven, asthma is thought to be hereditary. The majority of asthmatics tend to have asthmatics in the family. In most cases, asthma usually is present at birth, although some cases have developed after age forty (Mayo Clinic Family Health Book "Asthma" 466-467)

A flare up of asthma is generally referred to as an asthma attack. An asthma attack starts with the a spasm and constriction of the muscles in the bronchial passages; there is also an inflammation of the mucous lining. This will cause breathing to become laboured and cause a wheezing sound. (Mayo Clinic Family Health Book "Asthma" 933).

Answers: A is a formal letter of the transactional genre. B is an advertisement and is persuasive. C is a poem and belongs to the poetic genre. D gives information and belongs to the expository genre.

Parts of Speech: compound nouns

Compound nouns are made up of two or more words. Some are separate words, others are hyphenated and a third type of compound nouns are joined as one word. As language is always changing it is often difficult to know which compound nouns are hyphenated or not as there are no definite rules, and American and British English also have differences. It is useful to check a dictionary to determine what is acceptable these days. Remember that the first syllable of each word is always stressed.

In a compound noun the first word usually tells the *kind* or *purpose* and the second word tells us *who* or the *general name* of the noun. There are many different combinations of words. Here are *some* compound noun types to think about.

Types of Compound Nouns (noun + noun)		
Separate Words	Hyphenated	Joined
Christmas tree	tooth-brush	football
Santa Clause	self-esteem	bedroom
winter nights		toothpaste
fire place		sunset
coffee mug		teapot

Types of Compound Nouns (noun + verb)		
Separate Words	Hyphenated	Joined
movie goers	merry-go-round	sunrise
heart attack	film-making	snowfall
bus stop	fund-raiser	haircut
hand shake		firefighter

Types of Compound Nouns (gerund + noun)		
Separate Words	Hyphenated -only when used as adjectives	Joined
swimming pool	stepping-stone	
washing machine	looking-glass	
sleeping pill	walking-stick	
looking glass	frying-pan	
steering wheel	mixing-bowl	
living room	writing-pad	

Types of Compound Nouns (noun + gerund)		
Separate Words	Hyphenated only when used as adjectives	Joined
decision making	mountain-climbing	housekeeping
problem solving	mischief-making	sightseeing
power steering		shipbuilding

Types of Compound Nouns (adjective + gerund)		
Separate Words	Hyphenated	Joined
hard working	dry-cleaning	—
	easy-going	
	free-standing	

Types of Compound Nouns (preposition & noun)		
Separate Words	Hyphenated	Joined
above ground	up-to-date	overcoat
after life	top-hat	inside
down stairs	on-screen	bypass

Types of Compound Nouns (adjective + noun)		
Separate Words	Hyphenated	Joined
electric light	five-year-old child	redhead
free trade	great-grandpa	blackboard
concrete idea	high-quality	software
black market	last-minute	sweetheart
half moon	long-term	grandfather
full moon	short-term	shorthand

1. Can you think of some compound nouns to add to the tables?

2. Use the compound words on this page to complete the gaps in the sentences.

a) The Australian Government decided to drop export and import taxes and allow _____ between our two countries.

b) Did you know they have two children only 14 months apart: a _____ son and an older three-year-old daughter?

c) She didn't sleep well and so she was having an _____ at work.

d) I get really nervous when I have to present information at office meetings: I hate _____!

e) My wife has been my _____ since secondary school, when were used to study together.

f) Nowadays you rarely see a _____ in schools because we use whiteboards instead.

g) Whenever I ask my mum how to cook something she tells me to do it any way I want: she's _____.

h) If you are outside at _____ you will need to wear sunscreen to avoid sunburn.

Answers: a) free trade b) two-year-old c) off-day d) public speaking e) sweetheart f) blackboard g) easy-going h) midday

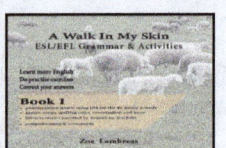

Grammar: linking or copula verbs

Some verbs link the subject to more information and do not actually do any action. These are known as copula or link verbs. In these cases copula verbs are not used as action verbs, although they may show action in other sentences.

A Linking verbs that can be used in front of adjectives to describe people/things:

| be | appear | feel | look | prove | seem | smell | sound | taste |
| become | come | fall | get | go | grow | keep | remain | stay | turn |

subject + link verb + adjective

The dog became thin after his surgery. ("Became" links the subject, the dog, with information about him, that he became thin.)

We are happy.   We ~~are being~~ happy.

They seemed upset with us.   They ~~were seeming~~ upset with us.

I appeared asleep but I was actually awake.   I was appearing asleep but I was actually awake.

subject + link verb + a + adjective + "one"

Our youthful memories were happy ones.

The park we visited proved a large one.

B Linking verbs that can be used in front of nouns to say that one thing is another thing:

| be | feel | look | prove | seem | sound | become | make | form |

subject + link verb + a noun (group)

She will make a great teacher.

It formed a great idea in her mind.

I feel a new woman, after my hair cut!

Look at the pictures and use a linking/copula verb, to write your own sentences.

  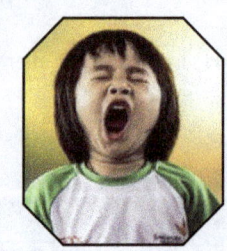

_____
_____
_____
_____

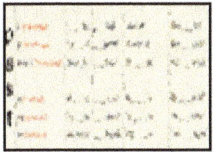

Verb Tenses: conjugation of "to study"

Complete the table using the correct tenses.

TENSES	Present Simple	Present Continuous	Present Continuous "wh" Questions	Present Continuous "to be" Questions	Present Continuous Contracted Negatives
1st person singular **I**	I study				
2nd person singular **you**		you are studying			
3rd person singular **she/he/it**			Why is she studying?		
1st person plural **we**				Are we studying tonight?	
2nd person plural **you**					You aren't studying tonight.
3rd person plural **they**					

Answers: present simple: you study; she studies; we study; they study. present continuous: I am studying; she is studying; we are studying; you are studying; they are studying. present continuous "wh" questions: Why am I studying?; Why are you studying?; Why are we studying?; Why are you studying?; Why are they studying? present continuous "to be" questions: Am I studying tonight?; Are you studying tonight?; Is she studying tonight?; Are you studying tonight?; Are they studying tonight? present continuous contracted negatives: I aren't studying tonight; or I'm not studying tonight. You aren't studying tonight. She isn't studying tonight. We aren't studying tonight. They aren't studying tonight.

Chapter 8   ANZAC Day
Reading Comprehension

After reading Chapter 8 of *Speak English Like Australians!*, answer the following questions in full sentences, in order to improve your writing skills. This means, for each answer, you must repeat some of the words in the question. However, you might need to change the tense and the order of the words in your sentences.

1. When is ANZAC Day and why is each letter of this word a capital/upper case letter?
_____
_____

2. Where did the Diggers assemble before marching in the parade?
_____
_____

3. As more families arrived to wait along the main street, who felt very interested in the ex-soldiers?
_____
_____

4. As the ANZAC Day marchers followed the Hamilton Brass band, what did the people watching along Gray Street do?
_____
_____

5. Why do *you* think people were quiet, as marchers entered the oval? (The photo shows the entrance of the oval and looking at the monument.)
_____
_____
_____
_____

6. What was on the grassy ground of Melville Oval?
_____
_____

Answers: 1. ANZAC Day is on the 25th April and it is an acronym for the Australian and New Zealand Army Corps. 2. The Diggers assembled at the corner of Kennedy and Gray Streets before marching in the parade. 3. As more families arrived to wait along the main street, Peter, Voula, Jimmy and Andy Hadis' children, Peggy, Theo, Steven and John felt very interested in the ex-soldiers. 4. As the ANZAC Day marchers followed the Hamilton Brass band, the people watching along Gray Street, clapped and cheered. 5. People were quiet as marchers entered the oval, as a sign of respect. 6. On the grassy ground of Melville Oval were little white crosses, one for each fallen Digger from Hamilton and the surrounding area.

Reading: opinions, facts and statistics

Unlike other living creatures, it is in the nature of humans to have an **opinion**. Even from a young age, a child will want its own way and will argue with its parents to get what he/she wants! An opinion is easily recognised because it is debatable. Others may have a different view. For example, "beauty is in the eye of the beholder" and our opinions can vary as to what is attractive! Sometimes opinions are introduced by expressions like: I think, I reckon, from my point of view etc. But not in every case.

On the other hand, **facts** are supposed to be true, based on research, impartial analyses, surveys, questionnaires, etc. Most of the time people cannot argue against facts and usually agree that they are true and correct. However, how the information is gathered and which populations are investigated, is very important to know, because the data collected can result in completely different facts! There is a saying that "you can make facts say whatever you want" to prove your point of view!

A **statistic** is a number that shows something about a group or sample.
In statistics, a population is studied, but because populations are large, a smaller sample is taken and data collected. Statistics are often shown as percentages, fractions and ratios.

Read the text and underline the facts, while circling the opinions of the writer.

The Covid-19 pandemic is causing widespread confusion, besides the deaths and illnesses of people all over the globe.

There was some confusion over a change of name for this virus. Usually the name shows where the virus originated like the Spanish flu, the Ebola virus (from the Ebola River, Democratic Republic of Congo), the Marburg virus (Marburg, Germany) and so on. This current virus was originally named Wuhan coronavirus (Wuhan, China), then coronavirus-2019, next it was Covid-19 and now officially SARS-CoV-2. The International Committee on Taxonomy of Viruses decided on this name. (Lesney, 2020)

There is still some uncertainty as to whether or not children are carriers of the virus and whether or not they can be infected. It seems a rare thing for children to die from this virus, but information is hard to access. Some babies and children have died from this virus but very few indeed. The medical journal, The Lancet, stipulates that up till February 2021, in seven countries, in children aged 4 and under, there have been 0.00034% of deaths due to the virus. (Bhopal, Bagaria, Olabi, & Bhopal, 2021)

Another area of doubt is quarantine hotels, which have circulating air conditioning shared in their rooms. People are not confident to travel if it means quarantining in such hotels. Some people have become infected while waiting out their 14 days of quarantine in such hotels. Such outbreaks often lead governments to reduce the intermingling of individuals in order to stop the spread of the virus. Since November 2020, "three cities have entered snap lockdowns on the back of such infections, aiming to halt outbreaks at their source." (Mao, 2021)

In summary, the coronavirus pandemic is creating uncertainties about its name, as well as how the virus impacts our children's health and how to conduct quarantine measures.

Works Cited

Bhopal, S., Bagaria, J., Olabi, B., & Bhopal, R. (2021, March 10). Children and young people remain at low risk of COVID-19 mortality. Retrieved from The Lancet: https://www.thelancet.com/journals/lanchi/article/PIIS2352-4642(21)00066-3/fulltext

Lesney, M. (2020, February 25). SARS-CoV-2: What's in a Name? Retrieved from Medscape: https://www.medscape.com/viewarticle/925710

Mao, F. (2021, February 8). Covid: Why Australia's 'world-class' quarantine system has seen breaches. Retrieved from BBC News: https://www.bbc.com/news/world-australia-55929180

Questions:

1. What statistics are given in the text? _____
2. Is there some more information you would like to know about the sample this statistic came from?
_____

3. Can you find an opinion in each of the second, third and fourth paragraphs?
_____
_____
_____

4. Do you agree with each of these opinions? Explain your reasons.
_____
_____
_____
_____
_____

5. What are some facts in the second paragraph? _____
_____
_____

6. Are these facts true? Please explain. _____
_____

Answers: 1. 0.00034% of deaths 2. Yes, from which 7 countries did the sample come from and how many people were investigated? 3. 2nd paragraph= the Covid-19 pandemic is causing widespread confusion 3rd paragraph= There is still some uncertainty as to whether or not children are carriers of the virus and whether or not they can be infected. 4th paragraph= People are not confident to travel if it means quarantining in such hotels. 4. Learner's may or may not agree with the opinions in the text, as long as an explanation is plausible. 5. Usually the name shows where the virus originated like the Spanish flu, the Ebola virus (from the Ebola River, Democratic Republic of Congo), the Marburg virus (Marburg, Germany) and so on. This current virus was originally named Wuhan coronavirus (Wuhan, China), then coronavirus-2019, next it was Covid-19 and now officially SARS-CoV-2. The International Committee on Taxonomy of Viruses decided on this name. 6. Yes the facts cannot be argued with as it is a matter of historical record.

Speaking: jig-saw activity

Divide the class into four groups and give each group member the same part of the story to read together, and to discuss sentence by sentence, and to look up any words they don't know. Slang will need teacher explanation.

Then re-group students, so each of the four parts can be shared in the new group. Although they may refer to their written part, they are to speak their part and not to read it out.

Learners listen to each speaker in turn, and ask him/her questions to clarify their understanding.

Part 1

It was April 25th, ANZAC Day and Argyro and Theo were waiting together with other people outside Lucas Cafe. They were all waiting to watch the returned World War 1 and World War 2 soldiers, march along the main street. They were called Diggers. They marched wearing their ribbons and medals on their chests. As the soldiers marched in the ANZAC Day parade, their children often marched proudly beside them. It is still an Australian tradition and they still march in Hamilton to this very day. (You can check on the Internet for the ANZAC Day notice in Hamilton, and the times of different events.)

Part 2

In the 1960s the returned soldiers got together at the corner of Kennedy and Gray Streets at 9:45am. It was always the same every year. Then, at 10 am they would start marching, led by a brass band in full uniform. Some men, with Scottish bag pipes and drums, marched along with them too. They joined together with the Hamilton Brass band. Also, it was an important event and many people watched them marching. They wanted to clap for them and to show their respect for the returned soldiers.

Part 3

As more families arrived to wait along the main street, everyone was getting excited. Peter, Voula, Jimmy and Andy Hadis' children, Peggy, Theo, Steven and John felt very interested in the ex-soldiers. Voula watched their faces and they looked very serious, because they were remembering their friends, who had died and could not march with them.

Part 4

They always looked important in their medals! Argyro and Theo had told them that the returned soldiers had fought for our freedom, and way of life, here in Australia, and in Greece too. Australian soldiers were in Greece, fighting during both World Wars. The Greeks helped to hide them, from the Germans, when they were in danger, so many Aussie soldiers escaped. But very many Greek families were killed by the enemy, for helping the Aussie soldiers in Greece.

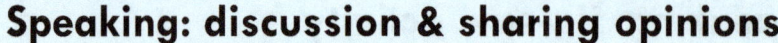

Speaking: discussion & sharing opinions

After Australia's involvement in the Vietnam War, interest in Anzac Day reached its lowest point. On 26 April 1975, *The Australian* newspaper reported on Anzac Day in just one short, single paragraph. The Anzac Day Parade was supported by very few by-standers.

However, terrible war is, we find men who became heroes because of their valour. The Internet provides the following information about a young soldier from Hamilton, who put himself in danger, to save the lives of many men in his platoon. For his fearlessness, the king of England (King George VI and father of Queen Elizabeth II) awarded him the highest medal for bravery, the Victoria Cross.

Edward "Ted" Kenna (1919-2009) won the highest medal possible for an Australian soldier, the Victoria Cross. He was born in Hamilton and when he returned from the war, the people of the Hamilton district raised sufficient funds, to build Kenna and his wife a house. The Kennas had four children. After the war he worked with the local council, and played Australian rules football for the local team. He attended many Victoria Cross reunions, in London, and led the annual Anzac Day March in Melbourne.

In the 1980s Kenna had his portrait painted by Sir William Dargie, and in July 2000 he was featured on a postage stamp, commemorating Australia's living Victoria Cross winners. His family later decided to sell his medals, including the VC, at an auction in July 2011. The medals sold for $1,002,000 to an unknown buyer. In 2013, a bronze statue of Kenna by sculptor Peter Corlett was unveiled, in the Sam Fitzpatrick Gardens in Lonsdale Street, Hamilton, his hometown in Victoria.

From Wikipedia

Pair Work
Discuss:

1. Do you think ANZAC Day is a good idea?

2. Do you believe in conscription?

3. Do *you think* humanity is in a constant state of peace, with periods of war, or the other way around? Explain your thinking to your partner. Use opinion expressions like:

"I reckon...", "I suppose that....", "I really believe that..."

Speaking: discussion & sharing opinions

The Victoria Cross (VC) medal, named after Queen Victoria, is the highest award that a British and Commonwealth serviceman can achieve. It is awarded for "gallantry of the highest order." There is a little metal "V" connecting the medal to the ribbon.

An additional famous Australian war hero is Edward "Weary" Dunlop whose statue is in the Royal Botanic Gardens, Melbourne. Poppy flowers are placed there on Anzac Day.

Another selfless hero was John Simpson, a medical doctor. He repeatedly risked his life to save the lives of many wounded soldiers, as he carried them to safety on his donkey. His statue is in the Australian War Memorial, Canberra.

Group Work: sharing opinions

1. Do you think you could put your own life in danger to save the lives of people you don't know?

2. What is true courage, in everyday life?

3. Should we forget about war heroes and get on with life without remembering them?

4. Can courage and fearlessness be taught, or is it something we are born with? Explain.

5. Are males naturally more courageous than women? Why/why not?

Chant: Soldiers Marching

Practise your pronunciation, by singing the verses until you can say them easily and keep the rhythm going. Stress the bold text to get the rhythm.

Soldiers **marching** in the **street**

Heads held **high** as they lift their **feet**

One and **two**, three and **four**

Can you **hear** the crowds appl**aud**?

Clap and **cheer** loud, for the **cor**ps

Watch them **swing** their arms once **more**

For our **heroes** play the **band**

In our **his**tory now they **stand.**

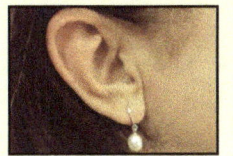

Listening: video of ANZAC Day

Please go to this website and watch this video to write the missing words.
https://www.youtube.com/watch?v=a0u4YTCqq2Y&ab_channel=BritishPath%C3%A9S

The narrator in the video speaks with a cultivated accent common to official reporting in the 1960s. However, no one speaks like that these days.
Begin the video at 15 seconds.

ANZACs march again. The heroes of two world wars swinging along with the same jaunty stride which carried them through the ¹_____ of France the deserts of Egypt, and the jungles of New Guinea.

There have been many Anzac Days, since that first one, the landing on Gallipoli. Some years the ²_____ has not been kind. But to the men who stormed the beaches to fight the Turks, and the men who ³_____ tropical downpours, in the jungles to Australia's North, unpleasant conditions mean little. The ⁴_____ and the widows of those who no longer march, watch their sons' and husbands' comrades, and rain cannot dampen the enthusiasm, with which the men of ANZAC march, in a ⁵_____ to comradeship, courage, and to those who've given their lives for their ⁶_____.

Let us look at Anzac Day 27 years ago. The ranks were not as thin then. For the passing years have taken their toll, and tens of thousands of old soldiers have faded ⁷_____. These were the days before World War 2, and among this huge crowd were thousands of young men, who were themselves to become ANZACs.

Now World War 2 is but a bitter ⁸_____ and the youngsters of Australia prepare in case they too must fight to preserve the ideals and the way of life, for which their fathers fought. This is not glorification of ⁹_____. This is not preparation for conquest. This is preparation for survival. For war is an ugly thing, and it leaves many scars. A former general and former governor of New South Wales, Sir John Northcott, sums it up this way. "I wonder sometimes, whether you ¹⁰_____ people growing up, realize that Anzac Day is something more, than just another day in our history. I want you to remember that the men who ¹¹_____, and the men who suffered from wounds and so on, paid the price, for the freedom, that we have today. And we hope and pray, that there will be no more war, but if there is, the responsibility for defending this ¹²_____, will be upon your shoulders, because you are growing up to take the place of the men, and the women, who fought and sacrificed themselves, for our freedom."

These are the grandchildren of the ANZACs. Some of them have ¹³_____ their fathers, and have only medals and memories. The children who lay these wreaths, are the generation for whom the sons of ANZAC fought. They will ¹⁴_____ a world, which has been torn by war, and which for years since, has lived, in uneasy peace. For two generations before them, the flower of Australia's youth has gone to war, so that this generation, and those that come may live in ¹⁵_____. Here on another Anzac Day, let us pray that these, our sons and daughters, may be spared the horror of another conflict. Let us pray, that those have died in battle, and those who still suffer as a result of war, may not have made their ¹⁶_____, in vain.

1. mud 2. weather 3. knew 4. mothers 5. tribute 6. country 7. away 8. memory 9. war 10. young 11. died 12. country 13. lost 14. inherit 15. peace 16. sacrifice

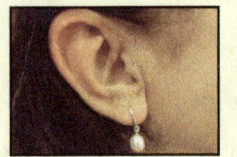

Listening: text cloze

Go to YouTube:Home on The Internet and search for Zoe Lambreas—Chapter 8 Anzac Day from the book *Speak English Like Australians!*
As you listen write the missing words. The answers are at the bottom of the page. Enjoy!

It was April 25th, ANZAC Day. Argyro and Theo were waiting together with other people outside Lucas Cafe. They were all waiting to ¹_____ the returned *World War 1* and *World War 2* soldiers, march along the main street. They were called *Diggers*. They marched wearing their ribbons and ²_____ on their chests. As the soldiers marched in the Anzac Day Parade, their ³_____ often marched proudly beside them. It is still an Australian tradition and they still march in Hamilton to this very day. (You can check on the Internet for the Anzac Day ⁴_____ in Hamilton, and the times of the different events.)

In the 1960s the ⁵_____ soldiers got together at the corner of Kennedy and Gray Streets at 9:45am. It was always the same every year. Then, at 10 am they would start marching, led by a brass ⁶_____ in full uniform. Some men, with Scottish bag pipes and drums, marched along with them too. They joined together with the Hamilton Brass Band. Also, it was an important ⁷_____ and many people watched them marching. They wanted to clap for them and to show their respect for the returned soldiers.

As more families arrived to wait along the main street, everyone was ⁸_____ excited. Peter, Voula, Jimmy and Andy Hadis' children, Peggy, Theo, Steven and John felt very interested in the ex-soldiers. Voula watched their ⁹_____ and they looked very serious, because they were remembering their friends, who had died and could not march with them. They always ¹⁰_____ important in their medals! Argyro and Theo had told them that the returned soldiers had fought for our freedom, and way of life, here in Australia, and in ¹¹_____ too. Australian soldiers were in Greece, fighting during both World Wars. The Greeks helped to hide them, from the Germans, when they were in danger, so many Aussie ¹²_____ escaped. But very many Greek families were killed by the enemy, for helping the Aussie soldiers in Greece.

the monument located at Melville Oval

Answers: 1. watch 2. medals 3. children 4. notice 5. returned 6. band 7. event 8. getting 9. faces 10. looked 11. Greece 12. soldiers

Listening: dictogloss

This is a task-based activity used to encourage learners to focus on the form of their language while also providing opportunities for communication; integrating listening, reading, speaking and writing. It also provides students with opportunities to talk about content and the language itself. This activity usually takes at least an hour to complete, depending on the abilities of the learners.

A. First, the educator prepares a text that contains examples of the grammatical form to be studied. Then the educator reads the text to the students at normal speed while they listen.

B. After that allow learners to make notes. If necessary, read the text again while they listen. Learners then work in pairs to paraphrase or to recall the text verbose.

C. Next they are organised into groups of four to prepare a summary of their work using the correct grammatical structures.

D. Finally each group presents their work to the class by tacking their sentences side-by-side onto a wall. While they help each other to correct their grammar with hints from the instructor, it is interesting for learners to note their linguistic similarities, as they approach closer and closer to native language.

E. Introduce each sentence by reading it at a steady pace without stopping mid-way.

1. In Australia there is another day to show respect for soldiers, Remembrance Day, also known as Armistice Day or Poppy Day, which is in November, on the 11th day, at 11am.

2. At 11 o'clock there was complete silence in Gray Street State School.

3. It started a couple of minutes before time, when the head master spoke over the speakers.

4. Everyone had to stop what they were doing and think about the soldiers, who had given their lives for Australia's freedom.

Dictations: aural & running dictation

Learners write the sentences as they are repeated by the instructor. Correction emphasises spelling and grammatical sentence structure.

1. It was April 25th, ANZAC Day. Argyro and Theo were waiting together with other people outside Lucas Cafe.

2. They were all waiting to watch the returned World War 1 and World War 2 soldiers, march along the main street.

3. They were called Diggers. They marched wearing their ribbons and medals on their chests.

Alternative Dictation: running dictation

(Please refer to *Chapter 3 Dictation* for an explanation and instructions.)

Learner A
Near the monument were hundreds and hundreds of little white crosses, pushed into the grassy ground. Each cross was for a killed soldier, from Hamilton and nearby areas.

Learner B
The children were soon free to walk about and read the names on the crosses, as well as to look at the flowers placed at the monument.

poppies at the Australian War Memorial in Canberra

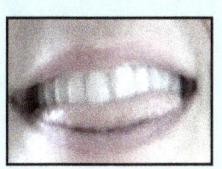

Pronunciation: linking sound /dʒ/

Sound 29 (refer to Chapter 1 Pronunciation) is often used to join words together when speaking.

Sometimes when we say two words, we link them with a new sound in the middle.

For example, when we have a /d/ sound followed immediately by a /j/ sound, we change them to make one linking sound: the /dz/ sound.

1. **Say and listen to the words below** *separately*. **Listen to the last sound of the first word and to the first sound of second word.**

    di**d**   **y**ou

    /d/   /j/

2. **Now listen to the words** *together* **as you say them quickly in one breathe.**

   di**d y**ou   ma**de y**oung   ai**d y**our   en**d y**ears

   /dʒ/   /dʒ/   /dʒ/   /dʒ/

Practise the linking sound by saying these sentences.

  a) Did you get there in time?   b) I am made young again with my grandkids.

  c) Did anyone aid your mum when she fell over?   d) It will end years of fun when you move away!

When is this linking sound used?

When we ask people to do something for us, we make a request. We often use words like:

  a) Would you ….? Would you please open the door for me?

  b) Could you …..? Could you get my pen for me please?

3. **Carefully repeat the above sentences, and listen to them as you say them smoothly and in one breath.**

4. **Now practise saying the sentences to a partner.**
   Make sure you say the /dʒ/ sound. Say each sentence in one breath.

Often, in spoken English, the "you" is shortened even more to "ya".

                                                          /jʌ/

  Mary: I went out for lunch today.

  Anna: Did ya really?

view video

    /dʒʌ/

5. **Practise saying the above two sentences, to each other, until you feel confident.**

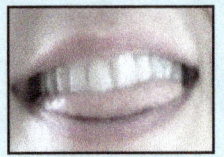

Pronunciation: minimal pairs /tʃ/ and /dʒ/

Practise saying and listening to the phonemes. /tʃ/ sounds are in the first column and /dʒ/ are in the second one.

Pair Work

Take turns with a partner to say *one* of each pair of words thrice quickly, until your partner can clearly understand if it is the first or the second word of each pair.

a) chin   gin
b) cherry   Jerry
c) match   Madge
d) Mich   Midge
e) cello   jello
f) chive   jive
g) choice   Joyce
h) choccie   jockey
i) check   Jeck
j) chill   Jill
k) Chester   jester
l) chains   Jane's
m) chain   Jane
n) batch   badge
o) lecher   ledger
p) choose   Jews
q) chew   Jew
r) cheap   jeep
s) cheer   jeer
t) cheering   jeering
u) chore   jaw
v) chest   jest
w) char   jar
x) chilly   Jilly
y) choke   joke
z) chess   Jess

Phonogram: "dge"

"dge" is used only after a *single vowel sound*.

Practise saying the words and the sound /dʒ/.

IPA for pronunciation of "dge"	/dʒ/
When you have the spelling of **"three letter j"** there is only one pronunciation: "j" for jam	badge
	edge
	fidget
	judge
	ledge
	midget
	nudge
	porridge
	pledge
	ridge
	wedge
	smidgen
	trudge
	dodge
	bridge

Tongue Twisters: "dge"

Practise saying these twisters until you can say them smoothly and easily, in a single breath.

1. Madge trudged across the bridge and dodged a badger on the ledge.

2. Judge Judy is a judicious and gentle judge with no jury.

3. Jumping Jack got the jitters when Jenny jolted him jokingly.

4. Jumping Jehoshaphat! Jack and Jill jostled Joseph and jarred his jaw!

5. Jeepers weepers! Jethro, Jade and James jived and jangled as they jaywalked.

Conversation Bits: fleet-footed! stalking me? milestone! Guinness Records! leisure!

Repeat the conversation until your intonation is native-like. Say the English expressions without pausing and in one breath. Practise with a friend as a role play.

Denis	I've never seen you shopping so fast before. It only took you 5 minutes, to buy a dress! You are **fleet-footed** today!
Glenys	Hi honey. I thought you were at the petrol station filling up. Are you **stalking me**?
Denis	No I decided to get petrol later, so I came into the shop to help you choose a dress, but I see you've already paid for it.
Glenys	Yeah I tried it on last week, so I knew what I wanted to buy after thinking about it.
Denis	Well this is a **milestone**. Maybe it should go in the **Guinness World Records** book, for the fastest woman shopper in the world! Will you always be so fast buying clothes from now on?
Glenys	I don't think so. Normally I like to take my **leisure**.
Explanations: fleet-footed = walking or running fast, moving very quickly stalking me = following someone who does not know you are doing that milestone = an important time or happening Guinness World Records = a book that records amazing things people do in the world leisure = to relax and not work	

Spelling: adding a suffix to word with a final "l"

Spelling Rule 1:

When a word ends in a vowel followed by the letter "l", double the "l" before adding "ed", "ing", or "er".

For example:

    travel > travelling   signal > signalling

Here are some more words:

funnelling	tunnelling	traveller	quarrelled
signalling	cancelling	labelling	enrolled
marvelling	councillor	repelled	enthralled

However, there are some exceptions where the "l" is NOT doubled like:
    paralleled, enrolment

Please note that in American English the "l" is not doubled. For example:

funneling	tunneling	traveler	quarreled

Spelling Rule 2:

When a word ends with two vowels followed by the letter "l" you do NOT double the "l" before adding "ed", "ing", or "er".

For example:

    steal > stealing   mail > mailed, mailing   deal > dealing, dealer
    heal > healing, healer   feel > feeling   cool > cooling, cooler
    school > schooling, schooled   sail > sailed, sailing, sailor

Write each word in a sentence.

prevailing _____
boiled _____
sailing _____
counselled _____
stealing _____
appealed _____
mailed _____

Vocabulary: match words to meanings

Join each word to its meaning.

rendition	Returned Services League
cenotaph	Australian and New Zealand Army Corps in World War 1
abide	to carefully examine something
wreaths	to wait with someone or to dwell, to live somewhere
inspect	a war memorial
RSL	performance, version
ANZAC	stroll, amble, walk
to wander	a circular arrangement of flowers

Here are the lyrics of the first and second stanzas (verses) of *Advance Australia Fair*, our National Anthem adopted in 1984, after a nation-wide poll in 1977 found that a majority of Australians thought it would be the best national anthem.

Write the meanings of any unknown words.

Advance Australia Fair

Verse 1

Australians all let us rejoice,
For we are young and free;
We've golden soil and wealth for toil;
Our home is girt by sea;
Our land abounds in nature's gifts
Of beauty rich and rare;
In history's page, let every stage
Advance Australia Fair.
In joyful strains then let us sing,
Advance Australia Fair.

Verse 2

With Christ our head and cornerstone,
We'll build our Nation's might.
Whose way and truth and light alone
Can guide our path aright.
Our lives, a sacrifice of love
Reflect our Master's care.
With faces turned to heaven above
Advance Australia fair.
In joyful strains then let us sing
Advance Australia fair!

Answers: rendition=performance, version; cenotaph=a war memorial; abide=to wait with someone or to dwell, to live somewhere; wreaths=a circular arrangement of flowers; inspect=to carefully examine something; RSL=Returned Services League; ANZAC=Australian and New Zealand Army Corps in WW1; to wander=stroll, amble, walk.

Vocabulary: acronyms and make a crossword

Find the meanings of these common words, expressions and acronyms.

diggers=

cenotaph=

"A time to be born, a time to die,… =

ANZAC=

AKA=

ASAP=

PTO=

RSVP=

AWOL=

CYA=

F2F=

FAQ=

LOL=

RSPCA=

Refer to the bottom of the next page for the answers.

Create a crossword using vocabulary from *Speak English Like Australians!*, **Chapter 8 ANZAC Day. Some of it has been done for you. You may choose your own words that fit in the squares.**

¹m	a	²r	c	h	³i	n	⁴g		⁵p
e		e			n				r
l		s			s				o
v		p			t				c
i		e		⁶	i		⁷		e
l		c			t				s
l		t			u				s
e					t				i
		⁸			i				o
⁹					o				n
					n				
									¹²
		¹⁰		¹¹					
			¹³						

Don't forget to write your own clues. When you finish, give it to a friend to figure out!

DOWN

1 the name of the oval

2 to honour, to pay _____

3 an established practice, part of the culture

4

5 a group of people or vehicles moving forwards in a line as part of a ceremony

7

8

9

10

11

12

ACROSS

1 striding, walking in formation

6

8

10

11

13

Figures of speech: anaphora

In anaphora, a word or a phrase is repeated at the start of neighbouring clauses in order to *emphasise* or *add meaning* to something. For instance, in the Bible, in the book of Ecclesiastes Chapter 3 and verse 2:

<u>A time to</u> be born, and <u>a time to</u> die;

<u>a time to</u> plant, and <u>a time to</u> pluck up that which is planted;

Anaphora, in a speech about ANZAC Day, by former governor of New South Wales, Sir John Northcot, in 1962.

<u>This is not</u> glorification of war. <u>This is not</u> preparation for conquest. <u>This is</u> preparation for survival.

1. Underline the anaphoras used by the Black Rights activist Martin Luther King, Jr. in his speech on August 28, 1963. (Only a part of his speech has been reproduced.)

http://en.wikipedia.org

I have a dream that one day this nation will rise up and live out the true meaning of its creed: "We hold these truths to be self-evident, that all men are created equal."

I have a dream that one day on the red hills of Georgia, the sons of former slaves and the sons of former slave owners will be able to sit down together at the table of brotherhood.

I have a dream that one day even the state of Mississippi, a state sweltering with the heat of injustice, sweltering with the heat of oppression, will be transformed into an oasis of freedom and justice.

I have a dream that my four little children will one day live in a nation where they will not be judged by the colour of their skin but by the content of their character.

I have a dream today!

Answers for this page: The anaphoras are: "I have a dream," and "sweltering with the heat of".

Answers for previous page: Diggers=soldiers; cenotaph=a monument built as a memorial to people killed in war; "A time to be born, a time to die,...." =everything in life happens given the right time; ANZAC= Australian and New Zealand Army Corps; AKA=also known as; ASAP=as soon as possible; PTO=please turn over; RSVP=répondez s'il vous plaît (French for 'please respond'); AWOL= Absent Without Official Leave (American soldiers who leave without permission); CYA=see you; F2F=friend to friend; FAQ=frequently asked questions; RSPCA= Royal Society for the Prevention of Cruelty to Animals

Figures of speech: anaphora (continued)

2. Please explain which anaphora Martin King used in his speech to achieve his purpose of supporting civil rights for black Americans.
_____
_____
_____

3. How did the anaphora make you feel?
_____
_____
_____
_____

4. In your view, was his use of anaphora successful in emphasising the need for equality between black and white Americans?
_____
_____
_____
_____

Proverbs: comfortable

Write the meanings of each proverb, in your own words.

1. There's no place like home.

2. Keep your friends close and your enemies closer.

3. It is better to be a free man in a small house than a slave in a big one.

4. To a friend's house the road is never long.

5. The house with an old grandparent harbors a jewel.

6. Bricks and mortar make a house, but the laughter of children make a home.

Answers: 1. Your own home is the most comfortable place to be. 2. Pretend to be friends with your enemy instead of openly fighting with them. In this way you can watch them carefully and know if they are planning something against you. 3. A free man with little is happier than a slave without freedom although in a palace. 4. When you anticipate being with a friend, then travelling to their house doesn't seem to take long. 5. The family with a grandparent is rich. 6. A house is not warm and homey unless it contains happy children.

Writing: opinion – organising your own two or three paragraphs (persuasive genre)

ANZAC Day, is sometimes written in capital letters because it is an acronym for Australian and New Zealand Army Corps. Here the word *corps* /kɔ: / refers to a World War 1 army corps or unit. A corps usually composed of two or three divisions, and normally included from 10,000 to 15,000 men.

%%%

During the 1970s and 1980s, people were sick and tired of Australia's involvement in the Vietnamese War and not many Australians turned out to watch the ANZAC Day procession. People felt that ANZAC Day glorified war. Diggers marched on nearly empty streets for some years.

However, by the 1990s Australians desired to honour the soldiers who had paid the ultimate price and many people turned out for the ANZAC Day Dawn Service and to watch the marching.

Today we know we are not glorifying war, but rather remembering and honouring those who died, so that we can live in our land as free people and maintain our way of life. Many Australians travel to Turkey and France to visit the cemeteries where WW1 soldiers are buried. The Australian Government has built an The Sir John Monash Centre on the site of the Australian Memorial in Villers-Bretonneux in northern France, so that young Australians can visit the site and connect to their history and ancestors.

159 words

Expressions for sharing your opinion include:

I personally feel/believe that …
I suppose …
I reckon …
To my mind …
As I see it …
As far as I can tell …
It seems to me that …

I honestly feel …
In my opinion …
From my point of view …
It strongly believe that …
It appears to me that …
Personally, I think …
I think …

Writing: opinion (organising your own two or three paragraphs) continued

Please write two or three paragraphs, from 100 - 150 words each, stating your opinion about what you think of ANZAC Day. Also, should soldiers who fought *against* Australia be marching in the ANZAC Day Parade, as they do nowadays? Use the <u>expressions for sharing your opinion</u>. Show your writing to an instructor or to a friend.

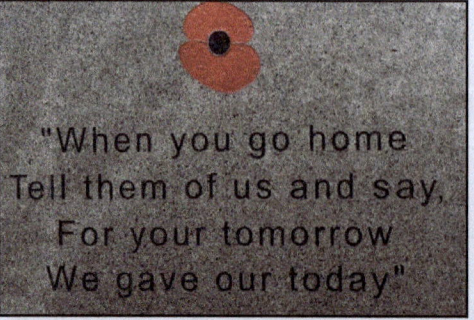

"When you go home
Tell them of us and say,
For your tomorrow
We gave our today"

Writing: a speech (transactional genre)

When thinking about what to write for your speech, know who your audience is! It will be different if you are speaking to children, factory workers or doctors. So you must choose the suitable tone for your speech and remember that because people will be listening to you, your vocabulary should be easy to understand and the grammar fairly simple as you don't want to "lose" your audience. Try to include a story as it is easier to remember than a lot of boring information!

Mrs Sanders, the President of a charity for mental health called *The Blues*, is invited to make a speech at a golf club, to raise money. The speech will aim to inform listeners what her charity does and that the money they donate will not be wasted. The speaker will try not to bore the listeners and will aim to gently flatter them, as she wants them to help her charity. Listeners will get involved as they silently answer a rhetorical question in the speech.

formal start	Ladies and gentlemen, it is a great honour to be invited here today to talk to you about the important work of The Blues.
gentle flattery	I know you are very busy people, so I will keep my presentation brief. I have some flyers here about The Blues and what we do, and I am happy to answer questions later and individually.
no details and brief summaries	The Blues started 15 years ago, because many young people and isolated older people suicide in our city. We have community houses in eight locations that are open 24 hours a day, 7 days a week. They are run by professional social workers and psychologists, who give advice and encouragement. We also have trained volunteers who answer the phones and make appointments. At every location we give out free lunches, every day for those who are in need, and then they can join in our organised activities to make friends and to get the help that they need. We also have some temporary accommodation to help the homeless. Every year more and more people are coming to us.
Use reasons that your audience will like.	I'm sure many of you would like to have help for a son or a daughter who lives far from home and might begin to feel lonely and depressed. This is what we do. It can be short-term or long-term professional assistance, until people get back on their feet or can work again. As their quality of life improves, their future becomes brighter too.
Show it is a respectable charity that deserves help.	We get State Government funding that covers 50% of our costs and our accountants keep a record of all our spending, so not a single cent is wasted. Our finances are open to public scrutiny in the release of our Financial Statement every July.

future plans	We plan to open three new centres next year with government funds that will pay for these buildings. So we need your aid to pay for more staff and to buy more housing accommodation for clients too. You know the great need that The Blues continues to fill.
gentle flattery	We appreciate that your golf club has been generous to The Blues in the past. You are well known for helping in our community, so I appeal to you most sincerely for your continued support. We cannot keep going without such generosity.
polite and confident finish	Thank you very much ladies and gentlemen for your time and attention.

~~~~~~

Guided Writing

You are a supervisor of some workers in an office. You want to thank and farewell a long-term employee who is retiring. You want to set the tone for rewarding good workers and for encouraging others to work hard too. Use the ideas on the left to help you write a short office speech.

farewell the worker

office motto: "serve others and you serve yourself"

been loyal to the company

worked well with colleagues

helped customers

planned farewell dinner & bonus money

happy retirement & keep in touch

Page 218

Parts of Speech: infinitive and distributive nouns

An infinitive can be an adjective, an adverb or a noun, depending on how it is used in sentence. An infinitive always starts with the word "to" followed by the base of the verb. E.g. to run, to march, to prepare, to read, etc.

Let's take a look at the types of infinitive <u>nouns</u>.

A) The **subjects** of these sentences are infinitive nouns.
To swim is fun. **To work** makes me tired. **To depart** now would be considered rude. **To hear** the choir was an enjoyable opportunity.

B) The **direct objects** in the sentences are infinitive nouns.
Molly loved **to write** songs. I like **to read**. The passers-by were asked **to donate** to the hospital fund.

C) Infinitives can also be **predicate nouns**, that refer to the subject and follow a linking verb—often "to be".
His best tennis skills were **to hit** backhand but not forehand. My favourite hobby is **to collect** stamps.

Identify and decide the type of infinitive noun in each of the sentences.

Underline the Infinitive Nouns.	Is it a subject, object or predicate type of infinitive noun?
1. He decided to leave home.	
2. To read is a relaxing pastime.	
3. Mary greatest hope is to climb Mt Kosciusko one day.	
4. Her idea was to grow vegetables in the garden.	
5. To travel expands your horizons.	
6. The quartet played music to entertain the wedding guests.	

Answers: 1. to leave=object 2. to read=subject 3. to climb=predicate 4. predicate 5. to travel=subject 6. to entertain=object

Parts of Speech: infinitive & distributive nouns (continued)

Distributive pronouns show how many of a particular larger group. If they refer to separate single things of a larger group they are always followed by a singular 3rd person verb. For example: every, each, all, both, half, neither, either.

Each refers to one person or thing at a time and takes a singular verb.
Each of us wants to holiday in different places.
She gave Christmas gifts to **each one of** her grandchildren.

Either and *neither* refer to two people only.
Either cake is delicious but I prefer the apple cake. (*Either* is also an adjective to the noun *cake*.)
Neither Jack **nor** Ben will win the trophy, because **neither** is in the final round of the tournament.
Either one of you should go and help grandmother.

If referring to more than two people or things, we use: any, no one, none, each of.
Everyone is here now, so we can start dinner.
All of them *know* how to play guitar. (*All of* refers to plural people and takes a plural verb.)
None of our neighbours are coming. (The meaning may be *none of them*, so it takes a plural verb. However, if the meaning is *none of it*, then it takes a singular verb.)
None of the *information* is correct. (A <u>single verb</u> for an *uncount noun*.)
None of it <u>is</u> true!
Half of the food was frozen.
No one arrived before me. **No one** <u>is</u> here yet.
Is **anyone** bringing the music for the party?
Any person with suitable qualifications is able to apply for the job.
Each of them is/are trying to win her heart.

Cross out the incorrect distributive pronouns.
1. Does **anyone/all** here know how to change a tap washer?
2. The parked car could belong to **any/each** person in the restaurant.
3. **Each of/No one of** them can ride a bicycle.
4. **Neither of/Both** of the dogs is trained to retrieve.
5. **None of/Neither of** them are invited to the wedding.
6. **None of/Neither of** them is invited to the wedding.
7. **Either/Both** of you need to do your homework.
8. **Neither/Either** she or he should come to the birthday party but not both.
9. **Neither/Either** she nor he should come to the birthday party.
10. **All of/Each of** the chairs are damaged.

Answers: the following are INCORRECT. 1. all 2. each 3. no one of 4. both 5. neither of 6. None of 7. Either 8. Neither 9. either 10. each of

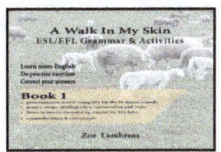

Grammar: informal use of "though" & "but"

When we speak we sometimes use "though" and "but" at the end of a sentence. Compare these examples:

I'm ready to go but you're not! > I'm ready to go. You're not *but*!
Though I'd like to stay, it's getting late. > I'd like to stay. It's getting late *though*.

*Note that a single sentence becomes two sentences.

Re-write the sentences to end them with "but" or "though".

1. We've seen each other a few times but we don't really know each other.
___

2. She had a daughter but I haven't heard the baby's name yet.
___

3. We've had a lot of rain this year, though I think we still have water restrictions.
___

4. The electrician came to repair our wiring yesterday, but I'm not sure of the cost.
___

5. I finished my assignment though it was late by a day.
___

6. Mary has a new hair colour but I don't like it much.
___

7. Our garden looks colourful and healthy though we haven't watered it for months!
___

Answers: 1. We've seen each other a few times. We don't really know each other but. 2. She had a daughter. I haven't heard the baby's name yet but. 3. We've had a lot of rain this year, I think we still have water restrictions though. 4. The electrician came to repair our wiring yesterday. I'm not sure of the cost but. 5. I finished my assignment. It was late by a day though. 6. Mary has a new hair colour. I don't like it much but. 7. Our garden looks colourful and healthy. We haven't watered it for months though!

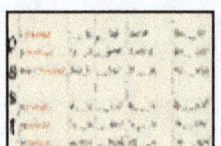

Verb Tenses: the 12 verb tenses

In English there are three main verb tenses: present, past and future. The present, past and future tenses are divided into four aspects: the simple, continuous, perfect and perfect continuous. Therefore, there are 12 verb tenses that English learners must know. Here is a table that quickly summarises them. The blacked out tenses are rarely, if ever, used.

The 12 English Verb Tenses

TENSE	ACTIVE VOICE	PASSIVE VOICE
Present simple	She cooks it.	It is cooked.
Present Continuous	She is cooking it.	It is being cooked.
Present Perfect	She has cooked it.	It has been cooked.
Present Perfect Continuous	She has been cooking it.	
Past Simple	She cooked it.	It was cooked.
Past Continuous	She was cooking it.	It was being cooked.
Past Perfect	She had cooked it.	It had been cooked.
Past Perfect Continuous	She had been cooking it.	
Future	She will cook it.	It will be cooked.
Future Continuous	She will be cooking it.	
Future Perfect	She will have cooked it.	It will have been cooked.
Future Perfect Continuous	She will have been cooking it.	

*Modals like "can, could, would, might, may, should, ought to" can also be used to express possibility or advice. In these cases the verb following the modal verb is in the base form, the same as for "do, does, did". (i.e. use the infinitive verb form and remove the "to" E.g. ~~to~~ have, ~~to~~ write, ~~to~~ think, etc.)

For example:

   She *might* have been cooking it. (present perfect continuous)
   She *could* cook it. (future)
   It *would* have been cooked by then. (future perfect in passive voice)
   He *ought to* cook it. (present simple)

Underline and name the tenses.

1. The work is finished now, because everyone worked very fast today.

2. Our children had been playing outside until we called them in for lunch.

3. The fruit trees were being pruned expertly by our friend who is a horticulturalist.

4. By now the computer will have been uploading all our overseas photos, for two hours!

5. Why does she like cooking so much?

6. Susan might have been cooking all afternoon to get this dinner ready for us!

Answers: 1. is finished (present simple-passive voice); worked (past simple) 2. had been playing (past perfect continuous); called (past simple) 3. were being pruned (past continuous-passive voice) 4. will have been uploading (future perfect continuous) 5. like (present simple) 6. might have been cooking (present perfect continuous)

Verb Tenses: stative verbs cannot be used in the continuous tense

Some verbs are not usually used in continuous tenses, because they have no physical action that you can see being done. But, some of these verbs have a second meaning: one with a physical action, so that meaning can be used in the continuous tense.

Here is a list of verbs that are not normally used in continuous tenses and no physical action.

admire	adore	appear	astonish	be	believe	belong	concern	consist	contain
deserve	desire	despise	detest	dislike	doubt	envy	exist	fit	forget	guess
hate	have	hear	imagine	impress	include	involve	keep	know	lack	last
like	love	matter	mean	owe	own	please	possess	prefer	reach	realise
recognise	remember	resemble	satisfy	see	seem	sound	smell	stop	suppose
		surprise	survive	suspect	understand	want	wish		

Collins Birmingham University International Language Database. (1994). Collins Cobuild English Grammar. London: Harper Collins

For example we say:

"I **believe** you!" *not* "I am believing you."

"Stuart Diver **survived** the deadly landslide at Thredbo. *not* "He was surviving the landslide at Thredbo."

"They **appeared** unhappy with the results." *not* "They were appearing unhappy with the results."

"We **have seen** them twice." *not* "We have been seeing them twice."

"My dad **will be impressed** with my grades." *not* "My dad will be impressing with my grades."

"Our neighbour **is satisfied** with his garden." *not* "Our neighbour is satisfying with his garden."

In some meanings, which are <u>dynamic</u> as they refer to action, the <u>continuous tense</u> is used.

For example we say:

3. "She **is smelling** the flower in her garden."

But when the sentence shows a <u>condition or state</u>, we can say:

1. "He **smells** because he hasn't had a shower yet." *not* 2. "He ~~is smelling~~ as he hasn't had a shower yet."

Sentences 1 and 2 above do not refer to any activity by the *subject, and so cannot be used in the continuous tense.* Sentence 3 shows action and has a different meaning.

Practise using the stative and non-stative verbs by crossing out the incorrect tense in each sentence.

1. The box **contains/is containing** some of my special photos and memories!
2. It's very nice to see that her son **pleases/is pleasing** her whenever she asks him to help.
3. It **pleases/is pleasing** to see such a well-behaved child.
4. My friends and I **remember/were remembering** our childhood yesterday at our get-together.
5. You **remember/are remembering** me don't you?
6. The car **belongs/is belonging** to me but I let my son drive it too.
7. I **know/am knowing** a lot of things since I started my English class.
8. When I was younger I didn't think about it but now I **believe/am believing** in God!
9. I **remember/am remembering** you from last year at the cafe.
10. It **matters/is mattering** a lot to me that you are working so hard!
11. We **want/were wanting** to buy a house so went to an auction yesterday.
12. With his calculator he **guesses/is guessing** how much money he will get from the bank.
13. They were **astonished/admonishing** to hear they had won TattsLotto!
14. We **wish/are wishing** you a happy birthday for tomorrow.
15. Sorry that I **owe/am owing** you a lot of money and I will pay you back soon.
16. He **resembles/is resembling** his mother I think.
17. I felt **surprise/surprising** when I heard the phone ring at 2 a.m.
18. She **surprises/is surprising** her husband tonight with the news that she is pregnant!
19. I **hear/am hearing** loud music and I think it's coming from across the road.
20. She **seems/is seeming** to enjoy the tennis game.

Answers: 1. contains 2. pleases 3. is pleasing 4. were remembering 5. remember 6. belongs 7. know 8. believe 9. remember 10. matters 11. want 12. is guessing 13. astonished 14. wish 15. owe 16. resembles 17. surprise 18. is surprising 19. hear 20. seems

Index

B

Being a good listener 40
Board Game about Marriage 70
Board Game Monarchy or Republic? 174

C

Chant: Assimilation 42
Chant: Cultural Misunderstandings 9
Chant: Proxy Marriage 72
Chant: School 121
Chant: School Rituals 146
Chants: Family 96
Chants: Old English Nursery Rhymes 175
Chant: Soldiers Marching 200
Chapter 1   Coming to Australia 1
Chapter 2   Becoming an Aussie 38
Chapter 3   The Marriage Proposal 69
Chapter 4   Family 94
Chapter 5   School 118
Chapter 6   School Ceremonies and Rituals 143
Chapter 7   Imperial Australia 167
Chapter 8   Anzac Day 194
Character Attributes 81
Class Debating Rules 170
Conversation Bingo 35
Conversation Bits: a fair go 51
Conversation Bits: dilly-dally! lift my game! I was mortified! 126
Conversation Bits: fleet-footed! stalking me? milestone! Guinness Records! leisure! 208
Conversation Bits: it's up to you! 151
Conversation Bits: photobombed! some random! 181
Conversation Bits: she'll be right; oodles; no worries 19
Conversation Bits: What a coincidence! What a fluke! 78
Conversation Bits: what a stereotype; no surprises there 102
cultural misunderstandings 9

D

Debating Outcomes 171

Describing People 80, 81

Dictation: a different running dictation 123

Dictation Alternative: running dictation 148

Dictation: aural 14, 98

Dictation: dictogloss 178

Dictation: in pairs 98

Dictation: listening to "chunks" of prose 47

Dictation: running dictation 74

Dictations: aural & running dictation 148, 204

E

Expressions for opinion 40, 215

Expressions for polite disagreement 169

Expressions for when you don't understand 7

F

Figures of Speech: allusion 56

Figures of speech: anaphora 212

Figures of Speech: antithesis 84

Figures of Speech: merisms 155

Figures of Speech: simile 23

Figures of Speech: similes revised 130

Figures of Speech: synecdoche 105

Figures of Speech: tautology 184

G

Grammar: determiners 115

Grammar: determiners [articles and specific & non-specific determiners] 164

Grammar: gerunds & infinitives 89

Grammar: indirect questions – to ask politely 161

Grammar: informal use of "though" & "but" 221

Grammar: linking or copula verbs 192

Grammar: the patterns of sentences 139

Grammar: uncount/mass and count nouns 30

Grammar: word order in sentences 60

Grammar: words to use with count & uncount nouns 31

Group Work: opinions 144

Group Work: sharing opinions 199

L

Listening: a jig-saw activity 10
Listening: aural text cloze 43
Listening: being a good listener 40
Listening: cloze activity 97
Listening: dictogloss 203
Listening: follow the text along 122
Listening: Go to the Internet to watch and listen to a YouTube video of The Queen 177
Listening: shadow reading in chunks 176
Listening: text cloze 73, 147, 176, 202
Listening to a song for general meaning 46
Listening: video of ANZAC Day 201
Listening: write the missing words 11

O

order of adjectives 82

P

Part of Speech: collective nouns & male/female/young animals 160
Parts of Speech: a definition of nouns and determiners 28
Parts of Speech: collective nouns 159
Parts of Speech: compound nouns 190
Parts of Speech: count and uncount nouns revision 136
Parts of Speech: determiners 29, 112
Parts of Speech: infinitive and distributive nouns 219
Parts of Speech: infinitives & gerunds 87
Parts of Speech: nouns 59
Parts of Speech: verbs and preposition 113
Peer Checklist for the debate 173
Phonogram: "ch" 125
Phonogram: "ci" 150
Phonogram: "dge" 207
Phonogram: "i" 180
Phonograms: "ai", "au" & "ar" 50
Phonograms: "augh" and "ough" 77
Phonograms: "aw", "ay", "c" 101
Phonograms: how used in this series of text books 18
Physical Attributes 80

polite questions 161
Pronunciation: /dz/ as a linking sound 205
Pronunciation: linking sounds /r/ & /ə/ 100
Pronunciation: linking sounds /w/ & /n/ 99
Pronunciation: minimal pairs /iː/ and /ɪ/ 179
Pronunciation: minimal pairs /s/ and /z/ 49
Pronunciation: minimal pairs /ʃ/ and /tʃ/ 149
Pronunciation: minimal pairs /tʃ/ and /dʒ/ 206
Pronunciation: plural nouns & present simple verbs 48, 49
Pronunciation: plural "s" 124
Pronunciation: reminder 179
Pronunciation: Stressing and Grouping Words Together 75
Pronunciation: the Schwa 17
Pronunciation: using IPA symbols for sounds 15
Proverbs: A good woman is hard to find. 106
Proverbs: birds 185
Proverbs: Birds of a feather... 185
Proverbs: comfortable 214
Proverbs: Customs are stronger than laws 57
Proverbs: know and do 57
Proverbs: learning 156
Proverbs: No man is an island. 131
Proverbs: relationships 131
Proverbs: short, well-known expressions that share advice and truth 24
Proverbs: The pen is mightier than the sword. 156
Proverbs: There's no place like home 214
Proverbs: travel 85
Proverbs: woman 106

R

Reading Comprehension Chapter 7 ACSF 2.03 & 2.04 167
Reading Comprehensions – refer to 'Chapter'
Reading: opinions, facts and statistics 195
Reading: word attack skills 2
Reading: word attack skills - phonics 3

S

Speaking: arranged marriages 70, 71
Speaking: board game 120

Speaking: board game - Monarchy or Republic? 174

Speaking: class debate - monarchy or republic? ACSR 3.07 & 3.08 168

Speaking: cultural misunderstandings ACSF 2.07 & 2.08 8

Speaking: cultures 39

Speaking: discussion & sharing opinions 198

Speaking: expressions for polite disagreement. *See* Expressions

Speaking: getting a listener's attention 95

Speaking: I don't understand 7

Speaking: indirect questions–to ask politely 145

Speaking: jig-saw activity 197

Speaking: learning and school 119

Speaking: modals express possibility 144

Speaking: public speaking in a debate 170

Speaking: reading about arranged marriages 71

Speaking: sharing personal information 41

Speaking: sharing points of view 174

Speaking–speed dating 145

Speaking: stressing and grouping words together 75

Spelling: adding a suffix to word with a final "l" 209

Spelling: adding suffixes to silent "e" words 79

Spelling: "c" spelling rules and pronunciation 152

Spelling: "er", "en", "est" and "y" suffixes [word endings] 182

Spelling: plural nouns 20

Spelling rule for "ei" & "ie" 179

Spelling: silent e rules 127

Spelling: The 350 Most Commonly Used Words in English 52

Spelling: when to use double "s" 103

Survey your friends for their information. 41

T

Tongue Twisters: "a" 18

Tongue Twisters: "ai" 50

Tongue Twisters: "dge" 207

Tongue Twisters: "f" 77

Tongue Twisters: "i" 180

Tongue Twisters: "r" 101

Tongue Twisters: "s" and "z" 49

Tongue Twisters: "s" & "ch" 125

V

Verb Tenses: conjugation of "to study" 193
Verb Tenses: "do" and "have" in questions 35
Verb Tenses: "Do you ever...?" & "Have you ever...?" 36
Verb Tenses: have got 116
Verb Tenses: list of irregular verbs, bases & participles 63
Verb Tenses: making questions with the simple tenses–conjugation 117
Verb Tenses: present participles 91
Verb Tenses: present simple & present continuous 141
Verb Tenses: present simple & present continuous tenses 92
Verb Tenses: present simple tense 62
Verb Tenses: revision present continuous tense 165
Verb Tenses: stative verbs 223
Verb Tenses: the 12 verb tenses 222
Verb Tenses: the base verb for instructions & directions 34
Verb Tenses: the base verb for questions & negatives 33
Verb Tenses: to be, to have & to do 32
Verb Tenses: use the correct forms of the verbs 166
Vocabulary: acronyms and a crossword 211
Vocabulary: acronyms and make a crossword 211
Vocabulary: crossword 21, 129, 153, 183
Vocabulary: match words to meanings 210
Vocabulary: order of adjectives 82
Vocabulary: synonyms 22, 55, 80, 104
Vocabulary: unfamiliar words 55
Vocabulary: word families 154

W

Writing: a childhood recount or an imaginary recount (expository genre) 107
Writing: a letter to a friend (transactional genre) ACSF 2.05 & 2.06 186
Writing: a paragraph 58
Writing: a personal letter (transactional genre) ACSF 1.05 & 1.06 157
Writing: application for a course (persuasive genre) 134
Writing: a speech (transactional genre) 217
Writing: building sentences 25
Writing: comparing & contrasting (persuasive genre) ACSF 3.05 & 3.06 187
Writing: genres–six types 188
Writing: imaginary recount (expository genre) 108
Writing: joining sentences together. 27

Writing: opinion – organising your own two or three paragraphs (persuasive genre) 215
Writing: two contrasting paragraphs (persuasive genre) 86
Writing: Two Supporting paragraphs (persuasive genre) 132

www.ingramcontent.com/pod-product-compliance
Lightning Source LLC
Chambersburg PA
CBHW060458010526
44118CB00018B/2461